CHURCHILL'S PIRATES

THE ROYAL NAVAL PATROL SERVICE IN WORLD WAR II

CHURCHILL'S PIRATES

THE ROYAL NAVAL PATROL SERVICE IN WORLD WAR II

BY
JON SUTHERLAND AND DIANE CANWELL

Pen & Sword
MARITIME

First published in Great Britain in 2010
and reprinted in this format in 2020 by
Pen & Sword Maritime
An imprint of
Pen & Sword Books Ltd
47 Church Street
Barnsley
South Yorkshire
S70 2AS

Copyright © 2010, 2020 Jon Sutherland and Diane Canwell

ISBN 978 1 52679 651 6

Typeset by Acredula

Printed and bound in the UK by CPI Group (UK) Ltd, Croydon, CR0 4YY

Pen & Sword Books Ltd incorporates the Imprints of Pen & Sword Aviation, Pen
& Sword Family History, Pen & Sword Maritime, Pen & Sword Military,
Wharncliffe Local History, Pen & Sword Select, Pen & Sword Military Classics,
Leo Cooper, Remember When, Seaforth Publishing and Frontline Publishing

For a complete list of Pen & Sword titles please contact
PEN & SWORD BOOKS LIMITED
47 Church Street, Barnsley, South Yorkshire, S70 2AS, England
E-mail: enquiries@pen-and-sword.co.uk
Website: www.pen-and-sword.co.uk

Contents

Introduction

The Royal Naval Patrol Service, variously nicknamed Harry Tate's Navy, The Lilliput Fleet or Churchill's Pirates, was a very special service. It had its own rules and regulations, its own silver badge, and its fleet consisted of literally hundreds of requisitioned vessels. These Minor War Vessels, as the Admiralty called them, consisted of drifters, paddle steamers, trawlers, tugs, whalers and yachts.

If they were armed at all they had vintage weapons. Their headquarters was the unlikely municipal gardens of the Sparrow's Nest, close to Lowestoft High Street and boasting a concert hall, an open-air stage and conservatories. It first became HMS *Pembroke X*, a rallying point and base, initially for men of the Royal Naval Reserve and later for the Hostilities Only Men, who would become known as the Royal Naval Patrol Service. It was an assembly point for these men who were rapidly organised into crews and despatched to vessels scattered amongst the ports around Britain, to serve around the world. The Sparrow's Nest ultimately became HMS *Europa*, a landlocked major naval vessel and the administrative headquarters for more than 70,000 men and 6,000 vessels.

As the majority of the men were reservists the Royal Naval Patrol Service became 'a navy within a navy'. It quickly acquired its unofficial titles. The term 'Harry Tate's Navy' was an unofficial one and probably derived from the Scottish comedian Harry Tate. There

1

are many theories as to how the service acquired this name. Undoubtedly Harry Tate was used as a slang term, possibly connected to the Merchant Navy title for the mate, or chief officer. Hence it may be linked to cockney rhyming slang. More broadly, it was a phrase used to describe something rather amateur. Harry Tate would often play a clumsy man who could never get to grips with contraptions. The Royal Navy used the term as a way of poking fun at the drifters and trawlers, although in time they would begin to appreciate one another and have a special camaraderie.

Because of the Royal Naval Patrol Service's unwavering support from Winston Churchill the service readily accepted the second nickname of 'Churchill's Pirates', since the men were predominantly more civilian than service orientated. They were proudly independent and coped with conditions on tiny vessels that were more reminiscent of the privateers than a regular naval force.

Lord Haw Haw dubbed them the 'Sparrows' because of their connection with the Sparrow's Nest, but it was meant in a derogatory way. Others called them the 'Lilliput Fleet', focusing on the size of the vessels rather than the immense job that they would perform throughout the course of the Second World War.

The service can trace its roots back way beyond the First World War, when it had been recognised that small ships were ideal for minesweeping and other wartime duties. For generations Britain had a massive fishing fleet, with thousands of trained seamen that could, in times of hostility, act as a ready reserve for the Royal Navy.

The Royal Naval Patrol Service, in its launches, fuel carriers, converted trawlers and drifters, naval seaplane tenders, corvettes and specifically-built vessels would serve in all theatres of the war, from the Arctic and the Atlantic, across the Mediterranean, the Indian Ocean and to the Far East. Perhaps their most significant contribution was to ensure that the coast of Britain was as clear of mines as was humanly possible.

It is difficult to estimate exactly how many vessels were deployed by the Royal Naval Patrol Service, but it is certainly around 6,000, of which there were at least 1,600 different types. In excess of 260 were lost in action in the Second World War, and around 15,000 Royal Naval Patrol Service personnel were killed. Nearly 2,400 of them have no other grave than the sea.

Although there was just one winner of the Victoria Cross from the service, Lieutenant Stannard, who was awarded it whilst in command of the trawler *Arab* during the 1940 Norwegian campaign, there were thousands of others who were given other awards for outstanding acts of bravery. Alongside them were many thousands more unsung heroes whose courage was never formally recognised.

The Royal Naval Patrol Service lives on, as does HMS *Europa*, in the form of the association's Stannard Room Museum, still situated amongst the buildings in the municipal park in Lowestoft. In the walls of the Europa Room some 850 men who won honours during the Second World War are listed, in addition to a list of over 200 more that were mentioned in despatches.

HMS *Europa* was decommissioned in 1946, and in October 1953 a memorial was unveiled by the then Admiral of the Fleet, Sir Rhoderick McGrigor. On its base were seventeen bronze panels, bearing the names of the 2,385 officers and men of the Royal Naval Patrol Service who died in action during the Second World War. A granite memorial, with a replica mine at the top, was unveiled in August 2009; seventy years after the service had been established. This was a fitting tribute to the forgotten fleet and the exploits of Churchill's Pirates.

CHAPTER ONE

Royal Naval Reserve

In many respects, the traditions and origins of the Royal Naval Patrol Service can be traced back to the seventeenth and eighteenth centuries. Back then, there were never enough men that would voluntarily agree to join ships in time of war, let alone in peacetime. As a major maritime power, England needed fully manned vessels to be patrolling the world's seas, to mount raids on rival powers, protect merchant shipping and resupply far-flung outposts of the empire.

Although by Second World War standards the ships were primitive, lacking in firepower, range and effectiveness, these vessels ensured that England remained and continued to grow to become the pre-eminent naval power in the world. Drastic measures were needed to find the 'volunteers' to man the ships. Jails were often emptied and men were literally impressed into service. In fact impressments were where the bulk of the naval personnel were acquired.

By the end of the second decade of the nineteenth century, the global situation had changed to a large extent. England's greatest danger since the time of the Spanish Armada, Napoleon's France, had been defeated. Ships were laid off or mothballed awaiting the next major global conflict. The need for large numbers of volunteers had temporarily passed. However, it dawned on the government that it was one thing to have vessels mothballed and preserved to ensure that they would be serviceable when needed, it was quite another to have sufficiently trained and available men to sail them.

Solutions were sought, notably with organisations such as the Royal Naval Coast Volunteers (RNCV): these were seamen who were prepared to serve on board Royal Navy vessels in time of war and who also made themselves available during peacetime. In 1859 the Royal Naval Volunteer Act was passed and later the Royal Naval Officers Act. Under these acts financial and training provisions were made to train up to 10,000 experienced seamen in naval gunnery. These men would be drawn from the merchant and fishing fleets for use in time of war. For many years, the men would be known as the Royal Naval Volunteers, but later as the Royal Naval Reserve. The Royal Navy provided them with ships moored around the coast so that both men and officers could brush up on their basic training. It was a feature of the officers in particular that many of them were either senior officials in the shipping industry or government, or often captains of very large commercial ships.

By the beginning of the twentieth century there was a massive expansion in the size of naval forces in Britain. It was readily apparent that enormous numbers of men would be required to man the dreadnoughts. Even with the Royal Naval Reserve there would be too few such men. By 1903 a new programme was introduced: men could now train on a part-time basis with the Royal Navy. The vast majority of these men were civilians, many with no connections to the sea at all. The Royal Navy set up special provision for them to train at shore establishments. Effectively this created the Royal Naval Volunteer Reserve (RNVR). By 1914 there were some 30,000 officers and men in the RNVR.

Once the First World War broke out in August 1914 the men of the RNR were quickly posted to the fleet, operating aboard Q-ships, auxiliary cruisers, destroyers and submarines. Many thousands found themselves actually serving as infantry with the Royal Naval Division and saw action on both the western front and in Gallipoli. Throughout, however, they maintained their naval customs, ranks and traditions. Another group of men served with the Royal Naval Air Service as pilots, flying aircraft and airships.

No sooner had the armistice been signed in November 1918 than the RNR and the RNVR began to be cut back, both in terms of manpower and administration. But there was an understanding that these men could well be needed again, so a more streamlined programme was designed. Regular opportunities with the Royal Navy were made available to the volunteers. Across the country, training centres were opened and men would serve for a short period of service every year. In return, they would be paid after meeting certain obligations.

By the mid-1930s there was another review of the numbers of men that would be needed in the Royal Navy in the event of a war. In 1936 this led to the formation of the Royal Naval Volunteer (Supplementary) Reserve, the RNV(S)R. Many of the men that were attracted to this organisation were those who had a keen civilian interest in the sea, typically those that owned pleasure boats and yachts. This was to attract a broader group of men; age was not a particular concern and neither was where they lived, which often made it difficult for them to attend training centres.

When war broke out in September 1939, the Reserve Naval Forces were immediately mobilised. RNR officers took command of sloops, frigates, destroyers, submarines and landing craft. Others found themselves posted to larger vessels, such as aircraft carriers, cruisers and battleships, where their specialist skills in gunnery and navigation were much needed. Others were posted to convoy duty, where their merchant navy experience was invaluable. The initial group of individuals that reported in 1939 amounted to 1,000 RNVR officers and 7,251 men. During the war around 95 per cent of all of the coastal force craft were commanded by RNVR officers and they won at least 1,781 decorations. By the end of the war 48,000 reserve officers were serving.

There was, however, also an entirely different organisation: a navy within a navy, with its own silver badge and a fighting fleet of whalers, trawlers and drifters. The vessels were armed with obsolete guns. Where the fishing catch was once stored men now ate. Nets were stripped out of the vessels to be replaced by minesweeping gear. The organisation's headquarters was in the unlikely location of a municipal garden in Lowestoft, Suffolk. Its fleet initially consisted of hundreds of different types of requisitioned vessel, although later a small number of Admiralty-built trawlers were added.

To begin with, these men of the Royal Naval Patrol Service were taken from the Royal Naval Reserve. The crews were fishermen, tug men and others with little or no connection with the sea. Naval discipline was observed and enforced by a small number of Royal Navy regulars. Over the course of the Second World War many thousands of men reported to HMS *Europa*, the official name of the municipal gardens, known colloquially as the Sparrow's Nest. Many of the men had never been to sea before and it was a fisherman's navy. The men were stubbornly independent, the vessels were weather-beaten, but they would face German aircraft, surface vessels, U-boats and mines. They would brave the seas across the world, operating on the US east coast, the Indian Ocean, the Far East, all around the African coast, in the Mediterranean, the Arctic, the Channel and the North Atlantic. The force, which was variously known as Harry Tate's Navy, the Sparrows or Churchill's Pirates, began with a force of 6,000 men and 600 vessels. By the end of the war it had grown to 66,000 men and 6,000 vessels.

The deployment of fishermen and others in wartime was not a new thing; it had been used to good effect during the First World War. Britain had always been, as we have seen, a major naval power; not just a military naval power, but a commercial one too, hence there was always going to be a large number of highly skilled men available to be called up as reserves.

Towards the end of the nineteenth century it had been recognised that the raw material for a naval reserve of experienced men could be split into two categories. The inshore fishermen were used to working in open boats near the land. They were the successors of those who had always fished in estuaries, lakes and rivers. They were used for short sea trips and would tend to avoid bad weather. The other major group were the deep-sea fishermen. They were used to going further afield in either sailing or steam vessels. These men sailed out of Grimsby, Great Yarmouth, Hull, Lowestoft, Scarborough, Whitby, and Ramsgate and into the North Sea. Others operated in the English Channel out of Brixham and other places. In 1887 it had been estimated that two large fleets of smacks and three small fleets operated out of Hull, employing 2,200 men in the summer months and 2,900 in winter. They operated around the Dogger Bank. Two more large and several smaller fleets operated out of Grimsby; 2,750 men fished between Heligoland and the Sylt Estuary in the summer and around the Dogger Bank in the winter. Not only were these men very used to sea life, but they also knew the sea itself incredibly well, with years of accumulated experience on voyages lasting for eight weeks or more.

In a way the fleets themselves even had their own command structure. One of the most experienced skippers, with the best knowledge of the fishing areas, was given the title Admiral of the Fleet. He would command up to fifty other vessels and was supported by a Vice Admiral with almost as much experience. So the men were used to working under discipline and their training made it relatively simple to convert them into real Royal Navy men.

In the First World War the main fishing vessels that were used were the steam trawlers and the steam drifters. They were supplemented by smaller vessels, such as sailing smacks, sailing drifters, open boats and motor vessels. Steam trawlers were designed to cope with the worst of weather. They were normally around 150ft long and would weigh around 250 tons when fully laden with coal, ice and stores. They were perfectly capable of a voyage of 1,000 miles or more to fishing grounds. A later steam trawler, built around 1916, was not quite as long, being around 117ft, and the Admiralty would hire one of these for around £132 per month.

Steam drifters were designed for shorter voyages and were rarely out for more than a week. Many of these operated out of Brixham, Ramsgate and Lowestoft. Steam drifters were around 60ft long.

The Germans hoped that mines would paralyse the Royal Navy and British seagoing commerce. However some time before the war broke out the Royal Navy had bought steam trawlers at Grimsby, Fleetwood and North Shields, to be used for minesweeping. Steps had also been taken to organise a reserve of 100 steam trawlers. The nucleus of this fleet was soon enlarged as more vessels were added. By mid-August 1914 there were 107 of these vessels, variously known as 'Special Service Vessels' or 'Trawlers Commissioned'. The Navy also intended to use eight obsolete torpedo gunboats. This Trawler Section had 140 skippers and 1,100 men but this was just the beginning. By the start of 1917 the Royal Naval Reserve employed 2,500 skippers and as many as 100,000 fishermen. By the time the war had been raging for two-and-a-half years, three-quarters of British fishing vessels were on Admiralty service.

Trawlers and drifters were hired on specified terms and the requisitioned fishing vessels were paid for, with the liabilities also covered by the Admiralty. The trawlers and drifters were ideal choices for dealing with mines and even trapping German submarines. A single drifter could extend its nets to a distance of two miles. It is worth bearing in mind that from Great Yarmouth alone, where the majority of the drifters operated, around 1,000 craft worked across the whole of the North Sea and all the way to the Continent. As a result, German submarines had to operate underwater, not daring to come too close to the surface for fear of being entangled in the herring nets.

The Royal Navy recommended that minesweeping be carried out by pairs of trawlers. They would tow a sweeping wire between them, which would catch and hold the steel mooring wire of a mine. The mine would then be drawn to the surface and shot at with a rifle. In the last two weeks of December 1914 a large number of mines were cleared off Scarborough in precisely this manner. This was an operation fraught with danger and not inconsiderable loss. Some of the trawlers were destroyed when they collided with mines, whilst others were badly damaged. Mines were not the only hazard for these converted fishing vessels. They were attacked by German surface ships and sunk by U-boats. In one short three-month period alone Grimsby lost twenty-seven trawlers, with eighty-three men dead and 128 taken prisoner. All of these losses were from direct attacks.

A prime example was the *Balmoral*. She left Grimsby on 23 January 1915 and was never heard from again. Amongst the crew was the deckhand James Coleman. During the war the Colemans lost James the father, while one son was washed overboard from a trawler and drowned and a second son died in France.

On a Sunday afternoon in April 1915 the Grimsby trawler, *Vanilla*, was hit by a torpedo from a submarine without warning. The *Vanilla* was blown to pieces. Another Grimsby trawler, *Fermo*, made for the *Vanilla*'s position. She steamed amongst the wreckage and found no survivors, then a German U-boat suddenly appeared and fired a torpedo at her from 500m. Fortunately it missed. The *Fermo* now tried to escape, chased by the U-boat. It was only the skill of the skipper that allowed her to get home safely to Grimsby.

By March 1917 some twenty-eight fishing vessels had been sunk or captured and nineteen more were lost to mines. The Germans now allowed unrestricted operations by their U-boats and this meant that in March and April alone seventy-eight British fishing vessels were sunk. By the end of the year this total had reached 167.

It was not just the North Sea that saw large losses. In the winter of 1916, for example, sixteen fishing vessels were lost off the relatively quiet west coast. Attempts were even made by German airships to sink them. One of the reasons for targeting these small boats was the fact that trawlers coming into harbour would often report sightings of Zeppelins out at sea; hence the airships' attempt to eliminate them before they could raise the alarm.

Trawlers also succeeded in making many daring rescues. The battleship HMS *Formidable* was sunk by a torpedo fired from a German submarine on New Year's Day 1915. Many crewmen, 600 from 800, were lost; but more would have died had it not been for William Pillar, skipper of the trawler *Provident*, operating out of Brixham. The *Provident* brought home seventy-one survivors, and the Admiralty wrote:

> The battleship *Formidable* was sunk this morning in the Channel, whether by mine or submarine is not yet certain. Seventy-one survivors have been picked up by a British light

cruiser, and it is possible that others may have been rescued by other vessels.

In fact the Admiralty knew that it had been the *Provident* heading back towards Brixham that had carried out the rescue. *Provident's* crew had spotted an open boat packed with survivors and on four occasions they had tried to get a rope to it. Eventually they succeeded; the survivors had been in the boat for twelve hours and were exhausted. They now had to jump or climb on board the fishing vessel in seas that were up to 30ft. It was a remarkable and brave act and the most serious injury was a man's fingers getting jammed between the cutter and the fishing boat. The last man to leave the cutter was torpedo gunner Hurrigan, by which time the cutter was full of water. *Provident's* skipper and his crew were later received by the king at Buckingham Palace, who congratulated them on their gallant and heroic conduct.

This was neither the first nor last time that trawlers would come to the rescue. The Lowestoft trawler, *Coriander*, along with two Dutch ships, had helped pick up a number of survivors from three cruisers, HMS *Aboukir*, HMS *Cressy* and HMS *Hogue*, on 22 September 1914. In October 1914 HMS *Hawke* and HMS *Theseus* were attacked by submarines in the North Sea and *Hawke* was sunk with the loss of over 500 men. However Skipper John Cormack and his crew of the trawler *Ben Rinnes* saved three officers and forty-nine men that had been picked up by a Norwegian steamer. The men were safely returned to Aberdeen.

There was a bizarre incident on the night of 31 January 1916. Zeppelins had attacked the east coast of England and one of them had been found floating in the North Sea by the Grimsby steam trawler *King Stephen*. The skipper and the crew found twenty-two Germans and they begged the trawler crew to save them, but the trawler was completely unarmed and there were only nine men on board. The skipper declined to put his men at risk, sailing away. But by the time the Royal Navy had been informed the airship had sunk and the twenty-two Germans had drowned.

However British fishermen did take enormous risks to rescue German sailors who had been shipwrecked. In a few instances their gallantry had been rewarded by specially inscribed binoculars and gold watches presented to them by the Kaiser.

Another amazing incident took place in the autumn of 1917. Lieutenant Thomas B McNabb, RNVR, was awarded the Distinguished Service Cross 'in recognition of his gallantry in going overboard and securing a line to a drifting mine after attempts to sink it by gunfire had failed owing to a choppy sea and considerable swell.'

Former Grimsby fisherman, Walter Wood, recalled another act of bravery, this time in the western waters of the English Channel:

A flotilla of minesweepers was sweeping between two given points when two mines exploded in the sweep which was towed by the second pair of minesweeping trawlers in the flotilla. The wire parted, and one of the two trawlers hove in the kite – the contrivance employed to keep the sweep at the required depth. When the kite had been hoved short up to the rollers it was seen that a mine was foul of the wire, and had been hauled up against the trawler's side; and not only that, but the outline of another mine was visible just below the surface. This second mine was entangled in the sweeping wire and was swirling in the eddy under the vessel's counter. The situation was one of most extreme peril and called for the greatest courage and promptness on the part of the officer in charge. Both were forthcoming. He ordered the trawler to be abandoned. That was but the beginning of one of the dramas of the sweeping service, it was, so to speak, the train that fired the powder. The senior officer in command of the minesweepers had no intention of letting the gallant little craft go. He led the volunteering, calling for a man to go with him. Having reached her they set to work on their perilous task. They cut the sweeping wire and the kite wire and both mines fell clear without exploding, and they were towed clear of the spot by means of a rope which had been passed to another trawler.

Two members of the Grimsby steam trawler *Exeter* were awarded the Albert Medal at Buckingham Palace on 14 November 1917. Both

Ernest Henry Outhouse and William Weldrick were from the Royal Naval Reserve Trawler Section. The incident that had led to their heroism had taken place almost a year before on 20 November 1916. The London-based ketch, *Frieda,* was sinking in the North Sea. *The Exeter* approached the spot and launched a small boat manned by Outhouse, Weldrick and two other men. The first rescue attempt failed as the small boat was badly damaged in the heavy seas and forced to return to the trawler. The *Exeter* now manoeuvred and threw lines held up by bladders. Three of the *Frieda's* crew jumped into the water and two of them were hauled on board, but the other man drowned.

The king also presented the Albert Medal to Herbert Powley, a deckhand. On this occasion there had been an explosion on board a motor launch. The launch was lying alongside the jetty and it was suddenly realised that Sub-Lieutenant Charles W Nash, RNVR, was buried underneath the wreckage. Powley and Chief Motor Mechanic Pooley were on board their own vessel about 50m away. By the time they got close the launch was burning furiously and it was clear that the petrol tank could go up at any minute. Oblivious to the danger the two men jumped on board and pulled Nash out with barely thirty seconds to spare.

Just as remarkable was an incident at 05.00 on a Monday morning in June 1917. A drifter, the *IFS*, commanded by Lieutenant H B Bell Irving, RNVR, was on patrol off Dover. Irving's crew encountered five enemy seaplanes and engaged them. They destroyed one of them and the pilot was rescued by another enemy aircraft. This aircraft then attacked the drifter but both pilots were taken prisoner in the fight. The remaining three enemy aircraft fled. The lieutenant was awarded the Distinguished Service Cross and Bar on 14 November 1917. The *IFS* had been built in Grimsby in 1908 and was registered and owned at Great Yarmouth.

Enemy aircraft were obviously not immune from attack from enterprising skippers of the RNVR. The commodore based at Lowestoft reported that at 20.00 on 9 July 1917, Lieutenant P Douglas, RNR, commanding His Majesty's armed trawler, *Iceland,* destroyed two German seaplanes and brought back four prisoners into Lowestoft harbour. One of the aircraft had tried to torpedo a steamer from the surface; it missed, by which time *Iceland* had come within striking distance. The German seaplane tried to make good its escape but the water was too choppy and it could not get into the air. The trawler's gun smashed the seaplane and it began to settle in the water. Suddenly a second seaplane arrived, but it too was hit by the trawler. The first two men were picked up and then Douglas set out to find the other seaplane. He found the aircraft broken in half and picked the men up, taking them prisoner.

One of the most celebrated fishermen of the First World War was William Thomas Baker, who became known as Submarine Billy. In his own words he described his exploits:

> It was nearly a year after the war began that I was fishing in the smack *Prospector*, about eighteen miles out, east-south-east of Lowestoft. By that time the war had made a lot of difference to fishermen and the North Sea fishing. Most of the ordinary fishermen, both fleeters and single boaters, had joined up for minesweeping and patrolling and war work in other ways, and those who went to sea to fish were either men over fighting age, like myself, or boys.

Baker went on to explain that an enormous number of modern steam trawlers and drifters had been requisitioned. This meant that old beam trawlers like the *Prospector* now had a new lease of life. The vessel carried a five-man crew and by his own accounts they were often the target of German attacks, either by submarine, surface vessel or even airship. He was also acutely aware of the fact that even though Britannia still ruled the waves it was impossible for the Royal Navy to protect them from German attack. By his own admission this meant that they were always terrified of running into the enemy:

> On the morning of August 10, 1915, I was on deck. The weather was very calm, so we hadn't our gear down. It was just before noon, and I was looking round pretty sharply, as you do in these days at sea, when I saw a German submarine quite

close to us. He must have seen us through his periscope and come to the surface, and there he was awash, like some ugly brute looking for prey. There was no mistaking him – I knew at once what he was, I had been fifteen years in the Royal Naval Reserve.

The *Prospector* was not alone and there were several other beam trawlers in the vicinity. Baker knew that there was nothing they could do to protect themselves against the submarine; they would just have to wait and see what was about to happen:

Almost as soon as I had spotted the submarine he came towards us, and the commander, as I took him to be, who was standing on the platform, shouted to us in quite good English, 'I will give you five minutes to leave your ship!' We chucked the boat out and got into it. We didn't bother to get our clothing or anything; we daren't, and there wasn't time. We were ordered to go to the submarine, and we pulled to her. When we got alongside three of our fellows scrambled on board, leaving me in the boat, where I was joined by two German sailors who carried bombs in their hands.

The German commander now ordered Baker to row the two Germans back to the *Prospector*. When they got back to the vessel the Germans went below with the bombs. The German commander was obviously scared that at any moment a British warship might appear. The two Germans were not below for very long and the three men got back into the boat and headed back for the submarine:

A very strange little thing happened while all of this was going on. The German commander said to our third hand 'I knew you in Yarmouth. I kept a shop in Millgate Street. They used to call me Peter.' The third hand said afterwards that he did not remember the German at all; but what he said may have been true, and he may have been one of the Germans who lived in England and waited for the war to come.

Fifteen minutes later there was a massive explosion and the *Prospector* began to sink; she disappeared beneath the water after about eight minutes. The Germans now ordered the crew of the *Prospector* to get back into their boat and make for another smack nearby, the *Ben Nevis*. The Germans had spared this ship so that it could take on board the crews of the other vessels that they were going to sink. One after another the Germans dealt with all of the other trawlers; they blew up the *Venture* and by the time the three crews were on board the *Ben Nevis* she was fairly full:

> We spent a wearying night, and very thankful we were when the morning came. Luckily a patrol boat, *The Retriever*, came up and pulled us inshore to the westward, and later a big minesweeper brought us into Lowestoft. It was good to be ashore again, after such a shaking. But I was soon to have a far worse experience than the bombing of the *Prospector*.

Baker was in no hurry to get back to the sea, but after a month he became the third hand on board another trawler, the *Boy Ernie*:

> On Friday, 10 September 1915, at five minutes to eight o'clock, when we were just outside the Long Shoal, I was standing by the cabin hoodway, threading a needle of black twine. We hadn't shot the gear, as we had lost our trawl through fouling a wreck, and we had bent a new trawl.

Baker spotted two submarines about half a mile away. No sooner had he seen them than they began to open fire. The skipper was sure that they were English, but Baker was adamant that they were German. The shots were fairly accurate and ripped through the sails, one just missing Baker and going straight through the superstructure of the boat. Reluctantly the skipper agreed to abandon ship. They could see what they believed to be a Dutch sailing vessel close by, but in fact it was a German vessel carrying fuel for the submarines:

> I started sculling the boat away from the smack, and we got about twenty yards astern very quickly, all the time under fire; but the Germans were not content with firing shells at helpless craft – they now turned a machine gun onto defenceless fishermen who were adrift in a boat in the open sea. There was

among us a little boy – William Collins, they called him, only fourteen years and a half. His mother was a widow, and he had four little brothers and sisters, 'get into the bottom of the boat Billy' I said, 'you'll be safe there.' The boat was actually getting riddled by machine gun fire – later on it was seen how she had been peppered and holed, so that it was wonderful she kept afloat – and before I knew what was happening I was struck by a bullet in the right thigh, and began to bleed dreadfully.

Baker had been incredibly lucky; the bullet had actually been stopped by a steel tobacco tin. Meanwhile the Germans bombarded *Boy Ernie*, blowing her to pieces. The submarines then sank down and disappeared. Baker and the others were soon picked up by a minesweeper and sent a message back to Great Yarmouth, confirming that all the crew were safe.

Baker remained onshore for twenty weeks until he joined a small fishing smack, *Waverley*. The *Waverley* had its own encounter with a submarine on the morning of 17 July 1916, some sixteen miles off Cromer:

My nerves had been broken altogether by the earlier experiences, and I was badly upset now when the Germans began to fire on the *Waverley*. The vessel was perfectly still, so that it was easy to get the boat overboard through the gangway. As soon as our little boat was afloat we jumped into her and pulled away from the vessel, leaving everything we possessed. A very strange thing soon happened. The submarine came up alongside the little boat, and the commander, who could speak very good English, astonished us by saying that he was very sorry for what he was doing; but he could not help himself – he was forced to do it. He was honest and he was certainly a gentleman.

The Germans looted the small vessel and then blew it up. Once again Baker was fortunate enough to be picked up, this time by HMS *Halcyon* after about five hours. By now Baker had become popularly known as Submarine Billy, but this did not put him off joining another smack after about two weeks; this time as a second hand on the *Francis Roberts*:

> About half past one in the morning of July 31 [1916] I was on watch, the rest of the crew being below. There was a thick fog over the water, but it was lovely and bright up aloft and the stars were out.

This time Baker did not see a submarine; instead he heard the ominous sound of an airship's propellers. Luckily, because of the fog, the Zeppelin could not see the trawler. But it was dropping bombs all around them and some exploded before they hit the water:

> Being on deck I got the full force of the fumes, while the rest of the crew, being below, were lucky enough to escape. Some of the other trawlers cut their gear and went away for home, and we got into the land as quickly as we could – thankful that there was just enough wind for that. By the time the fog had lifted and the weather was clear – we owed our wonderful preservation to being hidden. It isn't often you can speak well of a North Sea fog. After getting home I was lying on the couch for nine days, with one eye quite closed. The poison gas had turned me yellow as saffron, and I suffered cruelly. All the time, of course, I hadn't a penny coming in, and I could get no help from any fund; but at last the Deep Sea Mission set me up, and with a heavy heart I went to sea again, joining the *Glory*, this time as a third hand. I fully expected that something would happen again, and I was on the rack all the time; but, you see, she's safely home again, after a week's trip.

On January 1 1917 a Swedish steam ship, the *Carrie*, was attacked by a German submarine around twenty miles to the south of Wolf Rock Lighthouse, some four miles southwest of Land's End. The steam ship was on a voyage from Glasgow to Nantes carrying munitions. A German submarine ordered the crew into their boats but then the submarine disappeared. Shortly afterwards two armed trawlers, *Fusilier* and *Kinaldie*, arrived and picked up the crewmembers. The crew refused to get back on board the steam ship, so she was towed into Falmouth. There was considerable debate as to what was to happen to her and whether or not any salvage was due. After much legal wrangling each of the two sets of officers and crew of the trawlers was awarded £375.

It was not always possible to save vessels that were attacked by German submarines. In fact on the night of 3 August 1916 eight small motor herring drifters had been destroyed off the northeast coast by a single German submarine. The Germans had got into the habit of looting as much as they possibly could from their victims. Everything was plundered, including metal fittings and food.

Walter Wood described the events that took place on the night of 3 August 1916; this time the victim was the *Jane Stewart*. The skipper was David Stewart, operating out of Great Yarmouth:

> The night was exceptionally calm, it was spoken of as one of the calmest nights that the fishermen had ever known at sea. Things on board the *Jane Stewart* went well until midnight, then the lookout man called the skipper, and said he had heard an explosion in the distance and suspected that a submarine was at work. The sinister warning was not neglected for an instant. The sounds, it was judged, came from the *Volunteer*, a Musselburgh boat, with an English crew, which was about half a mile away. There was a second explosion and the lights of the *Volunteer* disappeared, and it was obvious that the vessel had been destroyed by a torpedo.

All of the other vessels in the area cut their nets and headed for home but before the *Jane Stewart* could follow a submarine made straight for her on a collision course. Miraculously she stopped with her bow touching the trawler. It was immediately obvious that the Germans intended to plunder the ship:

> The oldest member of the crew, a man named Hastie, of Cockenzie, was in his bunk when the Germans boarded the little drifter to destroy her. Hastie had an unusual stock of clothing on board, to see him through the ten weeks' fishing season, of which the vessel had completed about half. The

garments were a treasured property, and all the more valued because they included a Sunday suit. Hastie had not time enough to put on his boots; but determined not to part lightly from his belongings he went to the forecastle and there found the gallant German officer in the forecastle, placing a bomb.

Hastie was ordered off the boat but ignored the order. All of the time, the crew of the *James Stewart* were covered by German sailors holding revolvers. All of the crew barring Hastie were ushered below decks on the submarine. Hastie had stubbornly remained, hoping to retrieve his clothing but eventually he was forced to jump onto the deck of the submarine. Once the submarine had finished patrolling the area, hunting for more prey, the crew of the *James Stewart* was put on board a small vessel and left to their own devices. Hastie and the other men had lost everything. During that night alone the single submarine had destroyed eleven fishing vessels.

Throughout the First World War it was almost impossible for vessels to leave a British port without encountering the perils of mines, submarines and German surface vessels. It was a primary function of the requisitioned fishing vessels to keep the sea lanes open. Inevitably those on shore in the fishing ports around the British coast would hear terrifying explosions at night. Sometimes these were mines that had been deliberately set off, although in many cases it was the ominous sound of a fishing vessel striking a mine and then disappearing with its full complement beneath the waters. The minesweepers worked close inshore and far out to sea in all weathers and conditions.

In peacetime the North Sea was virtually a continuous line of shipping. It was possible to count forty or fifty vessels at any one time plainly within sight. From the cliffs of Scarborough or Whitby, steamboats, tramps and colliers could be seen. The sea lane extended all the way from the Tyne to the Thames. Vessels were continually arriving and departing and even when the German submarines began operating unrestricted warfare the numbers of vessels working their way up and down the east coast of England increased.

Of equal importance were the lanes between England and France. Millions of men were ferried across the Channel and tens of thousands of injured were brought back home for surgery and convalescence. Dover was a vital port and the sweeping was largely performed by drifters and trawlers.

There were heavy losses in the Channel: in the bitter winter of 1916/17 the bodies of German sailors on board the destroyer *V69* had to be dug out of the ice with axes. On 25 January 1917 the Ramsgate smack *Ethe* and the trawlers *Lucy, Gladys* and *Star of the Sea* were all lost. When the crews were finally recovered the men had been in open boats for seventeen hours. Survivors of incidents such as these had lost virtually everything yet they were quick to find fresh vessels and venture out to sea once again.

All of this gallantry and self-sacrifice seems to have gone largely unnoticed until the third year of the war. Up until that point over 300 Victoria Crosses had been awarded, primarily to the British army, but some to the Royal Navy. Some five Victoria Crosses went to the Royal Naval Reserve, of which the trawler section was a part. The first Victoria Cross was awarded to Skipper Joseph Watt, RNR, who had joined the naval service on 11 January 1915. In the *London Gazette* dated 20 August 1917 the exploits that won him the Victoria Cross were detailed:

> For most conspicuous gallantry when the allied drifter line in the straits of Otranto [the line that connects the Ionian Sea to the Adriatic Sea] was attacked by Austrian light cruisers on the morning of May 15 1917. When hailed by an Austrian cruiser at about 100 yards range and ordered to stop and abandon his drifter, the *Gowan Lea*, Skipper Watt ordered full speed ahead and called upon his crew to give three cheers and fight to the finish. The cruiser was then engaged, but after one round had been fired a shot from the enemy disabled the breech of the drifter's gun. The guns crew, however, stuck to the gun, endeavouring to make it work, being under heavy fire all the time. After the cruiser had passed on, Skipper Watt took the

Gowan Lea alongside the badly damaged drifter *Floandi* and assisted to remove the dead and wounded.

This brief description of the engagement only scratches the surface of what actually happened. Deckhand Frederick Hawley Lamb, RNR Trawler Section, had his leg shattered but continued to work the gun throughout the engagement. Lamb was awarded the Conspicuous Gallantry Medal. His leg was broken in two places yet the Fraserburgh man refused to give in.

This had not been the first dangerous engagement that Watt's crew had endured. In the previous December a shell had passed straight through the cabin of the vessel. The funnel had been blown off and several of the crew had been killed. The crew had lowered a boat and had put the ship's compass on board but then the boat had also been hit and sunk. Watt and the remainder of the crew still on board the *Gowan Lea* were unable to locate themselves as they now had no compass. Watt saw a patrol vessel heading towards him but believed it to be an enemy vessel and made off under full steam.

In this dangerous stretch of water alone there were other trawler section heroes. Skipper William Bruce had stayed on board the *Quarry Nowe*, a drifter, trying to save her until she finally blew up. Skipper Robert Stephen and Skipper William Farquhar respectively of the *Taits* and the *Admirable*, had also stayed on board under heavy fire until both of their vessels were finally sunk. Skipper Robert Cowe of the drifter *Coral Haven* engaged enemy vessels, firing four rounds until his ship was smashed to pieces. The skipper of the drifter *Floandi*, Dennis John Nichols, whose crew had been picked up by Watt, had 'remained at his post in the wheelhouse, steering his ship, and although wounded himself, assisted in removing the more severely wounded members of his crew.' In fact Nichols had been able to plug the holes in the drifter and managed to get all the way back to port.

In the same area of operations Engineman Charles Mobbs, RNR, had remained at his post after the main steam pipe had been shot away. He managed to put out the fires and then clambered aboard a small boat and began plugging holes in the side of the vessel, allowing her to reach port. Second Hand John Turner, RNR, was awarded the Victoria Cross when his vessel came under fire. The enemy was firing at the wireless telegraphy apparatus, so he climbed aloft to strike the topmast, irrespective of the fact that shells were passing between the mast and the funnel. Joseph Hendry, RNR, was awarded the Conspicuous Gallantry Medal after he refused to leave his sinking vessel when the rest of the crew had abandoned her and been taken prisoner. Eventually Hendry's drifter sank and after spending several hours in the water he was picked up by another drifter.

When the drifter on which Engineman Walter Watt was serving was captured by an Austrian cruiser Watt had no desire to become a prisoner of war. He jumped overboard from the enemy ship but was recaptured. He jumped overboard again and remained in the water for over an hour until he was saved by another drifter.

Skipper Watt, who had won the VC, was a typically modest man. He had become incredibly famous and had been decorated by the French, Serbian and Italian governments. When he returned to Fraserburgh he was to be given the welcome of a hero. But he arrived on the last train on a dark November night; no one knew what he looked like and he managed to get home to be reunited with his wife without fanfare. He was awarded the Victoria Cross by the king on 6 April 1918.

The trawlers were also at work off the Turkish coast, in the Dardanelles. Skipper Woodgate of the *Koorah* described the type of work there:

When we were up in the Dardanelles, there was what we call three groups – 1, 2 and 3 – and each group had to go up, one at a time. The vessel I was in belonged to the second group. The night we were going to make the final dash in the Dardanelles, up to the Narrows, we went, no lights up, everything covered in. They let us get right up to the Narrows, and as we turned round to take our sweeps up, one of our number was blown up. Then they peppered us from each side, from one and a half to two miles. We heard cries for help. I said, 'we shall have to do the best we can to go back and pick up'. There was no waiting, no saying who shall go? As soon as I called for volunteers, three jumped in. I kept the vessel as close as I could to shelter them. I did not think any would come back alive, but no one was hit, and I said, 'now we'll get the boat in'. Just as we got the boat nicely clear of the water, along came a shot and knocked it in splinters. I shouted, 'all hands keep under cover as much as you can!' and I got on the bridge and we went full steam ahead. I could not tell you what it was like, with floating and sunken mines and shots everywhere. We got knocked about, the mast almost gone, rigging gone, and she was riddled right along the starboard side. One of the hands we picked up had his left arm smashed with shrapnel.

In fact the trawlers were very much in evidence in the Dardanelles and the Gallipoli landings. The first landings north of Gaba Tepe had a squadron that included fifteen trawlers and the landings on the extreme south of the Gallipoli Peninsular utilised fourteen trawlers.

One last mention needs to be made of the *Floandi*, which we recall was involved in operations in the Adriatic. The rear admiral commanding the naval forces forwarded the wireless telegraph log to the Admiralty, along with the following note:

This log was found in this condition in the wireless operating cabin of HM drifter *Floandi* after an attack on the drifter line by three Austrian cruisers in the Adriatic on May 15 1917. The wireless operator, Douglas Morris Harris AB RNVR, continued to send and receive messages, although the drifter was being riddled by shells, until he was killed by a piece of shrapnel whilst writing in the log. The piece of shell perforated the log, and the line made by his pencil when he was hit and collapsed can be seen on the page upon which he was writing. The operator was found dead in his chair, lying over the log.

To put this kind of gallantry into perspective a number of skippers were awarded silver or bronze medals by the king of Italy. Fishermen serving with the Royal Navy between 1 January and 31 December

1917 included eleven skippers being awarded the Distinguished Service Cross, forty-eight second hands, engineers and deckhands receiving the Distinguished Service Medal, and seventeen skippers and forty-four other ranks mentioned in despatches. Two skippers were given the Distinguished Service Cross after actions with enemy submarines, one deckhand the Distinguished Service Medal and five skippers were mentioned in despatches. All of these men were members of the Royal Naval Reserve.

During the First World War the fleet had built up from a tiny group of twelve vessels to something approaching 3,300 by the end of the war. Some 60 per cent of Britain's fishermen served in the Royal Naval Reserve. Lloyd George, the then Prime Minister, paid tribute in the House of Commons in late 1917, illustrating the type of courage that the trawlers and their crews had exhibited. Lloyd George mentioned one trawler, armed with an antiquated 3-pdr, that had been attacked by a German submarine. The skipper refused to haul down the flag even after he had both of his legs shot off and the bulk of his crew either killed or wounded. He shouted a last instruction 'throw the confidential books overboard and throw me after them.' The skipper went down with his trawler.

The prime minister paid tribute to the men, recognising that they were not trained for war, but were fishermen. He also recognised that they had rendered great service to their country. The First Lord of the Admiralty, Sir Eric Geddes, in his maiden speech on November 1 1917, said:

> I would wish to mention the work of the minesweepers and minelayers and of their gallant crews, largely recruited from our hardy fishermen. Both these duties may be offensive as well as defensive. Is it not an offensive measure to lay mines at night in the tortuous channels of the enemy minefields, with the possibility of attack from his patrol craft or discovery and bombardment from his land guns? Similarly, is it not an offensive measure for the minesweeper to go into the enemy minefields, which are protected, to sweep a passage, as they have done, to enable their comrades of the submarine or light service craft to follow in the next night?

25

Geddes went on to put the activities of the auxiliary naval services into perspective. He noted that in a recent month Royal Navy battleships, cruisers and destroyers operating in home waters had covered over a million nautical miles. Over the same period vessels of the auxiliary forces had covered six million.

Watt was not the only skipper to win the VC during the First World War. Skipper Thomas Crisp, RNR, was posthumously awarded the Victoria Cross on the same day that his son, Second Hand Thomas William Crisp, RNR, was awarded the Distinguished Service Medal. The Crisps were Lowestoft men and on board the smack *Nelson*. The skipper was below, packing fish. When he came up one of the deckhands pointed at an object in the distance. The skipper, looking through his binoculars recognised it as a submarine. Almost immediately they came under shell fire. The fourth shell went straight through the port bow, just below the water line. The seventh shell struck the skipper; it passed through him, through the deck and out through the side of the ship. The skipper's son took charge and manned the gun, whilst giving orders to send off an urgent message for assistance. It is now clear that this is the incident that was referred to in the House of Commons, as the skipper's last words were to abandon ship and throw the books overboard. The skipper's son realised that his father was too badly injured to be moved and reluctantly he was left on deck whilst the others took to a small boat. A quarter of an hour later the *Nelson* sank below the waves. Walter Wood takes up the rest of the story:

> By this time it was nearly dusk. Throughout the night the crew of the boat pulled. Towards morning they were blown out of their course by a freshening wind; but all that day they continued pulling, having hoisted a pair of trousers and a large piece of oilskin fastened to two oars to attract attention. Once a vessel was seen and once a group of minesweepers, but they passed out of sight. The weather became finer at night, and this was something to the advantage of the weary men who continued toiling at the oars. During that second night the boat's crew went on pulling until daybreak, and at half past ten

o'clock in the morning they found a buoy and made fast to it. By afternoon they were sighted and rescued.

By the time the armistice was signed in November 1918 the Royal Naval Reserve Trawler Section, which had begun as a force of just 1,200 men, had expanded to 39,000, and they were manning 700 vessels, the majority of which were deep-sea trawlers and drifters. Around 200 of these had been sunk during the war, many of which had been lost in the east coast waters. During the war the Germans had laid 43,636 mines; more than half of them had been sewn around Britain's coast. Around seventy mines a month during 1917 had been laid in the Dover area alone. Clearing them was a dangerous and tiring task for the minesweepers. In fact in six months one flotilla of minesweepers had swept a distance equivalent to steaming around the world three times.

Even after the ceasefire the war was not over for the trawler men. They spent the next twelve months clearing what remained of the German minefields, along with dealing with the so-called northern barrage. This was a vast belt of 17,000 allied mines that had been laid between the Orkneys and the Norwegian coast, extending for 230 miles.

By the end of 1919 the bulk of the trawlers were not only back at their home ports, but had also been returned to their original owners. It was at this point that the Royal Naval Reserve Trawler Section was reconstituted. It was renamed as the Royal Naval Reserve Patrol Service. Understandably the number of men and vessels dwindled in the post-war years. They were based around HMS *Boscawen* at Portland and HMS *Osprey*, a training establishment.

It had been decided that the fishing industry would be needed again in the event of another world war. The men would now be trained in anti-submarine warfare and dealing with torpedoes and mines. The director of torpedoes and mining wanted 400 trawlers, with 454 skippers and 3,733 ratings. As it was, the approved figure was settled at around 300 vessels, but by the time the Second World War broke out they were woefully under strength.

CHAPTER TWO

HMS *Europa*

Situated barely a kilometre to the northwest of Lowestoft Ness, the most easterly point of Britain, is the Sparrow's Nest. Little did the Suffolk fishing port and holiday resort realise that it was about to become the centre of frenzied activity and would greet literally thousands of men, becoming one of the strange and peculiarly British HMS 'land-based ships' of the Royal Navy.

The Sparrow's Nest, at the time, as indeed it is today, was a walled municipal garden. It had been the private gardens of a grand house; it had green lawns, bowling greens, flowerbeds and a lily pond. It was a favourite place for holidaymakers, where they could enjoy the weak summer sun whilst listening to music from the bandstand and relax in Britain's most easterly town.

The Sparrow's Nest, Lowestoft would become the Royal Naval Patrol Service's central depot and was requisitioned on 23 August 1939. Staff began arriving the following day. Telegrams had been sent off to reservists up and down the country. Trawler men that were already in port were the first to arrive; they were already members of the Royal Naval Reserve.

One of the first was William Thorpe, whose Lowestoft trawler had just docked. Thorpe's experience was no different from the thousands of men that would follow him over the next few years. The first men were housed in the concert hall after the seats had been taken out. Beds were stowed and blankets were begged, stolen or borrowed. That first night for Thorpe, 24 August, went on until midnight; such was the amount of work that needed to be done. More men began arriving steadily.

It was an incredible feat of organisation and the first draft of men were sent out by 27 August. Everywhere across the North Sea steam trawlers were being told to come home. On 29 August a general mobilisation was called across Britain. But by then the inhabitants of Lowestoft could see that the Sparrow's Nest sported a new flag: the white ensign. Lowestoft railway station was packed with Royal Navy Reserve men, each train was full to capacity, and the harbour was crammed with trawlers and drifters from every corner of the British Isles. From even the most remote fishing grounds experienced sailors were converging on Lowestoft.

It is important to make the distinction from the outset that the men passing through the Sparrow's Nest were somewhat different from those of the Royal Naval Reserve. The RNR was the Royal Navy's first professional reserve after its own fleet reserve. The Royal Naval Reserve was actually split up into general servicemen and the patrol service itself. The general servicemen would be expected to congregate either at Portsmouth, Chatham or Devonport; hence there was a need for a separate depot to handle the patrol servicemen. These men were exclusively from the fishing industry. They would not serve on warships as such and neither were they trained to operate on them.

In order to control and organise this vast pool of experienced men a depot needed to be set up to pay them, supply them, keep records, deal with casualties and replacements and countless other administrative duties. Lowestoft was chosen as it was relatively central and well served with a railway service. Representatives belonging to the Admiralty Surveyor of Lands had visited Lowestoft and had decided to requisition the Sparrow's Nest, almost on the seashore. The property had originally belonged to the Marchioness of Salisbury and in 1939 had a dilapidated manor house, some conservatories, a concert hall and an open-air stage or bandstand. It was all set in around seven acres of land. It was initially given the name HMS *Pembroke X* and it had been used to mobilise men in

1938, during the Munich crisis. The initial staff and senior officers of the new base were all relatively local, and Captain Basil H Piercy, a retired naval officer, was selected as commander.

Across the country, in shipyards, harbours and ports, deep-sea fishing trawlers were being converted into miniature warships. The Trade Division of the Admiralty had already put the process in motion, having earmarked suitable vessels and yards that would handle the work. Under the terms of the Reserves and Auxiliary Forces Act around 15,000 naval reservists were liable to call up. The general servicemen had begun to receive their call up orders in June 1939. These men were to man the destroyers and cruisers of the Reserve Fleet. Vice Admiral Sir Max Horton, the Flag Officer of the Reserve Fleet, was able to report by early August that his fleet was fully manned. Captain Piercy and other selected staff officers had received a coded telegram on 23 August, telling them to make for the Sparrow's Nest at Lowestoft.

So it was that by the time the general mobilisation was called an enormous number of naval reservists were already *en route*. The Sparrow's Nest now had Royal Navy sentries, with fixed bayonets, guarding its gates. The Royal Naval Reserve Patrol Service was already ahead of the game when the Germans invaded Poland in the early morning of 1 September 1939 and war now seemed inevitable.

As their wartime record would reveal, the British trawlers were as hardy and irrepressible as their crews. British fishing trawlers were sturdy vessels, ranging from around 115ft to 170ft in length. They had a beam of between 22 and 28ft and could weigh anything from between 275 to 590 tons. The ships were coal burners, with an average speed of between 7 and 10 knots. Most of them had short forecastles, one or two masts and a single funnel. Their trawls were operated by powerful steam winches and they had large fish holds. There was very little room for the crew and on many of the vessels this space appeared to be something of an afterthought. The vast majority of the space inside a trawler was designed to hold refrigerated fish.

For generations the fishing industry had relied on men capable and willing to withstand the worst possible conditions at sea, to live in cramped and claustrophobic cabins below deck and to brave the worst that the sea and the elements could throw at them. When the vessels returned to their home port they would become a hive of activity of a different kind, with riggers, joiners, shipwrights, engineers and others carrying out vital maintenance and repair work. Periodically the vessels would be brought into dry dock, which would give the repairmen an opportunity to overhaul the vessel and refit it.

It was another whole set of headaches to turn these trawlers into miniature warships. In many cases the hulls and the decks had to be strengthened in order to hold the gun, often a 12-pdr or a 4-inch weapon. Others were given a pair of 0.5in machine guns, or maybe a Lewis or Hotchkiss gun to fend off enemy aircraft, while others might get a Bofors. Vessels that were designed for an anti-submarine role had to be given asdic gear and rails and depth charge throwers. The normal conversion was to strip out the trawl winch from the well deck and to transform the fish hold into the mess deck. Ammunition was stored beneath the mess deck and an all-purpose cabin was set up for the officers below the wheelhouse. A coal fired galley was put into the after deck house and some of the vessels might even have their own refrigerator.

On small vessels such as these even the most simple of tasks was a struggle. Trawlers rode the waves rather cut through them as larger ships did. Food had to be cooked in heaving conditions, eating was difficult, shaving a major hazard and there was little room for exercise. Nonetheless the men would be expected to spend weeks out to sea.

They were arriving now, converging on the Sparrow's Nest from points stretching from the Isle of Man to the Hebrides, from Brixham and Falmouth, from around the Scottish coast and from Milford Haven.

Britain, in its infinite variety of customs, dialects and traditions was forming the Royal Naval Patrol Service. Each of the men had to be processed, have a medical, be fed, be given a month's advance pay, have equipment distributed, have kit checked, bedding and gas masks issued and then be allocated to trawlers that were being feverishly prepared for active duty. The process went surprisingly smoothly given the number of men and the potential complications. In the vast majority of cases skippers and their crews were formed within hours and as soon as they could be organised they were entrained for their destination port to take possession of their unseen vessel. In fact by 3 September 1939 over 100 vessels were already converted and manned.

As in the First World War, despite the fact that the trawlers had defensive weapons, they would stand little chance against a determined German submarine or surface vessel. They were also relatively easy prey for the Luftwaffe and would be easily destroyed by German E-boats. Nonetheless, the men began their war willingly and without question. They were used to working up to seventy hours on deck without sleep. They could carry out the majority of their tasks without having to think. The men were used to taking orders from their skippers without question, and whilst the fishermen were tough the skippers were even more so, and stubborn too. Onboard discipline was maintained by the mates, perfectly willing to come to blows with the deckhands if necessary.

The majority of the men passing through the Sparrow's Nest would find themselves trawling not for fish but for mines. Others would face an equally demanding role hunting for submarines in the English Channel and in the North Sea. Others would guard the waters around Iceland and the Orkneys.

One such requisitioned trawler was *Northern Rover*. Paradoxically she was of German construction, having been built at Bremerhaven and launched in 1936 as part of the German reparation programme. She had been requisitioned in August 1939 and converted into an armed boarding vessel (ABV). She was based at Kirkwall and employed on contraband patrol. She was posted as being overdue on 5 November 1939, having disappeared between Iceland and the Faroe Islands. It was later confirmed, after the war, that she had been sunk by *U-59*.

The venerable, Mersey class Royal Navy trawler, *James McDonald*, which had been built in 1919 at Selby, was sunk by gunfire from a U-boat north of the Hebrides on 23 December 1939. The vessel had been renamed *Grand Fleet* and later *Barbara Robertson*. She was a minesweeper and it is probable that she was the second trawler to be lost in the war.

When the war broke out in September 1939 the Germans were believed to have around 100 contact mines. But they also had an undisclosed number of magnetic mines. The first of these was recovered by the British in the Thames Estuary in November 1939. It was stripped down in order to discover how best to deal with it. In the meantime, however, merchant ships were falling victim to this new peril. The only Royal Navy cruiser minelayer, HMS *Adventure*, was destroyed by one, as was the destroyer HMS *Blanche*. In the Thames Estuary alone nine merchant ships were sunk in a matter of days. The minesweeping trawler *Mastiff* was destroyed by a magnetic mine, the destroyer HMS *Gypsy* was badly damaged, and neutral merchant ships, including the Dutch *Spaarndam* and the Japanese *Terukini Maru*, were also victims.

From the outset the Royal Naval Patrol Service had powerful allies, and Winston Churchill as First Lord of the Admiralty recognised the important role that trawlers would have to play in helping sweep the Thames Estuary:

> We have deemed it necessary to call upon a large number of trawlers to assist in the dredging of our harbours. The effect of these serious dangers was sufficient to bring forward an overwhelming response from fishermen and trawler crews who were called upon to give their country assistance for, I imagine, only a short time. The offices at some of the fishing ports which remained open during the night were crowded and thronged out, and in a very short time the full complement was made up by these fisher folk eager to serve their country in a manner which they felt would be really effective.

In fact many of the newly requisitioned wooden-hulled minesweepers and their crews were set to work on the dangerous task of towing a magnetised iron bar at the end of a line to attract the mines. So swiftly were the men deployed to deal with this threat that there was no time to put them into uniform. The skippers of each of the vessels were given an Admiralty warrant, effectively making them a temporary skipper in the Royal Naval Reserve. All the crewmen wore were armbands to denote that they were in the Royal Naval Reserve. This was yet another potential hazard, as the Germans had made it perfectly clear that civilians involved in direct war work would be shot on sight. Churchill was livid that nothing had been done beyond providing a woven arm badge and he was also concerned about the men working on anti-submarine duties.

Thus began the rapid quest to design a badge for the patrol service. The artist and medal designer Kruger Gray designed a shield showing a sinking shark impaled on a Marlin spike. In the background was a fishing net holding two German mines. Around this was a rope with a nautical knot known as the fisherman's bend. At the top was a naval crown and below a scroll with M/S–A/S, which stood for minesweeping anti-submarine. The badge was made of silver and the size of an old shilling. It had a pin at the back. The originals were struck by the Royal Mint and sent to the Board of the Admiralty and the king for approval.

Men in the patrol service were eligible for the badge after they had served for six months, or they would receive one immediately for meritorious conduct. As to the question of a uniform, the Royal Naval Reserve men already had theirs, but the others would have to wait. There was far too much work to be done, as upwards of a third of the Luftwaffe was engaged in dropping mines around the British coast.

Whilst the trawler minesweepers were required to clear the shipping lanes for the merchantmen it was the role of the anti-submarine trawlers, supported by whatever vessels could be spared from the regular fleet, to protect the convoys. The trawlers themselves, either as escorts or minesweepers, were under flag and had naval officers in charge. Men from the Royal Naval Reserve, the Royal Navy or the Royal Naval Volunteer Reserve became group commanders. Some of the commanding officers were Royal Naval Reserve skippers. Each of the groups was based at a particular port and comprised between four and six vessels. The minesweepers were charged with keeping the channels in their immediate area clear. The escorts would be responsible for protecting merchantmen along their particular part of the sea lane.

Further north, between the Faroe Islands and Iceland, were other groups. These were either of anti-submarine trawlers or armed boarding vessels. Although the vessels may have been comparatively safe close to the British coast this was not the case further out to sea, particularly in the North Sea, where Luftwaffe Heinkel bombers, operating in pairs, would attack even the smallest of the trawlers, sensing an easy target. Although the trawlers always fought back as best they could they often lacked the armament, the speed and manoeuvrability to effectively defend themselves.

Not all of the men reporting to HMS *Europa* (as HMS *Pembroke X* was renamed) were fishermen. Some of the Royal Naval Reserve fishermen found themselves grouped with individuals who had never been to sea in their lives. Undoubtedly the skippers, coxswains, chief engineers and other men were hardened fishermen. But often there would be raw men straight out of training from the Royal Navy Volunteer Reserve.

The last of the fourteen trawlers and drifters to be lost in 1939 was *Loch Doon*, which went down on Christmas Day, with the loss of fifteen men. She had struck a mine while minesweeping off Blyth. She was a Hull based trawler that had been built at Southbank on Tees and launched in 1937. She had been requisitioned in August 1939 and converted to anti-submarine duties.

One of the smallest vessels to have been lost in 1939 was the *Ray of Hope*, which had been mined in the Thames Estuary on 12 October 1939. She was just 98 tons but her loss, of course, was hugely overshadowed by that two days later of the battleship HMS *Royal Oak*, at over 29,000 tons, torpedoed by a U-boat at Scapa Flow.

The *Ray of Hope* was part of a small and select group of vessels. Skipper Sidney White and five other Royal Naval Reserve skippers had been ordered to report to Commander Charles Hammond, DSC RN, in a ramshackle building on the dockside at Lowestoft. Beforehand White and the other skippers had been told that they could pick their own crew of twelve men and that their mission was to be a secret one. When they turned up to see Hammond they were shown six tiny wooden herring drifters. White took command of *Silver Dawn*, and the other five drifters were the *Ray of Hope, Jacketa, Lord Cavan, Formidable* and *Fisher Boy*. They were to become the Mine Recovery Flotilla and were under direct orders from the Royal Navy's research establishment at Portsmouth, known as HMS *Vernon*. Each of the tiny drifters was fitted with a small trawl and the crew were given a handful of rifles. Their job was to bring in intact magnetic mines so that they could be dismantled and examined. They were to be based at Margate, although they were supposed to go anywhere that it had been reported that magnetic mines had been laid.

The Mine Recovery Flotilla became known as *Vernon*'s Private Navy. Undoubtedly they were carrying out the most hazardous fishing devised. In late November they recovered two mines on mudflats in the Thames Estuary and presented them to HMS *Vernon*. By December 1939 they were operating out of Ramsgate. White, along with the skipper of the *Ray of Hope*, Walter Hayes, volunteered to try and clear a channel five miles to the east of the main convoy route. They began sweeping in an area where it was reported that parachute mines had been dropped. The *Ray of Hope* ran out of luck; the sweep stuck to the ocean floor and Hayes heaved on the winch to draw his tiny vessel backwards, but she passed over a magnetic mine. The mine was triggered by the magnetic field from the boat's fittings and engine. Hayes was blown from his bridge and only he and his second hand, John Bird, survived.

Commander Hammond, following the loss of the *Ray of Hope*, called a meeting in Ramsgate harbour and offered the men of the flotilla a way out, realising just how dangerous their role was proving to be. He gave each man the option of returning to Lowestoft for reassignment. Six men left and their places were quickly taken by new volunteers.

In the meantime, the Naval Research Section was working on the thorny problem of the magnetic mine. An engineer officer in Grimsby came up with the idea that ships should reduce or control their own magnetic field. This was known as 'degaussing'. The first ships to be fitted with their own magnetic field had to have some three miles of copper wire around their scuppers. However this proved to be rather too delicate, and ultimately, a single wire, powered by the ship's dynamo, was put in a casing around the outside of the ship. Hammond and the skippers had also come up with a new way of sweeping that would be less hazardous. A pair of drifters would now tow one trawl between them. If something had been picked up one of the vessels would pass their end of the trawl over to the other. They would then slip both ends of the trawl attached to a wire with a buoy. A dinghy party would then haul up the trawl and examine what had been found.

The trawler *Calvi* was built at Beverley and launched in 1930. She was originally known as *Galleon* but had been renamed in 1938. She was requisitioned in September 1939 and converted to a minesweeper. She was operating out of Dover in the minesweeping role and primarily involved in operations in the English Channel. She was hard at work around noon on 9 January 1940, just off the North Foreland. It was routine work for her until she saw a large convoy slowly pass her by. All of a sudden there was a massive explosion. The 10,000-ton liner *Dunbar Castle* had triggered a magnetic mine and it went up directly under her bridge. She sank in moments, very close to the North Goodwin Lightship. In fact her mast would be clearly visible throughout the whole of the war. The *Calvi* was one of the many vessels that rushed to aid the stricken ship. There were two lifeboats with seventy-three people on board, including firemen, two nuns, and women and children. The body of the liner's captain was also on board, as well as a man in a severe state of shock, who refused to move and died where he lay. The *Calvi* took on as many people as possible.

The trawler herself would not see another January, as she too was lost off Dunkirk on 29 May 1940, during Operation Dynamo, when she was targeted by German aircraft.

There was an incredible incident on the South Goodwin Sands in early January 1940, which would win the skippers of the trawlers *Cayton Wyke* and *Saon* Distinguished Service Crosses. The two trawlers were working as part of the Dover Patrol. There was a known gap in the Goodwin Sands and a vessel could get through it if there were a good tide. It was protected by an electric loop cable. It was a dark night and the coastguards alerted the trawlers that something had crossed the loop. Together with a small destroyer the two trawlers steamed up and down the break in the sands, dropping over eighty depth charges. Up came a U-boat. Skipper William Mullender, commanding the *Saon*, explained:

> We went in and saw the U-boat stuck fast on the sands, but we could not approach it because of the strong gales. A cable ship came out and joined us as we waited for the weather to ease before trying to save the U-boat, for it would have been a great prize captured intact, the first of the war. But as we watched and waited, the sands slowly swallowed the U-boat up, and its crew.

Meanwhile, back in Lowestoft, the landladies of boarding houses were being desperately called back to the area. The Royal Navy had declared the port depot a restricted area and now the landladies were needed again to provide billets for the ever-growing numbers of men congregating around the Sparrow's Nest. Hundreds of men moved through Lowestoft, being fed in boarding houses. The men were ordered to walk along the seafront to prevent congestion on the high street.

The increasing numbers of men were the new 'hostilities only' groups, who were only liable to serve for the duration of the war. But as Lowestoft was pretty much a front line town many of them wondered, as the Luftwaffe swept above the port, whether they would even get to sea before they were killed or injured. Many of the men had in fact volunteered, for example, naval trainees from Skegness were so desperate for action that they opted to join the Royal Naval Patrol Service. Some may have transferred to escape the appalling conditions there. The campsite, known as HMS *Royal Arthur*, a Butlin's holiday camp, was freezing cold and several ratings actually died there.

One of the men that had made the trip from Skegness to Lowestoft was Seaman Robert Muir. He was told to report to Dover to join the *Nautilus*. She was a small fishing drifter and her armament was a Lewis gun and two rifles. Her job was to protect paddle sweepers and her crew would use their limited armament to shoot at mines. They were also involved in helping to deal with magnetic mines. The *Nautilus* was chosen for a very secret mission, as Muir explained:

> We had been selected to put the block ships into Zeebrugge. Our job would be to lay the DANS after the sweepers up to the mole, after which we were to carry on to the mole, go alongside and find out if the lock keeper was a fifth columnist. If he was, we were to shoot him and give the block ships the go ahead.

As it was, the *Nautilus* was not up to making the journey. On one occasion they got about twenty miles out but were recalled. On their third attempt the Navy decided she was too slow. Muir wondered for years whatever happened to the lock keeper.

A civilian coming into the service had to quickly adapt to the new way of life and muck in with a crew of ex-fishermen. One such individual was telegraphist Thomas Burn. On the trawler he was attached to, the cook sold the carpet out of the skipper's cabin to buy beer. He even sold his hammock. There were other problems too:

> The crew had no idea of naval discipline. In harbour we were supposed to keep deck watches in case of prowlers, but they never did – I think I was the only one to stick to the rules. Luckily I was deck watchman late one night when two of the crew fell over the side as they were coming aboard drunk; I

called the rest of the lads and we fished them out, or they'd have been gonners.

In the early months the use of depth charges often meant more danger to the trawler and crew than to a submarine lurking beneath the waves. There were instances when depth charges were dropped and blew half the stern off the trawler. Some of the skippers had no clue how to even come alongside a jetty. One of the trawlers did £9,000 worth of damage at Harwich and after that many of them were ordered to tie up to buoys midstream. Many of the older trawlers were not even watertight; it was not uncommon for there to be six or more inches of water lying around at the bottom of the ship, and when the ship rolled the 'deep end' could be as much as three feet. Lavatories did not work so the crews often resorted to having their ablutions over the side.

The tough work dealing with the mines continued all around the coast of Britain. A prime example was that carried out by former Hull fishing vessels operating to the northeast of Aberdeen. Amongst the group working in February 1940 was the *Thomas Altoft*, commanded by Skipper Thomas Lowery, the *OHM* commanded by Skipper Edmund Chilton, the *Robert Bowen* (Milford Haven) with Lieutenant-Commander E King and with Skipper Lieutenant John Clark in command, and Aberdeen's *Fort Royal*, commanded by Chief Skipper William Craig. The four trawlers were sweeping in an H formation with lookouts, Lewis guns at the ready and their 12-pdrs ready to be fired in an alarm. It was a few minutes before noon and the cooks were busy preparing the midday meal when suddenly two Heinkel 111s appeared overhead. The men manned the guns as the aircraft came in at barely 500m height. The first target was the *Fort Royal*. The first bomb narrowly missed the trawler, but the second bomb in the stick hit *Robert Bowen*. In a matter of seconds the tiny vessel broke in half and sank, taking her entire crew with her. The Heinkels peeled away under fire and then the German pilots came in for a second attack, again aiming at the *Fort Royal*. This time they hit her, causing extensive damage, and within three minutes she was gone. The survivors managed to get onto a raft. There were just two trawlers left and the next German attack was different. One of them made for the *OHM* and the other the *Thomas Altoft*. As the Germans closed they passed through a curtain of fire. One bomb exploded alongside the *Thomas Altoft*, and five others fell near the *OHM*. This was the last attack and the Germans now headed away and out of sight. By the time the two remaining trawlers returned to Aberdeen their narrow escape was plain to see. Their hulls were dented, the wireless transmitters wrecked and they would serve no longer with the Royal Naval Patrol Service. Four officers and eighteen other ratings had died in the space of just a few minutes.

A similar fate awaited the trawlers *Ayreshire* and *Fifeshire*. They were now part of the 11th Anti-Submarine Fighting Force based at Rosyth. They had not yet even reported to base. It was a cold day with low cloud and they were steaming at around 8 knots half a mile apart. Without any warning the *Fifeshire* shuddered after three explosions. In seconds she was gone. Sub-Lieutenant Dixon then saw two Heinkels heading for him on the *Ayreshire*. They lined up as the *Ayreshire* began taking evasive manoeuvres. The first stick of bombs fell into the sea barely 10m away and the Heinkels tried on four more occasions to destroy the vessel, riddling the bridge, wheelhouse, deck, hull, lifeboat and wireless cabin with bullets and cannon shells. Dixon continued to zigzag the *Ayreshire*. Inside, hatch doors had been blown off and bolts were loosened. The crew had a solitary Lewis gun to fend off the German aircraft. Frustrated, the Heinkels circled and then made off to the east. The only man to survive from the *Fifeshire* was Seaman Albert Blowers.

Another miraculous survivor of such an incident was the 300-ton *Solon*, who was sweeping a channel off the Norfolk coast, near Great Yarmouth in early February 1940. She had a 12-pdr gun, a Lewis gun and minesweeping gear. Her commander, Lieutenant-Commander Gillett, was a retired Royal Navy officer. She usually operated with three other minesweepers and was normally based at Sheerness. There was poor visibility that day but she was spotted by two Heinkels. In moments the trawler's crew manned the 12-pdr and the Lewis gun and began firing at the raiders. The Heinkels hurtled in at around 80m. Explosive bullets hit the Lewis gunner and Gillett was also hit. The Heinkels swept in again, dropping bombs and machine-gunning; this time shattering the leg of the 12-pdr's gunlayer. The rest of the crew kicked incendiaries overboard. By the time the attack was over the deck was littered with debris, bullets and unexploded incendiaries. Second Hand George Shaul, who had been the 12-pdr's gunlayer, was sat at the wheel, and Signalman Wells guided the ship home to Great Yarmouth. Incredibly the *Solon* had withstood an hour of attack. The Heinkels had dropped over twenty bombs and 2,000 incendiaries in a desperate attempt to sink her.

CHAPTER THREE

The Ships

In 1939 there were only a handful of drifters and trawlers ready to go out to sweep mines. Ultimately there would be a wide range of different variations of mine to tackle. They would have to deal with moored mines, magnetic ones, acoustic ones then magnetic-acoustic and moored magnetic-acoustics.

It took at least two years, from September 1939 to September 1941, for the Naval Building Programme to even catch up with the losses that were being suffered every day. It has been estimated that around 10 per cent of the entire minesweeping force, including the Royal Naval Patrol Service, was being lost each month.

Whilst the Royal Naval Patrol Service was in operation throughout the entire war it was the first eighteen months that were the most crucial. Without them, British ports would have been closed to the escorted convoys that were being brought across the Atlantic Ocean. As we will see in this chapter, the tiny trawlers and drifters were gradually superseded by specifically built motor minesweepers and by the British Yard Minesweepers (BYMS), many of which were built in the United States. Without the little ships, the Lilliput Fleet, Britain may well have been strangled into submission.

For the Royal Naval Patrol vessels and the front line Royal Navy warships the principal danger was the mine, closely followed of course by the U-boat. With the exception of a handful of instances, the German surface fleet was as impotent and useless as it had been in the First World War, arguably even more so. Mines became the principle seaborne weapon that the Germans chose to try to nullify the Royal Navy and to prevent supplies of food, armament and ultimately men from arriving in Britain, to not only prolong the war, but to ultimately bring the fight to the Germans.

Trawlers and drifters served in the Royal Navy during both world wars. In truth the Royal Navy was ill equipped to cope with minesweeping, convoy escorts, anti-submarine patrols, auxiliary patrols and a host of other tasks that would be demanded of it. Mine warfare was not an invention of the twentieth century. In fact mines of a sort had been used as early as the late 1500s. They were used extensively during the American War of Independence, they were used during the Napoleonic Wars and the mine as the Royal Naval Patrol Service and others would know it probably dates back to the Russo–Japanese War in 1904.

During the First World War the mine was basically a contact weapon. It was a cylindrical drum with explosives in it. It was attached to a length of wire cable and the cable would be adjusted to the required length. Then the mine and a heavy sinker would be dropped over the side, effectively anchoring the mine just below the surface of the water. In effect it just lay there until something hit it. It had contact points, or horns, around it and when one of these was touched the mine would explode. The Germans and the British used them in enormous numbers during the First World War. Primarily they were placed around anchorages, along convoy routes or in entrances to harbours. One thing that could be pretty much guaranteed is that they would not be in deep water.

Britain was fortunate, just after the turn of the nineteenth century, that the Channel Fleet was commanded by Lord Charles Beresford. He appreciated the importance of mines and in 1907 he had put forward a plan to use fishing trawlers to experiment with minesweeping methods and equipment. Somewhere along the line the connection had been made between the normal peacetime duties of a trawler or drifter hunting for fish and the fact that this technique could be adapted to hunt for mines.

Beresford went up to Grimsby to look for himself. There were literally thousands of trawlers and drifters in the fishing ports around Britain. The men were used to hard and dangerous work and the vessels, although small and dissimilar in so many ways to a Royal Navy vessel, were equally as sturdy and seaworthy. Trawlers routinely operated within the Arctic Circle and in equally inhospitable stretches of water. Beresford put his ideas to the Admiralty and they readily accepted his suggestions, buying two trawlers to be converted to minesweeping duties.

The first two vessels, *Algoma* and *Andes*, arrived at Portland in February 1908; others were to follow and the Admiralty was also looking at using some of their smaller warships for minesweeping duties. Once the initial trials had taken place and many of the problems dealt with, it was decided that trawlers were ideal for the task. Plans were put in motion to requisition trawlers and their crews in the event of wartime. The initial arrangement was to charter 80, but soon this was increased to 150.

We can also trace the history of the Royal Naval Patrol Service from about this time. Whilst it had been recognised that the trawlers were ideal for the job, the Admiralty also needed to be assured that they had sufficient trained men to man them. In 1910 the Trawler Section of the Royal Naval Reserve was created. The Admiralty looked for experienced officers and trawler men. The officers were given the rank of Skipper Royal Naval Reserve, which was broadly equivalent to the regular rank of Commissioned Warrant Officer. Similarly, the other ratings were graded as second hand, engineman, deckhand and trimmer; all broadly equivalent to regular service ranks.

The men would have to be between twenty-five and forty-five; they would have to agree to be in the Trawler Section for at least five years, with a maximum of twenty years for officers and twenty-five years for ratings. They would have to spend two weeks each year on minesweeper training.

So it was that the system was in place before the First World War. The Admiralty called up its trawlers and they began to arrive ready for conversion. The trawlers were organised into command areas, and within each command area groups were created, responsible for specific geographical areas. Initially 150 vessels were requisitioned and 1,200 reservists were called up. The vessels were quickly refitted and armed, but few could have predicted just how crucial anti-mine warfare would be in the First World War.

The very first time that the Royal Navy fired shots in anger during the First World War was at the German minelayer *Konigin Luise*, thirty miles off the east coast, near Aldeburgh. This was on 5 August 1914. Just the following day the Royal Navy lost its first vessel to a German mine when the scout cruiser HMS *Amphion* entered a freshly laid German minefield thirty-five miles off Aldeburgh. Nearly half of the ship's company was lost.

There would always be a problem in calling up for war duties enormous numbers of trawlers. Not only were there the obvious logistical issues, but there was also the fact that the peacetime occupation of the trawler was needed to contribute towards the feeding of Britain. Hence, as would be the pattern in both world wars, an enormous variety of different vessels was requisitioned – not just the trawler and the drifter. Some of these were simply not up to the job, while the sheer variety of vessels also made it incredibly difficult to ensure that repairs could even be attempted. In the First World War some of the requisitioned minesweeping trawlers actually became minelayers instead.

Towards the end of 1916 the Admiralty decided that in order to avoid stripping the British fishing fleet to dangerously low levels, they should begin to build their own trawlers. The first ten were being constructed as peacetime fishing vessels and were bought before they were even completed. A few adjustments were made to them and then the Admiralty began looking for vessels of comparable size that were being constructed around the country. So successful was the whole operation that by the time the armistice was signed in November 1918, the original 150 vessels and 1,200 men had swollen to 700 vessels and 39,000 men. Around 200 of the vessels had been lost, largely to mines, but also to surface attacks or to heavy weather.

As would be the case in the Second World War, the men had not taken to naval discipline particularly well, but they were used to the dangerous conditions and the seas. They were perfectly prepared to go out in even the worst weather to clear mines.

The First World War had had an enormous impact on the British fishing fleet. It had been estimated that the entire fleet in 1914 amounted to some 1,900 vessels. By 1917 the Admiralty had requisitioned 1,400 of them, although admittedly some for only short periods of time. They were also obliged to compensate for loss of earnings and, in the worst-case scenario, the loss of the vessel itself. In addition to the fishing fleet losses, other requisitioned civilian vessels were also being sunk in alarming numbers by German U-boats. So it was that in May 1917 all remaining trawler fishing vessels were requisitioned. This included the bulk of foreign trawlers in British ports. This group of trawlers was officially known as the Fishery Reserve and they were amongst the first to be demobilised when the war ended.

For many of the trawlers the armistice in 1918 meant very little. There were still thousands of mines to be removed and consequently many of the trawlers did not return to their owners until 1919 or 1920. After that the trawlers, of course, returned to their normal peacetime activities, but it had been proved that the men and the vessels were up to the job. They had not only been instrumental in winning the mine war, but they had also been vital as auxiliary patrol vessels and to add weight to escorts for coastal convoys. Others had been used for a variety of different purposes, such as ferries, moving stores, acting as barrage balloon vessels and other seaborne activities.

Post-war it was decided to reorganise and make the system even more efficient. The Royal Naval Reserve Trawler Section was renamed the Royal Naval Patrol Service and 300 vessels were earmarked for immediate call up.

Prior to the outbreak of the Second World War the Admiralty looked at the major trawler building yards. In 1935 the first Admiralty built trawler prototype, HMT *Basset* was launched.

Orders were also placed abroad, some in India, Canada and Burma. The Tree Class trawlers began to appear towards the end of 1939, the Dance Class and Shakespearean Class in 1940, along with the Isles Class. In 1941 a number of classes began to be launched including Hills, Fish, Round Table and Military. In India the Basset Class ships were being launched and Portsdown or Portuguese Class trawlers were being built. In New Zealand there were the Castle Class and there were also trawlers being built for the Royal Navy in Brazil.

Despite the enormous number of ships that were either being requisitioned or built specifically, a huge number of them were being lost. The largest number of new vessels entering service took place in 1942, but to a large extent even these replacements meant that the service was just maintaining existing strength.

The Royal Naval Patrol Service vessels were supposed to undergo a major overhaul and maintenance after they had steamed for 1,000 hours. In reality this rarely happened. Refits were a luxury and many of the trawlers were pushed to their absolute limits. The Isle Class trawler *Eday* steamed over 10,000 miles before it got a refit, by which time its propeller was virtually worn out. There was not a square centimetre on its hull that could actually be seen, as it was covered with every conceivable type of marine life. The *Eday*, which operated in the Mediterranean as well as around the British Isles, finally steamed over 70,000 miles during the war.

The tasks allotted to the Admiralty-built and requisitioned trawlers were incredibly varied and went beyond minesweeping and anti-submarine duties. Prior to the D-Day landings in June 1944 DAN layers were needed. These were vessels that laid marker buoys or DANs, which indicated safe passages or swept channels through potential minefield areas. Many of these were converted minesweeping trawlers and attached to minesweeping flotillas. Their work was invaluable to clear the way for the largest armada that the world had ever seen, which had to cross the English Channel for the liberation of France and beyond. Some of these converted minesweepers operating as DAN layers were sent to join minesweeping flotillas in the East Indies Fleet or the British Pacific Fleet.

Another vital role in the build up to the D-Day landings was preparation for Operation Neptune. Tens of thousands of vehicles would be transported across the English Channel in the first few weeks after the Normandy landings. It was essential that these vehicles had sufficient fuel. A large number of trawlers were converted into fuel carriers, or Essos, and they tirelessly steamed to and from France. For the crews it was a dangerous job but a mercifully short one, as by November 1944 the Pipeline Under the Sea (PLUTO) had been established and the trawlers could now be used for other duties or returned to their owners.

Another group of trawlers operated as supply vessels. For this duty they were entirely suited, as they already had massive holds to take fish. During 1943 the trawlers *Transvaal*, *Lapageria* and *Quercia*, amongst others, operated in the Mediterranean and became known as Walt Disney's Navy.

Yet another group of trawlers were used for wreck disposal or for wreck location. These vessels had no armament and were specially converted, normally Admiralty built, to carry out this hazardous task.

More trawlers had been converted into armed boarding vessels. It was their job to intercept merchant vessels and examine their paperwork and their cargoes. Once France had fallen in 1940 many of these vessels were redeployed.

Even the trawlers that were not very seaworthy found a role. Some were converted into barrage balloon vessels and most of these never even left the harbour. They were given large winches, and barrage balloons which they would send aloft if there were an air raid.

Another small group became boom gate vessels. These were also not very seaworthy. They were attached to an anti-submarine net in harbour entrances and would open and close the net when a vessel wanted to enter or leave the port.

A handful of trawlers were also used as controlled minelayers. They would be responsible for small minefields that were laid just outside harbours. The mines could be activated or made safe by these trawlers.

As we have seen some of the vessels never left port, as they were either too old or too unreliable to risk sending out to sea. Many of them would act as harbour service vessels, ferrying personnel, stores and ammunition backwards and forwards from anchored ships. They would also be responsible for degaussing vessels, or dealing with any demagnetising protection.

A large number of the vessels were also used for what became known as 'buttoning' and 'unbuttoning'. This was the task of handing over convoys between groups of escort vessels as they sailed up and down the coast. The patrol vessels would meet up with large convoys and escort a small number of merchantmen to a specific port so that they could be unloaded (unbuttoning). They would also escort these ships back to their main convoy (buttoning).

It would be a confusing and impossible task to even try to categorise the enormous number of 3,000 or more requisitioned trawlers that were employed either by the Royal Naval Reserve or the Royal Naval Patrol Service during the wars. It is a slightly less hazardous and confusing task to look at the Admiralty-built trawler classes. It is worth bearing in mind of course that many of the classes that were originally instituted during the First World War were still in operation for the Second World War. However the focus in this final section of the chapter is on the Second World War.

The first group were known as the Armentiers Class. There were just twelve of them and they were built as part of the Admiralty programme in 1917. By the Second World War most of them were lightships, but *Ypres*, which had been built in Canada, was rammed and sunk by HMS *Revenge* off Nova Scotia on 12 April 1940.

The Axe Class were actually Russian vessels seized in the White Sea in August 1918. Some of them found their way back into Russian hands and others were handed over to the French. Just four of them survived long enough to serve in the Second World War.

As previously mentioned there was also the Basset Class, the first of which was launched in 1935. Only two were built in Britain and the rest were built in Canada, India and Burma. Most of them proved to have major engine problems.

A sub-class of the Isles and Fish Class trawlers was the Bird Class. There were five of these mine-laying trawlers. A similarly small group were the Brazilian Class. As this name may suggest they were built in Brazil for the Royal Navy, but before they were completed Brazil joined the allies in the war and they were transferred to the Brazilian navy.

The Castle Class was a huge group of 197 vessels built in British yards, plus 9 built in India and 60 in Canada. These were First World War vessels, although a large number of them saw service during the Second World War. The Dance Class came into existence in 1939 and was a group of twenty trawlers. Only one was lost during the war, *Sword Dance*.

All ten trawlers of the Fish Class were built at Selby. They were anti-submarine vessels and only *Mackerel* failed to survive the war, being lost in the Atlantic in late January 1943. The eight steam powered Hills Class vessels were all built at Beverley, primarily for anti-submarine convoy escort duty. Two of these vessels were lost during the war. The Isles Class was another large group. 145 of them were built and they served across the globe as escorts, minesweepers and anti-submarine trawlers. Four were mine layers and fourteen others were DAN layers. Thirteen of them were sunk during the Second World War.

A number of Mersey Class trawlers that had been built from 1917 were, by the Second World War, commercial fishing vessels. A number of them served during the war under their new civilian names. The Military Class was another First World War group, most of which operated as minesweepers and some as Q ships. A number of these older vessels that had started being launched as early as 1914 were once again used, and some lost, during the Second World War. There was a specific group of Military Class trawlers built between 1942 and 1944. They were used as anti-submarine vessels and all nine of them survived the war.

In order to take the pressure off British shipyards orders were given to the neutral Portuguese to build fifteen trawlers. Not all of them were actually built, mainly due to the problems that Portugal was experiencing in finding sufficient building materials. All six that were completed survived the war. The second group of another six, made of steel and slightly longer, also got through the conflict unscathed.

The Round Table Class consisted of eight trawlers to be used as minesweepers. They were all built in Aberdeen and survived the war. There were twelve vessels in the Shakespearean Class and nine of them were launched in 1940, with the balance the following year. Three of these were sunk during the conflict.

Another vast group was the Strath Class, another element of the Admiralty's trawler building programme of 1917. The original order was for 145 vessels, but in the end 149 were built. They not only served throughout the First World War, but a number of them were requisitioned, now as civilian vessels, for the Second World War.

The Tree Class consisted of twenty Admiralty-built trawlers, launched between 1939 and 1940. Six of them were lost during the conflict. The Gem Group were those vessels that were bought whilst being constructed during the 1930s. There were two batches, the first consisting of ten, of which half were lost, and the second batch of five, of which two were lost.

As distinct from the Tree Class, there were also two groups of Admiralty-built minesweepers, each of ten vessels, known as the Tree Group. They were purchased between 1935 and 1939. The entire first batch survived the war but four vessels of the second batch were lost, namely *Alder, Beech, Myrtle* and *Tamarisk*.

There was also an enormous group of vessels that were minesweepers acquired under Lend Lease Agreement. They were variously known as either British Yard Class Minesweepers or, arguably, Brooklyn Yard Class Minesweepers. This difference in description has been much debated to no great conclusion. On 4 March 1941 the keel was laid for the first United States Yard Class Minesweeper. The initial order for a massive 561 would be built at 35 different locations around the United States. There were two main series: the first consisted of eighty 136ft vessels. They were given the numbers BYMS 2001 to 2080. Under the terms of the Lend Lease Agreement the United States was to build and transfer 150 of these vessels to the Royal Navy. The second series provided the balancing amount of seventy vessels. In 1941 alone the US managed to complete 134, with the second series coming on stream in 1942.

The wooden-hulled Yard minesweeper proved to be one of the most durable and versatile vessels of the war. Yard class vessels remained in service with the US Navy until 1969, by which time they also served, or were still serving with, twenty-six navies around the world. Only seven of them remain afloat at the time of writing although many of them were still being used well into the 1970s as pirate radio vessels, houseboats, restaurants, fishing vessels, yachts and even passenger ferries.

CHAPTER FOUR

Norway, Dunkirk
and the VC

Norway had managed to remain neutral during the First World War, but in April 1940 it was attacked by German forces. Only a handful of Norwegian army battalions had been activated and consequently the country was woefully unprepared for the onslaught. The Germans needed to ensure that the supply of iron ore from mines in northern Sweden continued to flow. The main Swedish port through which the iron ore was shipped was frozen in winter and for those few months the iron ore came by rail through Narvik, in the far north of Norway. The Germans were also concerned that the British were going to mine the coastal waters around Norway, which would prove to be a major hazard for their ore ships. The Germans seized Narvik, Trondheim, Bergen, Oslo and other Norwegian towns and cities on the first day of the attack (9 April).

The British were reluctant to throw their full weight behind the Norwegians to dislodge the German invaders. But they did identify Namsos, a small Norwegian town, as being a potential landing point. Namsos was at the head of the Namsen fjord, with a population of fewer than 4,000. It was ice-free and despite the fact it was a fishing port it was unknown to nearly every member of the Royal Naval Patrol Service. In fact when the Duty Commander of Combined Operations Headquarters, based at Donibristle in Fife, received the name as part of an order he had absolutely no idea where it was. In fact it was not even on his map. It was around 100 miles to the north of Trondheim. Namsos had been chosen because smaller warships and transports could get into the port and then an attempt could be made to liberate Trondheim.

Nonetheless, the Namsos campaign, as it would become known, would be the first major operation of the Royal Naval Patrol Service in the Second World War. Around thirty trawlers were to make their way across the North Sea in support of the Royal Navy and the British Expeditionary Force that was being hastily assembled. The trawlers would provide vital anti-submarine protection and they were also to help in ferrying troops from larger vessels into the port of Namsos itself.

The vessels involved belonged to a number of anti-submarine striking forces and groups. The 11th Anti-Submarine Striking Force provided *Cape Siretoko, Argyllshire, Northern Pride* and *Wisteria*. There were four from the 15th Anti-Submarine Striking Force: *Cape Passaro, St Goran, St Kenan* and *St Loman*. The 16th Anti-Submarine Striking Force provided *Aston Villa, Gaul, Angle* and the vessel that would exemplify the courage of the new service, *Arab*, a trawler from Hull. The 12th Anti-Submarine Group provided *Stella Capella, Cape Argona, Cape Chelyuskin* and *Blackfly*. Other groups included the 21st Striking Force, with *Daneman, Lady Elsa, Man of War* and *Wellard*. The 22nd Anti-Submarine Group provided *Bradman, Hammond, Jardine, Larwood* and *Warwickshire*, and finally the 23rd Anti-Submarine Group *Berkshire, Indian Star, Melbourne* and *Rutlandshire*.

What initially appeared to be a half-hearted attempt to assist the Norwegians would turn out to be a miniature version of Dunkirk, which itself was not that far into the future. Some 5,000 allied troops landed at Namsos and as the trawlers arrived they came under immediate attack from German aircraft, as the bulk of the Norwegian airfields were already in enemy hands. The slow-moving trawlers were an easy target and they had very little in the way of defensive armament to fend off the marauders. The trawlers took to hiding during the day, draping tree branches and shrubs over their decks and only operating at night. However the losses would mount.

The trawler *Arab* was on patrol on 28 April 1940 in the fjord itself. The vessel was commanded by a thirty-eight-year-old Royal Naval Reserve, ex-merchant officer and the son of a master mariner. Lieutenant Richard Stannard had been educated at the Royal Merchant Navy School in Berkshire. He had joined the Orient Line as a first officer in the late 1920s and had joined the Royal Naval Reserve as a sub-lieutenant. Also on board was an anti-submarine specialist, Sub-Lieutenant Ernest Lees, an Australian. The watchkeeper was temporary Sub-Lieutenant R F Ellis, RNVR. The second hand and coxswain was David Spindler. All of the other crewmembers were Royal Naval Patrol Servicemen. The *Arab* was some 170ft long with a beam of 28ft and had been requisitioned in September 1939. This day was going to prove to be Stannard's and the *Arab*'s greatest achievement.

The fjord was a death trap, constantly under attack by Stukas, often as many as twelve at a time. Above them were Dorniers, dropping high explosives. Bombs were dropping everywhere and all around the pitifully inadequate anti-aircraft defences. Explosions were going off as supply dumps and stores were continuously being hit. The worst place was the fire on the pier, threatening to engulf hundreds of tons of much-needed supplies and ammunition. Stannard brought the *Arab* close beside the pier even as the paint on the side of the trawler was blistering and curling with the heat. Accompanied by two of his crew Stannard climbed onto the forecastle and they began to pump icy water onto the flames. Grenades were going off in the heat and the men had to douse themselves with water as their clothes began to smoulder. With blackened faces they continued to fight the fire. The German aircraft singled out the *Arab*: some sixteen Stukas came in to finish her, but Stannard was ready, and at the last moment he reversed the trawler as bombs dropped all around her.

The following day was no better; there were constant air attacks and there was talk of evacuation. By April 30 the Luftwaffe had returned in ever-increasing numbers, focusing on the sloop HMS *Bittern*. Stannard sailed to help and using *Arab*'s guns helped fend off the raiders. But later on the *Bittern* was hit and reduced to a mass of flame. Stannard and his men saved as many of the sloop's crew as they could.

The *Arab* continued to work tirelessly throughout the raids until the men were on the verge of collapse. By now over 130 bombs had been aimed at the trawler in some thirty-one air attacks. Stannard moved the trawler into the shelter of an overhanging cliff. He found stores in a cave and set up his Lewis guns for air defence. He established an air raid lookout post and sent his men ashore to sleep somewhat fitfully in the cave. They were joined by two other trawlers and the crews took it in turns to man the lookout post. Stannard used the post to warn other vessels and to open up on German aircraft as they emerged.

The *Gaul* was badly hit, as was the *Aston Villa*. Stannard got on board the *Arab* with two of his men and made for the *Aston Villa*, cutting her moorings to prevent her from destroying other vessels if she blew up.

After five days in the fjord the evacuation orders were finally given. The *Arab* escaped into open water amidst frenzied attacks by Stukas. One of the German pilots signalled to the *Arab* with a hand lamp, ordering it to steer east or be sunk. Stannard was furious at the impudence and he told his men to hold fire until the last minute. The German pilot, seeing that his instruction had been ignored, came down to destroy the trawler. At the very last minute Stannard ordered his men to fire and the Stuka was riddled with bullets, crashing into the fjord. A few days later the *Arab* and its crew were safely back at their home port.

Stannard was awarded the Victoria Cross and the rest of the crew also all received Gallantry Medals. (*See Appendix 2 – Stannard Report and VC Citation.*)

Three hundred miles to the north a number of trawlers had arrived at the operational headquarters, at Harstad. From the moment they arrived they could see that the port was in grave danger; half of the jetty had been destroyed and it was under constant air attack. The men were also told that German ground troops were not that far away.

57

The group of trawlers included *Northern Spray*, the group leader and one of five trawlers of the 12th Anti-Submarine Striking Force, with its captain, Lieutenant-Commander D J B Jewitt. Two of the trawlers were stationed in the main approach to Narvik. *Northern Spray* and *Northern Gem* took up patrol in Ofot fjord and were ordered to assist in intercepting German surface vessels heading up the fjord. They were enormously relieved to see that they were backed up by HMS *Warspite* and some destroyers. Jewitt was impatient for action and as one of the *Northern Gem*'s crewmembers, Sid Kerslake, recalled:

> On the evening of May 8 we were having tea in *Gem* when the alarm went and a German plane shot over the mountains on *Spray*'s side of the fjord. *Spray* fired a fierce burst at it, but by the time it was in sight of her it was also past her, as both ships lay within feet of the shore edge and were almost overhung by sheer rock walls. From *Gem* we saw that one of the plane's engines was on fire and smoking badly. We gave the plane a full broadside from our two twin Lewis guns, all we had time for before it passed over and disappeared beyond the steep rock wall, losing height rapidly.

A little later a small Norwegian motor fishing boat came alongside *Northern Spray*. Despite language difficulties they were able to tell Jewitt that the aircraft had gone down and they knew where it was and could take him there. Jewitt got a dozen men together armed with rifles and put them on board the Norwegian boat. They sailed down the fjord and turned to see the wrecked aircraft, which had crashed on the shoreline. Jewitt had told them to capture the pilots and retrieve any documents or maps that they could find. The men had to wade up to their waists in water to get to the wreck. One of the trawler men fired a few rounds with his rifle to scare the Germans out of hiding.

None of them could have expected what would happen next. A German machine gun opened up and instantly killed one of the trawler men. They dived for cover. They had not run into a three-man aircraft crew, but a thirty-five man German Alpine Unit. The trawler men were quickly overrun and captured and taken to an emergency camp. Kerslake continued the story:

> We had been in the camp for about three hours when we saw a British destroyer come in and land a party of Marines. At this the Germans decided it was time to be off. The Unteroffizier [equivalent to a sergeant] gave us German great coats to warm us, and ordered us to carry their equipment, including guns, boxes and bandoliers of ammunition, and the machine gun. We were warned that we would be shot if we tried to escape, after which we began a march inland across the hills.

They continued marching and reached the opposite coast. It was then that they saw that *Northern Spray* had gone around the island and was steaming off the shore. The trawler opened up and the Germans herded their captives into a shepherd's hut, along with one of the wounded pilots. They lay low whilst the *Northern Spray* shelled them. All of the other able-bodied Germans disappeared. The crew was found by British Marines and ultimately they were reunited with their fellow crewmen. But the fight for them was not over. They helped the Marines fight on against Germans in the area, constantly under threat from German aircraft.

The *Northern Gem* was later ordered to escort the Norwegian passenger ship, *Ranen*, back to Britain. The Norwegian vessel had been fitted out with anti-aircraft guns and had a mixed crew of naval men, Marines and soldiers, skippered by Commander Sir Geoffrey Congreve, RN. He had taken over the ship after his trawler, *Aston Villa*, had been sunk. The *Northern Gem* and *Ranen* made for Svolvaer, where they were challenged by what appeared to be an enemy trawler. After firing at them, it made off. The two vessels steamed into Svolvaer and destroyed the harbour installations and oil tanks. They were the last two vessels to leave the Narvik area. The Luftwaffe tried to sink the pair of them on their way back across the North Sea, but incredibly they both survived the attacks, even when an aerial torpedo was fired at the *Northern Gem*. The two vessels were supposed to head for Scapa Flow, but instead they made for Aberdeen.

Meanwhile, the *Northern Spray* had also come under constant attack. By the time the crewmen that had been captured and then found by the Marines returned there was blood all over the decks of the trawler. Several of the remaining men had been wounded. There were six badly wounded men on board and there was very little available in the way of medical supplies. Ultimately the wounded men were taken on board HMS *Resolution* and a large number of Marines boarded *Northern Spray* to be ferried to hunt for Germans up in the hillsides. *Northern Spray* would also finally escape from the fiasco of the Norwegian campaign and she would win fame in May 1943 in the Atlantic.

Some fourteen trawlers were lost during the Norwegian campaign, most of them to enemy aircraft. Some of them had been so badly damaged that they had to be sunk, but the Germans would salvage seven of them.

The Royal Naval Patrol Service's last loss of the campaign was *Juniper*. On 7 June 1940 she had sailed from Tromso, escorting the tanker *Oil Pioneer*. *Juniper* was commanded by Lieutenant-Commander Geoffrey Grenfell, RN. At dawn on 8 June they were spotted by German warships. Grenfell ordered the tanker to sail on while he turned to take on the German ships. One of the German ships was the *Hipper* and she blew the *Juniper* to pieces. Only four of the crewmen survived, along with twenty men from the tanker.

As if the Norwegian campaign had not been disastrous enough, both for the war effort and for the Royal Naval Patrol Service, there was worse to come on the mainland of Europe, following the collapse of France in May 1940.

Operation Dynamo involved the evacuation of upwards of 340,000 British and allied troops trapped against the French coast. Some 250 British warships transported troops from these beaches. Around half of them were trawlers and drifters belonging to the Royal Naval Patrol Service and about a third of these were sunk. Many of the other small craft that took part in the evacuation that were not actual Royal Naval Patrol Service vessels were also manned by men from the service.

One such example of this second group was Skipper Jack Wayman. He had fought in the Norway campaign and he was now a second hand, but given command of a Thames sand barge. The sluggish vessel was motor driven and capable of only 4 knots. It did not even have a compass. Wayman guided the vessel as close to the shore as he dared and on the first trip managed to get 400 men aboard. All around him bombs were dropping, as German dive bombers attacked. As Wayman moved away from the French shoreline he shot at a Ju 88 with his rifle. He managed to ferry the 400 men out to a larger warship and then went back and collected another 300 men. This time, bombs dropped so close that they turned the sand barge over, pitching Wayman and his passengers into the water. Wayman waded ashore about a mile from Dunkirk. Despite the heavy fighting going on all around him he made it into Dunkirk and headed for the docks. He got a lift back to Britain on board a destroyer.

Meanwhile, at Ramsgate, another group of five herring drifters, known as *Vernon's* Private Navy, were under the command of Lieutenant-Commander A J Cubison. They were ordered into the Channel and to make for Dunkirk. One of the vessels was *Fisher Boy* commanded by Skipper George Brown. The drifter was first into the harbour and they made for the mole, taking on 250 soldiers. Coming away they ran aground on a sandbank, but managed to get free. Cubison set up the *Lord Cavan* in Dunkirk harbour as a command vessel. He stood on the deck amidst the shellfire, directing operations. Meanwhile *Fisher Boy* had returned to Ramsgate, but was experiencing engine problems and was low in the water. *Silver Dawn*, one of the other drifters, damaged her propeller coming out of Dunkirk harbour but she managed to get back to Ramsgate, although this was her only trip. *Fisher Boy* continued to make journeys across the English Channel, timing their arrival so they got there at dusk. From the outset the drifters had been told not to take more than 100 men on board, but they never stuck to the rule.

The old minesweeping drifter, *Nautilus*, and the drifter *Comfort* headed out of Dover. They only got halfway across the English Channel when they were engaged by an E-boat. The *Nautilus* only had a Lewis gun but engaged the enemy craft. The E-boat sped off but shortly afterwards they heard a huge explosion and then saw men in the water. It was the remainder of the crew of HMS *Wakeful*: some sixteen of them. The E-boat had torpedoed her. At the time the destroyer had been full of troops that she had brought off Dunkirk and when she sank hundreds were drowned.

Comfort fell to friendly fire when she was later fired on by the minesweeper *Lydd*. The *Lydd* rammed the *Comfort*, which still had the captain of HMS *Wakeful* on board. He and the few survivors from *Comfort* were plucked out of the water.

Nautilus managed to find the cruiser HMS *Calcutta*, and passed on the soldiers that she had picked up. She then headed back to pick up more, constantly under air attack, and took them to a paddle sweeper before going back to the beach once more. *Nautilus* got to within 200m of the beach when Stukas sank her. Petty Officer Muir made sure that the crew snatched a jar of rum as they escaped. They made it to the beach and found an abandoned lifeboat. It was still just about working so they had a swig of rum and got it afloat. They then picked up eight soldiers and made for a paddle sweeper before turning round to get some more men. Once again they were sunk by Stukas, but luckily they saved the rum jar for a second time. They got back to shore, finished off the rum and went to search for another vessel. They came across a small naval landing craft that was picking up troops. Muir and one of the other men offered their assistance as crewmen and they made two or three trips backwards and forwards on the landing craft, picking up men.

By this time the conditions on the beach were almost intolerable. The landing craft was almost out of fuel and its commander offered to put Muir and one of his colleagues on board the paddle sweeper *Gracie Fields*. But Muir said he would rather go on the *Sandown*, which was an incredibly lucky decision, as *Gracie Fields* was sunk on her way back to Britain. The voyage back to Britain on board the

Sandown was no pleasure trip; it was packed with men and faced a mass attack from thirty-seven dive bombers. Incredibly none of them scored a hit, which would undoubtedly have sunk her.

One of the other paddlers was the *Emperor of India* and she made four trips to Dunkirk. On one occasion she had come out towing twenty smaller craft, which were either damaged, out of fuel, or otherwise unable to make their own way. The paddler *Brighton Queen* was lost, the *Brighton Belle* hit a wreck, *Devonia* was beached after having been bombed, but the *Medway Queen*, who had made at least seven trips to Dunkirk, survived, having brought back 7,000 troops.

The paddle sweeper *Waverley*, from Harwich, was not so lucky. She had 600 men on board when she was attacked by twelve enemy aircraft. A bomb cut straight through her and she began to sink. The order was given to abandon ship, but 400 men drowned. The survivors were picked up by some drifters and a French submarine. The *Marmion, Duchess of Fife* and *Oriole*, also paddle sweepers from Harwich, worked for four straight days, saving 5,000 men between them.

The *Crested Eagle*, however, also a paddle sweeper from Harwich, was to be involved in a desperate struggle for survival. It began when the Dover-based trawler, *Calvi*, moored alongside the jetty at Dunkirk with two other trawlers. Just ahead of *Calvi* was the destroyer HMS *Grenade*. The destroyer was badly hit by enemy aircraft and was on fire. *Calvi* assisted in pulling her away from the jetty. During this operation one of the other trawlers, *Polly Johnson*, was wrecked by air attack and then the Germans focused on *Calvi*. A stick of bombs landed across the trawler and one of the crewmen, Second Hand William Thorpe was knocked unconscious. When he came to he was on board the trawler *John Cattling*, already full of evacuated soldiers. Another one of the *Calvi*'s crew, Leading Seaman Ernest Yallop, managed to make it to the *Crested Eagle*, but it too came under enemy aircraft attack, which smashed it to pieces. She went down in a matter of minutes, taking 300 men with her. Moments later the *Calvi* sank too.

Gunner Amos Sumner was on board the armed fishing trawler *Gava*. The crew had not yet joined the Royal Naval Patrol Service. They had landed a catch at Fleetwood and were ordered to make for Ramsgate and then for Dunkirk. They got alongside the jetty, taking off French troops when they came under attack from Stukas. They managed to get off 376 French soldiers. Not content with this, they picked up the crew of a wrecked French destroyer outside the harbour. The trawler limped into Ramsgate with 500 men on board.

The unequal struggle continued through to 2 June1940, with the vessels of the Royal Naval Patrol Service the last ships to snatch men from certain capture. Now there was also the added peril of U-boats. Three trawlers were making their way across the Channel, checking the waters to protect the ships still coming out of Dunkirk. *Blackburn Rovers* was in the lead, followed by *Westella* and *Saon*. *Blackburn Rovers* made an asdic contact. There was confusion as to whether it was a wreck or a U-boat; it was neither. They had blundered into a British minefield. *Blackburn Rovers* hit one of the mines and broke in half and sank. Her depth charges went off amongst the survivors. *Westella* tried to help, but her bows were blown off when she hit a mine. Chief Skipper Mullender, on the *Saon*, had no option but to try and save what was left of the two crews:

> We saved thirty-six men in all from the two crews. Many of *Blackburn Rovers*'s survivors were suffering from internal haemorrhage as a result of being caught in the depth charge explosions. The mess deck of *Saon* was like a slaughterhouse, with blood running everywhere.

Fisher Boy was still hard at work and made her last visit to Dunkirk in daylight hours on 2 June. She was just coming into Dunkirk harbour when she saw a large troopship that had been hit by German bombers. It was lying on its side, on fire. In the water were 2,000 French soldiers and there were more standing on the hull. The men were under constant machine gun attack by German aircraft. There was no hesitation from *Fisher Boy*; they went straight in and began to grab as many of the men out of the water as they could. Their crowded ship managed to make it back to Ramsgate. More of the French soldiers had been picked up by another two drifters, *Fidget* and *Jacketa*

Meanwhile, *Lord Cavan*, with Cubison still on board, was hit and quickly sank, still in Dunkirk harbour. All of the crew were saved and returned to Dover by a destroyer. She was the last Royal Naval Patrol Service casualty of this operation. Cubison's force of drifters had saved over 4,000 men, *Fisher Boy* accounting for 1,350 of them.

There was one more evacuation that took place two weeks or so after Dunkirk. Around 100,000 British and French troops, including civilians, were trapped in the port of St Nazaire, in the Bay of Biscay. The Grimsby trawler *Cambridgeshire* was one of those sent to assist in their evacuation. She was an asdic trawler and was anchored off St Nazaire on the afternoon of 17 June 1940. There was a sudden explosion and the crew of the trawler could see the vast troopship, *Lancastria*, being smashed to pieces by German aircraft. There were some 6,000 people on board and she looked to be on the verge of sinking. The *Cambridgeshire* steamed to help. The liner sank within twenty minutes but the trawler's crew pulled out as many victims as possible. The trawler was almost capsized under the weight of 1,009 people. Despite this, as many as 4,000 people died in the disaster.

The day was not over for the little trawler, however. After passing on the survivors to one of the transports, *John Holt*, she steamed into St Nazaire itself in order to snatch army personnel from under the noses of the Germans, as the skipper, Billy Euston, recalled:

> I was not able to leave the bridge until we were several hours out of St Nazaire, and it was then I discovered that our passengers were, in fact, the General Staff of the British Expeditionary Force, headed by the commander of the Second Army, General Sir Alan Brooke. I jokingly asked if he and his staff could all swim, and when he asked why, pointed out that we had no life-saving equipment on board, having thrown every last thing we had to the *Lancastria* survivors. He just smiled and said, 'we shall not worry about that.'

The *Cambridgeshire* managed to make it back to Plymouth intact.

CHAPTER FIVE

Churchill's Pirates

With the European continent in German hands there were very real fears of an enemy invasion of Britain. The islands were very much alone; they were almost unarmed, in chaos and there were already rumours that the Germans were massing barges along the Belgian and French coasts, ready for the invasion force that was likely to be launched against the British shores.

Just before Dunkirk, Winston Churchill had sent secret, sealed orders to the various commands of the Royal Naval Patrol Service. The skippers were given these sealed orders. They were instructed not to open them, but curiosity often got the better of them. Inside were detailed instructions that in the event of an invasion which appeared to be successful, they were to steam across the Atlantic and make their way towards the United States or Canada to carry on the fight.

The Royal Naval Patrol Service trawlers were also issued with special recognition signals: a 6ft square of canvas, with red and white stripes. The trawlers, however, had no time to even prepare for the off chance that these orders would be confirmed. Many of them were transferred from their anti-submarine and minesweeping duties to become auxiliary patrol vessels. It was hoped that they would be the tripwire to warn Britain if an invasion fleet was on its way.

Meanwhile there was other work to be done. In the spring of 1940 three destroyers and six trawlers of the Royal Naval Patrol Service had been sent on a secret mission to cut the submerged telecommunication cables between Britain and Germany. There were six cables to tear up: one of them ran from Mundesley and Bacton, around ten miles to the south of Cromer, to Nordeney and Borkum in the East Frisian Islands. Another ran from Lowestoft to Nordeney and also one to Borkum. This was a highly difficult and dangerous job. The cables consisted of copper wire, protected by successive layers of tape and other material, with a lead sheathing. They were not the type of cable that we might imagine in these days, when fibre optics are relatively lightweight and flexible. These cables weighed 30 tons per nautical mile. Sections of the cable were at least 100 fathoms down and there was also the probability that the vessels would be targeted by enemy aircraft or surface vessels.

Lieutenant Albert Longmuir, RNR, commanded *Grampian*. The other trawlers were all commanded by men from the Royal Naval Patrol Service, all of them experts in minesweeping. The other trawlers were *Pelton, James Lay, Milford Queen, Milford Princess* and *Cape Melville*. The operations were codenamed Quentin, Quidnunc and Quixote.

The trawlers sailed out of Great Yarmouth on the night of 18 May 1940. At an arranged point each of the trawlers paired off with a destroyer and made their way towards their designated position. At around 03.30 on the morning of 19 May they stopped and threw grapples over the side to search for the cables. *James Lay* made the first catch, after eight hours. They hauled it up and then hacked through the armoured sheath and the copper core. They then threw the cable back into the sea. A similar process was taking place elsewhere, but by this time, with daylight, the destroyers were searching around and trying to cover the trawlers as they got on with their work. The trawlers had to also be very careful, as the area had already been mined by the Germans.

Suddenly HMS *Jackal*, one of the destroyers, spotted a vessel heading straight for them. The destroyer pulled alongside and a boarding party clambered onto the deck of the unknown vessel. There was not a soul on board; she was a Dutch salvage tug, *Hector*. She was towed back to Britain.

HMS *Javelin* also spotted a dinghy and managed to pluck five fortunate Whitley bomber aircrew out of the water. By nightfall the job had been done and communication with Germany had been severed.

In order to prepare for the potential invasion many of the trawlers were re-equipped and up-armed. *Fisher Boy* was a prime example. She now had two Hotchkiss guns and two Lewis guns, as well as a radio and transmitter. She was also armed with six mines. In those dark weeks of 1940 she and many other trawlers spent perilous nights off the coast of France, hunting for any sign of a German invasion force. On a number of occasions she was attacked by enemy aircraft, but always managed to fend them off with her First World War weapons.

Far away, on 19 June 1940, the trawler *Moonstone* was steaming on anti-submarine patrol off Aden. The little trawler was from Hull and had originally been called the *Lady Madeleine*. Although the crew were not Royal Naval Patrol Service men, as she had been commissioned in early 1939, she was carrying out typical trawler work. The destroyer HMS *Kandahar* had detected a submarine the night before and had chased it but had lost it. But now, the following day, just around noon, the asdic operator on *Moonstone* found the submarine. At first it escaped but an hour later the trawler detected it again and dropped depth charges. Suddenly a vast Italian submarine rose out of the water. The trawler steamed straight towards the enemy vessel, firing its guns and with the crew taking shots with their rifles. The submarine returned fire, but the shots from the trawler prevented the Italians from manning their large, deck mounted gun. One of the trawler's shells smashed the submarine's conning tower, causing a number of casualties. Immediately the Italians began waving white jackets in surrender. There were too many Italians for the small crew to guard so *Moonstone* covered the submarine and called HMS *Kandahar* for help. Together they had captured the *Galileo Galilei* and they towed her back to Aden.

Back in England, the Sparrow's Nest, having been dubbed *Pembroke X*, was now HMS *Europa*. Lowestoft was packed with not only 'hostilities only' men, who were just beginning to enter service, but also with all of the survivors of the Royal Naval Patrol Service vessels that had been lost during Operation Dynamo. HMS *Europa* was no less chaotic than it had been before, but there had been a transformation. Nissen huts were now being used for training classes, there were administrative offices, and schools around Lowestoft were being used to train the men. A secondary school had been converted into a makeshift, but fully manned, hospital. All around the Sparrow's Nest there were air raid shelters. Such had been the numbers of men passing through the Sparrow's Nest that the order 'muster on the lawn' no longer meant very much, as there was not a single blade of grass left.

Lowestoft itself was prepared for imminent invasion. The narrow passages between houses nearby, known as scores, had been mined and the two ravines, or narrow roadways, which led down to the Sparrow's Nest from the main road above, had rifle pits and defences built around them. All of the mines could be set off from the Commodore's office, called The Cottage. All of the new men coming in as hostilities only crew were enrolled straight into the Royal Naval Patrol Service, rather than the Royal Naval Reserve. Skippers of fishing boats were automatically given the rank of temporary skipper.

Amongst the enormous numbers now reporting to HMS *Europa* were chefs and stewards from commercial liners. There were also men arriving from Newfoundland: all experienced seamen. Added to this were Free French, Dutch, Belgians, Poles and Norwegians who were all found welcome in the Royal Naval Patrol Service. The service command itself was now working well, although overwhelmed at times, and it was growing day by day.

Serious consideration was given to actually moving from Lowestoft, but it was decided that the Sparrow's Nest was no more vulnerable than anywhere else and it was convenient. So it was that in May 1940 the Sparrow's Nest was confirmed as the Royal Naval Patrol Service central depot, with Captain Basil Piercy as its first Commodore. It also had its new, silver badge and motto, '*In Imis Ptimus*', which meant 'we search in the depths.'

It was abundantly clear to Piercy, however, that he would have to make do for a time, as there were insufficient funds to transform the Sparrow's Nest into a proper depot. The Sparrow's Nest would be the core of the depot but he would have to organise his own storage space and accommodation around it. Throughout the war Lowestoft would be one of the most bombed ports in Britain, but this did not prevent nearly 1,000 Lowestoft landladies from ensuring that sufficient billets were always available throughout the town.

By the end of 1940 some 22,900 men had reported to Lowestoft. This meant that additional accommodation was needed, as were more buildings that could be converted for training purposes. A school on St John's Road was turned over to navigational training for skippers and second hands, and the Roman Hill School, on Love Road, became a barracks. The sick quarters were moved into St Nicholas Orphanage and an engineering barracks was established at St Luke's Hospital. Engine men and stokers were sent to a training centre based at Oulton Broad. The main officers' mess was established at a house named Briar Clyffe on Gunton Cliff. The cricket ground was covered in huts for accommodation and the bowling greens also became home for training courses.

Most of the cooking was carried out by a naval cookery school, run by civilian women. The depot had its own electric galleys, where the ships' cooks were taught how to create filling meals on a coal-fired range. The training was masterminded by Grace Musson, who was the head of Lowestoft Technical College. She set up the school at Lowestoft Church Road School and found eleven domestic science teachers to do the training. The courses lasted for five weeks and catered for up to 160 men at a time. The other courses, organised by the Patrol Service central depot, included seamanship, drill, naval routines, minesweeping, use of depth charges, gunnery, and hygiene.

It is also interesting to note that regardless of where the men's ships were based the letter L for Lowestoft was added to their number on their service certificate, just as Royal Naval ratings would have C for Chatham, P for Portsmouth or D for Devonport.

As already mentioned, the Royal Naval Patrol Service gained its own badge, which helped reinforce its unique identity. The badge fulfilled a vital role, as it had been originally envisioned that the civilian fishermen brought into the service in emergency situations would be wearing their own clothes. Had they been captured by the Germans operating a warship in civilian clothing then they would not have had the protection afforded to military personnel as prisoners of war. The men were entitled to receive the badge after they had spent six months in the Royal Naval Patrol Service. General Service naval personnel could not wear it and patrol servicemen that were based onshore were not entitled to it. It became practice to wear the badge on the left sleeve, around four inches from the cuff. This was also the preferred position for officers.

The remainder of 1940 signalled some of the darkest days of the war. All around the coast German aircraft attempted to sink any vessel, regardless of its size or its purpose. All of the major and some of the minor ports also received the attention of the Luftwaffe day after day. The patrol service's minesweepers and anti-submarine trawlers had to make daylight sweeps just to ensure that they cleared the shipping lanes for the convoys that could now only move at night.

The situation was no better in the East Mediterranean. The waters off Egypt and Libya and particularly in the Suez Canal region required the presence of minesweeping trawlers. During the Battle of Britain period alone, in British waters thirty-four Royal Naval Patrol Service vessels were either sunk by mines or bombed by German aircraft.

There was work for the trawlers elsewhere. The Battle of the Atlantic was beginning and German U-boats were operating in wolf packs. In August 1940 no fewer than twenty anti-submarine trawlers were transferred from the northern waters and from Belfast to the North Atlantic. Henceforth all convoys would be accompanied by a pair of trawlers, in addition to other vessels.

November 1940 was the darkest month, with twenty-six trawlers and drifters sunk. One such victim was *Amethyst*. She was operating out of Parkeston Quay, near Harwich, covering convoys moving along the east coast. She hit an acoustic mine. The trawler took ten minutes to sink, but seven men were wounded and the crew was picked up by the trawler *Le Tiger* and taken to Southend Pier. The police promptly arrested them, as they had done with the crew of a small Dutch vessel that had also been lost that day.

By the time 1940 was over the Royal Naval Patrol Service had lost 140 vessels since September 1939. Even in the final days of 1940 there were tragic losses. On Christmas Eve an E-boat torpedoed *Pelton* off Great Yarmouth, and on Christmas Day *Scawfell* managed to sweep up twenty-five mines, but the paddle sweeper *Mercury* that was working alongside her, had a mine tangled up in her sweep. It went off astern and buckled *Mercury*'s stern. Despite the best efforts she could not get into Wexford, the nearest port. Reluctantly the crew abandoned her at 21.00 hours and she sank.

The acknowledged heroes that won the Battle of the Atlantic were the larger anti-submarine vessels, Coastal Command and the courage of the merchantmen. However, the Royal Naval Patrol Service, with its slow-moving, under-gunned vessels, played an equally important but unacknowledged role. A prime example was the anti-submarine trawler *Visenda*. The navy had requisitioned her in 1939 and she had only had two years of fishing before that time. She operated out of Kirkwall, with the Orkneys and Shetlands Command. Her commander was Lieutenant Ralph Winder, RNR, and the remainder of the crew had all passed through Lowestoft. She tended to operate between Kirkwall and Reykjavik, Iceland.

It was Sunday 23 March 1941, just before 08.00 hours. *Visenda* had spotted an unidentified merchant ship and was trying to catch up with her. She was around 150 miles to the southeast of Iceland. Eventually a signal from the trawler was responded to: it was a Belgian vessel, SS *Ville de Liege*. To the trawler's and no doubt the Belgian's astonishment, a U-boat emerged from the depths. The trawler was still four miles from the Belgian ship and there was a hasty signal of warning. It was the *U-551*, commanded by Captain-Lieutenant Robert Schrott, who had spotted not only the Belgian ship but also the trawler. He had not submerged because the trawler represented a danger to him. In fact he had determined to try to sink the pair of them.

The trawler's asdic got a good contact with the U-boat, now submerged, and depth charges were dropped. Nothing happened for a few minutes and then there was a massive air bubble. Another fifteen minutes passed but the contact was lost. Suddenly there was another contact and more depth charges were dropped. As another batch of depth charges was organised the thrower on the port side jammed and the contact was lost once again. After several tense minutes contact was made again and the trawler closed in on the position. Then there was a problem with the asdic recorder: the trawler was now blind. By 09.35 contact had been made once again and the trawler manoeuvred into position. She fired off a pattern of depth charges.

Meanwhile, on board *U-551*, the earlier depth charge attacks had caused significant damage to the U-boat. There were several leaks, the air was full of fumes and the majority of the lights were out.

The little trawler waited for seven minutes and saw air bubbles rising. The trawler stopped, hoping to pick up a trace and thinking that the Germans were trying to fool them. In fact everyone on board the *U-551* was dead and wreckage began to float to the surface: clothes, blankets, mattresses and some body parts. Four hours later the victorious trawler returned to Kirkwall.

The first three months of 1941 saw the Royal Naval Patrol Service lose more than thirty vessels. January's losses were almost exclusively down to mines. This was hardly surprising, since the Royal Naval Patrol Service trawlers, drifters and other vessels were now operating all around the British Isles, in the Atlantic and in the Mediterranean. Some were even posted further afield.

A large number of trawlers had joined the Mediterranean Fleet. This was at a time when British forces in North Africa had been pushed all the way back to Egypt and Tobruk was under siege. Amongst the trawlers operating in the region were the 169th Norwegian Minesweeping Group and whale catchers manned by South African naval forces. The inshore squadron, operating along the coast, were invaluable during the Tobruk siege. They helped bring in over 34,000 men, embarked over 32,000, evacuated 7,500 wounded and took out some 7,000 German and Italian prisoners. They also brought in tanks, guns and thousands of tons of stores. It was therefore not surprising that casualties were comparatively high. The anti-submarine trawler *Sindonis* and the minesweeping trawler *Stoke City* were both lost. The sloop *Flamingo* and the whaler *Southern Isle* shot down two out of sixty Stuka dive bombers that attacked them.

The Mediterranean was an incredibly dangerous place. There were mines all along the North African coast and at times crucial positions and bases, such as Malta, were completely hemmed in by minefields. At Malta was the 4th Anti-Submarine and Minesweeping Group, consisting of the trawlers, *Beryl*, *Coral* and *Jade* and the drifters *Margaret* and *Plough Boy*.

So loved was *Beryl* that she was nicknamed The Flagship of Malta. She would be the only vessel that would survive the entire naval and aerial siege of the island. She had been built in 1934 and had been a Hull trawler called *Lady Adelaide*. She was actually crewed by general servicemen of the Royal Navy. It is incredible to believe that *Beryl* survived so many air attacks and attempts by E-boats and submarines to sink her.

The crew on board *Jade* was no less courageous. She was another Hull trawler, built in 1933. She would routinely hunt for downed pilots, straying as close to the Italian mainland or the Sicilian coast as she dared. On one occasion in June 1941 she strayed perhaps a little too close and was attacked by a pair of E-boats. The First Lieutenant, Midshipman J C Creasy, RNR, was mortally wounded with the first volley of fire from the enemy ships. *Jade* fired back with her 4-inch gun and her third shot hit one of the 100ft E-boats so hard that it left the water. The commander, Boatswain William Fellowes, skilfully manoeuvred the sluggish trawler to avoid torpedoes fired by the second E-boat. The remaining E-boat was narrowly missed by a pair of shots from *Jade* and she broke off, allowing the victorious trawler to head back to Malta.

The damaged E-boat also managed to nurse its way back to base, but only a few days later the E-boats returned to attack Malta's Grand Harbour. They were pounced on by No. 185 Squadron's Hurricanes. Pilot Officer Winton was shot down in the counterattack and he bailed out, swimming towards the E-boat that he had machine-gunned. He climbed on board and saw the crew all dead from his strafing run. He went below to start up the engines, but just then *Jade* arrived and towed Winton in the E-boat back to the Grand Harbour.

British troops had been withdrawn from North Africa in order to reinforce Greek troops on the Greek mainland. But when the Germans attacked Greece through Yugoslavia and Bulgaria, British troops had been forced to evacuate, leaving most of their vehicles and equipment. Many of them were evacuated to Crete and some directly to Egypt. This meant that Crete was the next logical step for the German invaders. If British forces continued to hold Crete then they could threaten the much-needed German-held Romanian oilfields. If the Germans could capture Crete it would provide them with a base from which to launch air attacks against Egypt itself. Crete was blessed with a very important naval base in Souda Bay and it was here that five Royal Naval Patrol Service vessels operated.

Moonstone had been transferred from Malta and she worked alongside *Salvia*, *Syvern*, *Kos 21* and *Kos 23*, as well as the former Lowestoft trawler, *Lanner*. The final component of the group was originally the sloop *Derby*, which was to be replaced by the sloop *Widnes*. The little vessels had a wide variety of jobs: they had to fight fires, recover wrecks, and carry stores, as well as mount patrols and provide escorts.

One of the vessels that came under particular attention from raiding German aircraft was *Syvern*. She had been built in Norway in 1937 and was a former whale catcher. She had a 75mm gun and some machine guns. In command was Lieutenant-Commander R E Clarke, who was also in command of the 16th Anti-Submarine Group. Stukas attacked her at the harbour's entrance on 23 April 1941 and she suffered a number of casualties. Clarke was wounded in the stomach and command was passed to Lieutenant A R Tilston, RNR. Shortly afterwards she was attacked by Ju 88s and they dropped bombs all around her, machine gunning her and destroying the locker that held the ammunition. The air was filled with shell fragments as one exploded straight in the path of one of the Ju 88s. The pilot lost control and cut straight through the vessel's foremast before smashing into the sea. Half of the vessel's crew were casualties and by now *Kos 23* and *Widnes* had also both been beached after being too severely damaged to be repaired. Their crews replaced the casualties on the *Syvern*.

These air attacks were just the first phase of the Germans' attempts to subdue the island as a precursor to an airborne landing. German paratroopers and glider-borne troops dropped from the sky on 20 May 1941 and within six days the battle for Crete had been lost and evacuation orders were given to the allies.

The remaining Royal Naval Patrol Service vessels were told to make for Alexandria. They were to destroy any vessels that could not make it and their crews were instructed to march south, across the island of Crete, to the evacuation ports. At dawn on 27 May *Kos 22*, which had relieved *Moonstone*, along with *Syvern*, made for Alexandria. The skies were full of enemy aircraft, so it was prudent for them to only move at night. By dusk that day they had already been spotted, however, and for the next hour and a half they tried to fend off German aircraft attacks. *Kos 22* was badly hit and burst into flames then *Syvern* was also hit. *Syvern* was still afloat an hour later, but the crew abandoned her just before she blew up. The survivors of the two vessels now made their way towards Sfakia, the evacuation port on Crete.

Just as dangerous, if not more so, were of course the coastal waters around the British Isles. But there were victories too and more acts of outstanding heroism. Skipper T H Spall, RNR, was the commander of the *Stella Rige* in 1941. It was dark and he heard an aircraft engine. Spall was near the deck mounted anti-aircraft gun and as the German search aircraft flew overhead he opened fire. The Heinkel crashed into the sea about half a mile away; it had all happened in seconds. Spall was awarded the Distinguished Service Cross.

Casualties in 1941 reached a peak in May when the Royal Naval Patrol Service was losing a vessel on average every other day. One of the trawlers that survived potential disaster was *Young Mun*. She was an old drifter from Lowestoft. Walter Walker was her engineman:

> I was at my post at *Young Mun*'s engines when suddenly there was a terrific crash and water poured down through the engine room skylight. I stopped engines and ran up on deck to take a look. It was a fantastic mess. A Junkers 88 had crashed down on our deck, bringing down the mast and covering the ship with wreckage.

The drifter had been operating off Dover and had been attacked by a pair of German bombers. There were ten trawlers in the little fleet and they all opened fire. The Lowestoft drifter had been incredibly unlucky but fortunate to remain afloat. The mast was down, there was wreckage all over the deck and there was also the remains of the German crew to contend with.

From the Sparrow's Nest itself it was almost possible to see the loss of three of the patrol service's own vessels due to German bombing. The drifter *Uberty* was smashed to pieces just outside of Lowestoft harbour and the trawlers *King Henry* and *Ben Gairn* were also lost, whilst *Thistle*, another drifter, was lost to a mine.

A regular job carried out by up to five trawlers was to sweep ahead of the coastal colliers bringing coal from South Wales to power stations around the Thames. As soon as the convoy reached the Straits of Dover two of the trawlers would sweep at shortened depths and the other three would try to protect the flanks of the convoy. The trawlers would spend the night in the Medway and then try to run the gauntlet of the Straits of Dover the following night.

Although there were RAF Air Sea Rescue and Marine Craft Unit bases all around the British coast, the trawlers were often called upon to launch their own rescue missions. One such example in 1941 involved the SS *Westbourne*. She was just to the north of

Flamborough Head and had been badly hit. Joseph Willis was one of the crew and he had been in the water for nearly seven hours. Just after dawn a Royal Naval Patrol Service trawler plucked him out of the water.

Minesweeping work was not just being carried out by converted drifters and trawlers. Operating at North Shields was the 8th Minesweeping Flotilla, which consisted of eight paddle steamers. They had 12-pdr guns on their foredecks, a couple of Lewis guns around the bridge and some Bren guns and rifles if they were lucky. They were also armed with six depth charges. Towards the end of 1941 they were also given balloons, which they sent aloft when they were sweeping. Some of them also had a Holman projector. This fired Mills bombs into the air to try and fend off low flying enemy aircraft. The bomb was fired off using compressed air or steam from the boilers. It was an incredibly dangerous machine to the firer.

Collisions were also commonplace. The trawler *Marconi* was lost in a collision after having been badly damaged by German aircraft. The vessel had sailed from Harwich for its night's work of minesweeping. At around midnight it was anchored to a buoy and was sunk in a collision with a patrol ship out of Ipswich.

On the morning of 27 August 1941 a Hudson on anti-submarine patrol out of Iceland spotted a surfaced U-boat. It dropped four depth charges and saw the U-boat crash dive, or at least attempt to. The Hudson strafed the enemy vessel and the crew saw the U-boat commander hold up a white board, signalling that they had surrendered. A hundred miles away was Lieutenant N L Knight, RNR, on board the trawler *Northern Chief*. The trawler was instructed to make for the U-boat whilst allied aircraft kept a watch on it. The U-boat had been ordered to show a yellow light and the *Northern Chief* arrived just before midnight. Soon after, another trawler, *Kingston Agate*, arrived to help and at dawn two more, *Windermere* and *Wastwater*, along with two destroyers. Suddenly a Norwegian-piloted aircraft emerged from the clouds and it spotted the U-boat and dropped two bombs, narrowly missing it. *Northern Chief* opened fire on the aircraft and it disappeared again. Conditions on board the U-boat were dangerous, but the commander and crew seemed reluctant to evacuate. Attempts were made to come alongside the stricken craft but by now there was a gale that complicated matters all the more. Eventually, Jock Campbell and two other men from *Kingston Agate* got on board the U-boat. They spent five tense hours aboard, trying to get the Germans to come up on deck and prevent the vessel from sinking. Even then the U-boat commander and two of his officers still refused to abandon ship.

Back on board the *Kingston Agate*, the skipper, Lieutenant H L'Estrange, sent a signal saying that he would fire on the boat immediately if they did not abandon ship. The Germans finally conceded and thirty hours after the surrender the last German left the U-boat.

Kingston Agate made for home with the prisoners on board. The other trawlers worked to try to tow the U-boat towards Iceland. Eventually they managed it and beached her. Undoubtedly this was one of the greatest achievements by Churchill's Pirates so far.

As for the U-boat, it would become the only one in Royal Navy history to fly the white ensign, as HMS *Graph*.

CHAPTER SIX

Lady Shirley et al

The story of the trawler *Lady Shirley* and her encounter with the German submarine *U-111* is a classic Royal Naval Patrol Service tale, exemplifying the kind of seemingly insuperable odds that pitted a hastily converted vessel against another specifically designed to kill.

The *Lady Shirley* had been built in Hull. She was 63ft long with a beam of 27ft and was a relatively young trawler, having been launched in 1937. The skipper was an Australian, Lieutenant-Commander Arthur Callaway, RANVR. Second in command was Lieutenant Ian Boucaut, RANVR. The junior officer was Acting Sub-Lieutenant Allan Waller.

Pitted against them would be the *U-111*, a 740-ton submarine commanded by Captain-Lieutenant Wilhelm Kleinschmidt, who had served on E-boats and on two cruisers. He had volunteered for U-boat service in 1940 and this was to be his second trip. In his first the *U-111* had sunk 20,000 tons of allied shipping. His second mission took him into the South Atlantic, where he sank two merchant vessels. At the end of September the *U-111* was making its way back to the Bay of Biscay and its base at La Rochelle. The *U-111* was close to the Canary Islands when it received a signal telling it to meet up with *U-68* just to the south of the Canaries and to give *U-68* any unused torpedoes. The U-boat captain had hoped to hang on to some torpedoes, as there would be opportunities to sink allied vessels close to his home port.

The *Lady Shirley* was operating out of Gibraltar, with the 7th Anti-Submarine Group. She was heading north from Gibraltar along with the trawlers, *Erin* and *Lady Hogarth*. On 29 September 1941 *Lady Shirley* and *Erin* had been ordered to rendezvous 300 miles to the west-south-west of Tenerife with the Free French sloop *Commandant Dubac*, which was towing the SS *Silverbelle*, heading for Las Palmas. Accompanying the two trawlers was the *Maron*, which left them to the south of the Canaries to look for the tanker *La Carriere*, bound for Gibraltar from Barbados. *Lady Shirley* was told to look for three enemy tankers that might be trying to get out of Tenerife.

On the early morning of 4 October there was fine weather and the sea was calm. Sub-Lieutenant French was on watch when he spotted something and *Lady Shirley* altered course to investigate. The trawler was having problems with its asdic, but the crew made rapid repairs and then heard a ping. There was definitely something out there, and as they reached the position they dropped five depth charges. Seconds later a periscope appeared and Callaway ordered the ship to turn about and ram the target. Meanwhile he told the crew to open fire as soon as they had the opportunity.

Moments later the body of the *U-111* was clearly visible. They were around 500m from it. The submarine's conning tower hatch opened and German sailors scrambled out to man the guns. The *Lady Shirley's* guns cut them to pieces before they could reach their guns. The U-boat crew returned fire from the conning tower, hitting one of the trawler's gun layers. The 4-inch gun on board the trawler continued firing. Signalman Warbrick, standing next to Callaway on the bridge was hit, as were Seamen William Windsor and Sidney Halcrow, who were manning the machine guns. A shot from the U-boat ruptured the trawler's main steam pipe, while the lifeboat was holed and the deck and wheelhouse splintered. Even so, it was the *Lady Shirley* that was scoring the better hits. Three of the 4-inch rounds smashed into the U-boat. Sub-Lieutenant French then switched to shrapnel rounds to clear the decks of enemy sailors. After two more shots the Germans had raised their hands in surrender. By now the *U-111* was beginning to dip into the water stern first. All of this feverish activity had taken twenty-three minutes; just four minutes after the surrender the *U-111* sank.

The trawler picked up forty-five enemy sailors, including the captain. Seven of the crew of the U-boat had been killed and five of the prisoners were wounded. The trawler would take five days to reach Gibraltar; it was going to be difficult to contain the Germans for that amount of time. The *Lady Shirley* neared Gibraltar on 8 October and was met by the destroyer HMS *Lance*. She entered Gibraltar amidst the cheers and congratulations of all of the warships assembled there.

As soon as Winston Churchill learned of the exploits of the trawler he cabled his personal congratulations, awarding Callaway a Distinguished Service Order: 'For daring and skill in a brilliant action against a U-boat in which the enemy was sunk and surrendered to HM trawler *Lady Shirley*.'

Two of the officers on board were awarded the DSC. Seaman Halcrow, when he heard he had been awarded the Conspicuous Gallantry Medal, promptly fainted, although he was admittedly badly wounded. Six of the crew were awarded the Distinguished Service Medal and five other crewmen were mention in despatches.

Early in December 1941, though, there was tragedy for the *Lady Shirley*. The Admiralty released a communiqué: 'HM trawler *Lady Shirley* is overdue and must be considered lost.'

The crew by this stage was largely the same men minus the wounded and a couple of other replacements. Sub-Lieutenant Waller's place on board had been taken by a Polish officer. It was Waller's belief that the Germans had deliberately targeted the little trawler and that she had been sunk by *U-374* a few hours before dawn on 11 December 1941. In fact captured German documents after the war indicated that this was the case. Four officers and twenty-nine men went down with the *Lady Shirley*.

It can never be absolutely clear if this was the actual fate of the trawler, as not only was it difficult for U-boats to be absolutely certain of their victim's identity, but also that the records of the

U-374 went down with her when she was sunk a month later by the British submarine HMS *Unbeaten*.

There were also suggestions that a Spanish agent working for the Germans had planted a bomb amongst the *Lady Shirley's* depth charges. This would certainly explain why no wreckage of the trawler was ever discovered. There had been a precedent for this, as a Spaniard had put a time bomb amongst the trawler *Erin's* depth charges in Gibraltar.

Far further afield, other trawlers and drifters of the service were operating in other theatres. The trawler *Arthur Cavanagh* had not only served in the Mediterranean with the 91st Minesweeping Group, primarily around Tobruk, the Suez Canal and Port Said, but she was now in the Persian Gulf.

The little trawler was part of an operation designed to capture or destroy five German merchant ships and three Italian ships hiding in Bandar Shahpur. The attack force was a motley collection of vessels. The main troopship and headquarters vessel was the *Canimbla*, an armed merchant cruiser. There were two tugs, the Royal Indian Navy sloop *Lawrence*, the corvette HMS *Snapdragon* and a river gunboat that had operated in China, the *Cockchafer*. Accompanying this force was an Arab dhow and a Royal Air Force picket boat.

The operation was due to be launched on 21 August 1941 at 04.00 hours. The trawler *Arthur Cavanagh's* role was to assist in the capture of the tanker *Bronte* and then help take the *Barbara*. The German ships were anchored in the Khor Musa inlet. The allies also knew that there might be intervention in the form of a pair of Iranian naval gunboats, which were to be sunk if they did get involved.

As it was, the Iranian gunboats and the town surrendered immediately after three of the German vessels had been captured. The little trawler closed on *Bronte* and suddenly flames were seen on board the Italian vessel. The crew of the trawler sprayed the deck with water and Australian troops overwhelmed the Italian crew. The trawler now made for the *Barbara* that was also on fire, but once again the flames were put out and the vessel captured. Only one of the enemy ships managed to destroy itself in the operation.

For his part the skipper of the trawler, Tom Kirby, was awarded the MBE. This action, codenamed Operation Bishop, was part of a larger operation designed to prevent Iran, which was pro-German, from becoming a full German ally.

Way to the north, twelve anti-submarine trawlers were attached to Iceland Command to assist the escorting of convoys to Russia. A prime example of the kind of work carried out by these trawlers took place on 27 June 1942. Some thirty-seven merchant ships left Iceland, originally bound for Murmansk, but due to the heavy bombing of the port their new destination was Archangel. Amongst the escort were four trawlers, *Ayreshire, Lord Austin, Lord Middleton* and *Northern Gem*. The convoy, codenamed PQ17, was to the southwest of Jan Mayen Island, a volcanic island in the North Atlantic Ocean, some 950km to the west of Norway and 600km north of Iceland.

German aircraft launched their first attacks on the convoy on 2 July. On 4 July one of the merchant ships was sunk and at 21.00 German torpedo bombers began to swarm around the convoy. The Admiralty ordered the covering destroyers to fan out to screen against German surface forces, which were believed to include the *Tirpitz*. In fact the *Tirpitz* had already turned around and the danger was actually from lurking U-boats.

Between the German submarines and the aircraft they were to take twenty-three victims. One of the merchant ships had to return to port and it was due to the exploits of the trawler *Ayreshire* that four of the remaining thirteen reached their destination.

Commanding the trawler was Temporary Lieutenant Leo Gradwell, RNVR, and assisting him was Temporary Lieutenant R W Elsden, RNVR and the watch keeping officer, Temporary Sub-Lieutenant R Whyte, RNVR. When the destroyers left and the convoy was ordered to scatter Gradwell signalled to two merchant ships to follow him. In the early hours of the following morning another merchant ship joined them. By 18.00, in order to avoid U-boat attack, the four vessels were amongst drifting ice.

All through 5 July the vessels hid amongst the ice floes, scanning the skies for marauding German aircraft. But pack ice began to form around the hulls and they knew that they had to move on. Towards late afternoon the following day a German search aircraft flew overhead, but there was enough fog to hide the vessels. By 02.00 on 9 July they could see land ahead: it was Novaya Zemlya, a Russian archipelago separating the Barents Sea from the Kara Sea.

The vessels steamed into a fjord and anchored. They knew that they were still 500 miles from their destination. *Ayreshire* was resupplied with coal and water from one of the merchant ships. Gradwell determined to sail into the Matochkin Strait, which was some twenty miles south.

They entered the strait and one of the merchant ships ran aground. The trawler managed to pull her off and they continued on. They then saw a wireless station, but it was unclear whether it was Russian or German held. Luckily it was in Russian hands and they were told that there was better anchorage further up the strait. Gradwell picked up three lifeboats from an American ship that had been part of the convoy and moved on. By 13 July Gradwell was in contact with a British naval officer at Archangel. There was poor visibility and on 13 July, after not having managed to travel very far, another of the merchant ships ran aground. The *Ayreshire* went in search of her, accompanied by a Russian trawler, and they managed to get her refloated.

A week later, having been found by three British corvettes, the four vessels finally made it to Archangel.

On the morning of New Year's Eve 1942 the trawler *Northern Gem* was part of an escort for convoy JW51B, *en route* to Kola Inlet, in the Russian arctic. She was part of a force of six destroyers, two corvettes and a minesweeper and accompanying the trawler *Vizalma*. They were protecting fourteen merchant ships.

Heading to intercept them were the German cruisers *Admiral Hipper* and *Lutzow*, accompanied by six destroyers. As the Germans closed they pummelled the destroyer HMS *Achates* and badly damaged the destroyer HMS *Onslow*.

Northern Gem sailed to pick up as many survivors from HMS *Achates* as possible. By the time they had finished their work the trawler was crammed and the skipper, Lieutenant William Mullender, headed for the destroyer HMS *Obedient*, seeking a doctor for the injured. The surgeon managed to perform nine major operations in the wardroom of *Northern Gem* before they reached Kola Inlet.

On 6 August 1942 the Italian submarine *Scire* had slipped out of Leros in the Mediterranean, bound for Haifa harbour. This Italian submarine had been recently converted to carry two-man human torpedoes. It was under the command of Count Valerio Borghese, who had masterminded an attack on Gibraltar with human torpedoes, managing to sink or badly damage fourteen allied vessels. He had also launched attacks on Alexandria and on Malta. Also on board were Italian frogmen, who were under orders to fix limpet mines to British vessels in Haifa harbour.

Patrolling off Haifa was the anti-submarine trawler *Islay*, commanded by Skipper Lieutenant John Ross, RNR. It was around 14.00 hours on 10 August when the trawler registered a contact. Minutes later a number of depth charges were dropped. Contact was then lost and a new search initiated. Another contact was picked up and six more depth charges dropped. As the trawler turned to see the effect of its depth charge run, a submarine broke water. The trawler opened up with her 12-pdr gun and they fired seventeen rounds. Twelve direct hits were made. It was clear to Ross that they had done considerable damage, and to finish off the submarine as she sank below the waves, six more depth charges were dropped. On 14 August there was confirmation of the kill when the bodies of two Italian sailors washed ashore at Haifa.

Meanwhile, back in Lowestoft, men were still reporting for duty, training and eventual posting to vessels. Many of the men were shocked when they first discovered exactly what type of vessel they were going to be serving aboard. Many of the billets were hopelessly overcrowded and some woefully inadequate. Some difficult situations had been dealt with, such as on the one day of the week

Lowestoft landladies had to queue up for their pay, which meant no evening meal for the men on that day. Now they were being paid by postal order through the mail.

There were also some strange administrative duties, such as keeping the 'wet bed book'. It was often said that bedwetting was a combination of air attacks and beer. Bedwetting was particularly common on pay nights. Any man that had wet their bed was fined 2s 6d.

Commodore Daniel de Pass had taken over HMS *Europa* in April 1941. He had a great rapport with the men of the patrol service and consequently his fairness paid dividends, as the men in the service were not typical Royal Navy types. When the men had finished their training and had passed out they became part of the guard at the Sparrow's Nest until they received a posting. On one occasion the commodore himself tried to get into the Sparrow's Nest in civilian clothes. He was challenged by the petty officer in charge. The commodore knew that the man recognised him, but the petty officer told him that unless he proved who he was he would not be allowed inside. A week later the petty officer was awarded a silver badge.

The drafting of the men had caused an enormous amount of chaos. Men were given their station cards when they joined and they had to report each day until a vessel was allocated to them or vice versa. Some of the men waiting for a train at Lowestoft to go to a certain ship had switched cards with someone else in order to be with their friends. Others bribed drafting clerks to get onto particular vessels or operate out of particular ports. This meant that the wrong men could end up on the wrong ships, which had serious implications for pay, directing letters and in tragic cases when there were casualties or deaths on board. Eventually, with WRENs doing most of the clerical work, things began to settle down and the situation became far less confused.

Incredibly, throughout the war, although Lowestoft was hit on dozens of occasions during German air raids, the Sparrow's Nest was never damaged. The nearest damage was when bombs blew out two of the windows of the lighthouse above the Sparrow's Nest, close to Lowestoft high street.

For the men waiting for postings, the worst choice was to be transferred to the Northern Patrol and its cold and dreadful sea conditions. But little did they know that many of them would be destined to operate far from the British Isles; many of the men believed that the Royal Naval Patrol Service only meant coastal patrolling and minesweeping. They could not have been more wrong.

Some men had actually made the long journey to North Africa as early as 1941. One group had left on board the troopship *Cameronia* at the end of 1941. They had started off at Lowestoft and had travelled by train to Glasgow. After being held up for a week off Greenock, 5,000 men made the slow four-week journey down to Durban in South Africa. After a couple of days rest they then embarked on the *Mauretania*, bound for Suez. Once they arrived here they went by train to Alexandria.

One of the groups of Royal Naval Patrol Service men that took this trip found themselves in Sidi-Bish Transit Camp in February 1942. They were assigned to the old naval trawler *Moy*. She would see considerable action along the North African coast and off Tobruk. So often did the little trawler visit Tobruk that the crew agreed to pay protection money to a Bofors gun crew. The trawler crew agreed to pay them rum in return for the gun crew firing at any Stukas that were trying to sink the trawler. The trawler's crew also captured an Italian machine gun from an outpost in the desert. They fitted their gun to the deck and then realised they would have to go back to find ammunition for it. The trawler spent nearly forty weeks at Tobruk and eventually went for a refit at Alexandria. The trawler then spent a long period of time at Port Said but she was not the only vessel that was to win the hearts of other servicemen for their work in the Mediterranean.

Far to the east was the Indian Ocean, the hunting ground of Japanese submarines and German surface raiders. The enemy was also very much in evidence off the east coast of the United States and it was believed that the Germans had upwards of 250 operational U-boats. The US Navy had very few anti-submarine vessels at the time and in March 1942 the British Admiralty offered to loan them twenty-four anti-submarine trawlers. Many of these came from Hull or from Grimsby. Five of them would be sunk whilst in US service, but one of them sank *U-215*, and by October 1942 eighteen of them were on their way back home to operate in the South Atlantic.

Towards the end of 1942, on 10 November, two days after British and American forces launched Operation Torch, the trawler *Lord Nuffield* was heading from Oran to Algiers. She was part of the Gibraltar trawler force. It was an incredibly dangerous part of the Mediterranean: there were German and Italian submarines around, enemy aircraft and the danger of the Italian surface fleet. The trawler was on a 200-mile voyage alone and commanded by Skipper Lieutenant David Mair. Mair was a Royal Naval Patrol Serviceman, with solid fishing experience and an anti-submarine specialist. The trawler was about fifty miles from Algiers when they made a contact. It was about a mile ahead and moving slowly. Mair ordered the men to make ready the depth charges.

Steaming at full speed the trawler passed over the contact. Mair was just about to launch the first of the depth charges when there was a shout. He swung around to see a submarine coming up so close to the trawler that he thought they were going to collide. The submarine swung away and began to crash dive. At precisely that point the depth charges were fired. There was a series of huge explosions but the contact was now lost.

The asdic operator picked up a slight echo and Mair decided to search for the enemy, turning about with the crew ready for anything. Contact was picked up around half a mile away; they were about 900m from the target when they spotted the submarine beginning to rise out of the water. They saw Italian sailors rushing to man the guns.

The trawler fired first, followed by two more shots. The third shot hit the submarine and the crew could see enemy sailors falling into the water. The submarine fired back but the trawler hit the submarine with two more shots. They then began firing shrapnel. The Italians seemed to have had enough and abandoned their guns, waving their arms in surrender. But the submarine was already sinking and it slid beneath the waves, leaving only the bobbing heads of Italian naval ratings in the water.

The trawler picked up forty-nine Italians, including the captain. The Italian captain complained that he had chosen to ignore the vessel because he thought it was just a tugboat. Mair and his men had managed to destroy a 1,260-ton submarine measuring 290ft and called *Emo*. All the trawler had suffered was one slightly wounded man.

Way out east the Japanese were on the borders of India and were virtual masters of the Indian Ocean. The Pacific had been the graveyard of many of Britain's eastern fleet, and for vessels from the United States and a host of European nations.

It was 11 November 1942, a day after the exploits of the *Lord Nuffield*, when *Bengal* of the Royal Indian Navy was escorting the motor vessel *Ondina*. The captain of *Bengal* was Lieutenant-Commander William J Wilson of the Royal Indian Naval Reserve. Wilson and his seventy-man crew had not come via Lowestoft, but to all intents and purposes *Bengal* was just like a Royal Naval Patrol Service vessel. She was a minesweeper that had been built in Australia and launched in May 1942. She was due to join the 37th Minesweeping Flotilla of the British Eastern Fleet.

Her first port of call was to be Diego Garcia for refuelling. On 11 November the nearest land was the Cocos Islands, 500 miles to the northwest. At around 11.45 they spotted a ship off to port, and as they believed it was a Japanese vessel they prepared for action. It was around eight miles away and as it closed the men on board were convinced that it was a Japanese raider.

They then spotted a second ship ten miles away and approaching from the same direction. The ships were indeed Japanese raiders: the 10,493-ton *Hokoko Maru* and the 8,631-ton *Kyosumi Maru*. Each of them had five 5-inch guns, torpedoes and two aircraft.

There was little chance that *Bengal* could outrun them so Wilson decided to make straight for the enemy. The *Ondina* tried to head for Freemantle, firing her 4-inch gun as she sped away.

The crew of HMT *Flanders*, formerly the *Charles Antram*, which was requisitioned in August 1939 and operated as a minesweeper.

A visit by the Duke of Kent to the Sparrow's Nest in 1940.

HMT *Aston Villa*, sunk off Norway by German aircraft on May 3 1940.

Richard Been Stannard, a lieutenant in the Royal Naval Reserve, commanding HMT *Arab*, off Namsos in April to May 1940. For his courageous actions he was awarded the Victoria Cross. He was later mentioned in despatches and awarded the DSO and Bar..

The crew of HM Drifter *Salpa*.

Offshore defence works on Quivering Sands, between Southend and Queenborough.

Chief Engineer Harry S Sharman, DSM, who was awarded his DSM for services at Dunkirk onboard HM *Drifter Boy Roy*, which was bombed and beached. He was lost onboard HMT *Heyburn Wyke*, which was torpedoed by a submarine at anchor at Ostend on January 2 1945.

British troops being evacuated from Dunkirk in 1940 by a drifter. Note the Lewis gun on deck mounting.

Trawler inspection.

Skipper Tom Crisp, VC, DSC who was in the Royal Navy Trawler Section during the First World War. He was Lowestoft born and a skipper in the Royal Naval Reserve.

HMT *Clotilde*, December 12 1941.

Trawler crewmen shooting at mines with rifles.

HMT *Northern Spray*, whose 4inch gun was placed on a high platform for'ard.

WRENs in Lowestoft.

Charles Henry Brown was killed
whilst fending off a German air attack
in Great Yarmouth harbour, whilst
onboard the trawler *Their Meri*.

The doling out of the rum ration was guaranteed to get
the attention of all crewmen. These are stokers on
September 26 1942.

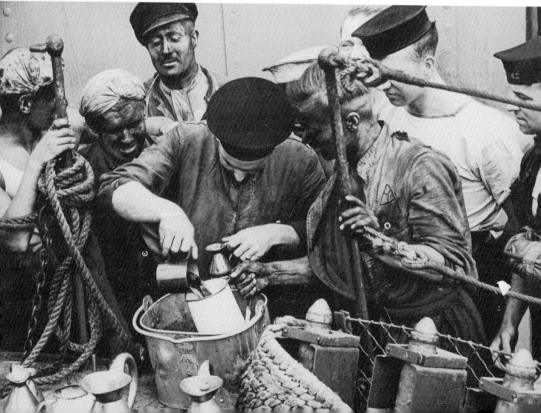

Officers on the bridge of BYMS 46.

Officer on the bridge of BYMS 46.

Officer of BYMS 46.

The mess deck onboard BYMS 46.

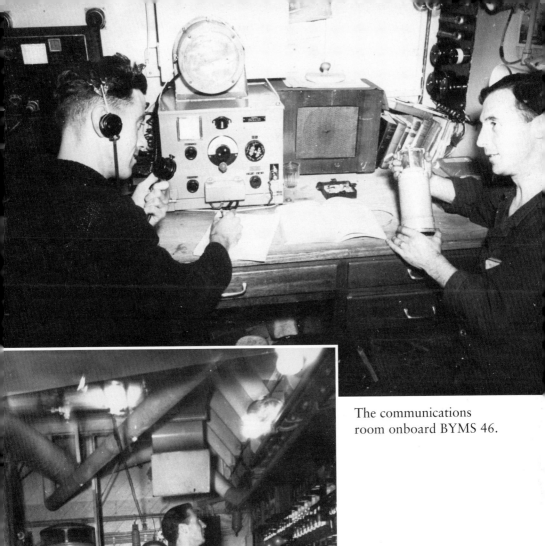

The communications room onboard BYMS 46.

The engine room onboard BYMS 46.

On deck on the BYMS 46.

The skipper and crew of the Great Yarmouth drifter *Youngcliff*, now a minesweeper.

BYMS 46 on a homeward bound sweep.

BYMS 46 on an
outward sweep.

HMT *Birch*.

The wheelhouse of HMT *Alcor..*

The crew of HMT *BenBhrackie*, Lowestoft, June 1 1942.

HMT *Andradite*, May 1942, possibly steaming into Great Yarmouth.

The crew of HMT *Rosemunde (Rosemonde)*, a Harwich based minesweeper that was sunk by U-203 in the Atlantic on January 22 1942. She was a former French fishing vessel.

At 12.12 the first Japanese ship opened fire, narrowly missing *Bengal*, who immediately fired back. By now the second raider was in range and she too began to fire. Incredibly, the sixth round from the *Bengal*'s 12-pdr hit the *Hokoko Maru*. It either hit her magazine or ammunition on deck, but either way she was badly damaged. The *Bengal* had only forty rounds, however, and as soon as these were used up she would be at the mercy of the Japanese.

As the ships continued to fire at one another Wilson found he was down to just five rounds. He decided to break off and make smoke. The largest of the raiders slowed down and did not pursue, but the smaller of the two continued to chase *Bengal*. She steamed westward, swerving to avoid the shellfire. All of a sudden there was an enormous explosion: the damage that the *Bengal* had done to the *Hokoko Maru* had been terminal and she had gone.

For the next fifteen minutes *Bengal* was chased by the *Kyosumi Maru* but eventually got away. It had been a narrow escape, but there was not a single casualty despite the fact that over 200 shells had been fired at her. *Odina* had not been so lucky: her captain had been killed and a number of the crew wounded. The Japanese had even tried to sink her after she had surrendered, but then had given up and had disappeared to the northeast. The crew of the *Odina* had clambered back on board and found that the engines were still intact. They managed to put out the fires and limped back to Freemantle, arriving there ten days later.

Wilson was awarded the DSO, six of the Indian crew the Distinguished Service Medal, and two more were given Orders of Merit.

CHAPTER SEVEN

The Turning Tide in 1943

The coastal waters around Britain were no safer in 1943 than they had been in the darker days of 1940. In many respects, the danger was even greater as the Germans began to perfect their blend of aerial attacks and swift raids by E-boats. In February, German E-boats mounted a successful attack against a convoy of ten merchant ships off Start Point, Devon, sinking three of them. They also boarded a crippled landing ship and took twelve prisoners before finishing off the vessel with a torpedo.

The Royal Naval Patrol Service trawlers were not immune either; E-boats claimed the whaler *Harstad* and the trawler *Lord Hailsham*. Another victim a few weeks later was *Adonis*, an Ipswich-based trawler when she was sunk off Lowestoft. One of the few survivors was T Roy Sparkes:

> Running out of Ipswich at that time were two flotillas of patrol vessels, each with an RDF-equipped master ship, one of which was *Adonis* and the other the *Norland*. The RDF (early radar) had a range of only six miles, and was a diabolical and misleading thing of false comfort. [We] sailed on the ominous date of Friday, April 13 1943. I had a premonition that something was about to happen, the feeling being so strong that I sewed a pocket into my old Mae West lifejacket, bought from a crewmate for a dollar of beer money, and into it stowed my wallet and a few personal photographs. On the night of the 14th, after manoeuvring my way across the pitching deck to

take over the middle watch, I had been settled down in the radar caboose astern for about an hour when I became aware of movement on the screen. There was a blip or two at about 6,000 or 7,000 yards. With the general conditions and the hand turned radar 'aerial' to contend with, the blip was at about 2,000 yards before I could make any really definite report. At 1.15 am I whistled up the old voice pipe to the bridge to report my suspicions, but they could see nothing. The range then closed to 1,700 yards. From the bridge I heard the muffled order given to fire star shells, a task for our foc'sle gun crew with their pride of weaponry, an old Japanese 14-pounder. Then all hell was let loose, Faintly I heard the gun's report, followed almost immediately by a huge explosion – the whole ship appeared to heave her guts and shudder. Up in my radar caboose, on its four spindly angle iron legs, I was flung violently forward, crashing my nose into the radar tube. All the lights had gone out and I felt the floor beneath me begin to tilt.

It still was not clear exactly what had happened and Sparkes could not contact the bridge:

There was a further lurch, the whole cabin tilting even more alarmingly towards the bows. At that moment a quiet voice spoke to me, seemingly out of the air. It insisted that I try the door again. With one mighty sweep of the palm of my hand I clouted each cleat in what seemed one movement. Destiny or luck was with me, the sinking movement carried the heavy door the right way and it swung away, the open space now rising above me. The night sky was lit by tracer flares. With an effort I clambered through the door on to the small cat platform, but a sudden lurch flung me down. I grabbed a rung of the narrow steel ladder which led to the deck and found myself twisting until I was hanging by one hand underneath the slope of the ladder.

There was nothing for it but for him to jump into the sea:

Then a rumbling noise arrested my thoughts and anchored my mounting panic: the depth charges astern were loose and threatening to roll in my direction. I let go and dropped into the icy North Sea, kicking and thrashing, catching my legs, and shins on floating wood and wreckage as I tried to make clear of the stricken ship. A large wave caused me to all but give up the ghost there and then for in spite of the lifejacket in which I had lived, eaten and slept, I was almost a gonner. Then I kicked out strongly and began to make headway through the seething black water, while around me I was aware of lads and men shouting, throwing up their arms and sinking from sight, and large timbers suddenly shooting up from out of the depths like huge rockets. I continued swimming. I then heard my first coherent conversation out of the chaos, voices crying out for guidance on freezing rafts or cutting a boat adrift from the fast sinking debris, though icy water, rusty cleats, and rope that had not been disturbed for months, resisted all their attempts. I swam on in no particular direction not caring so long as I cleared the two halves of *Adonis* which I saw standing starkly, bow and stern to the night sky.

Sparkes was not alone:

I saw a group of heads bobbing about and recognised one voice as that of a leading seaman. I struck out in that direction but then again that 'voice' I had heard in the radar cabin spoke to me clearly: 'No, no – this way.' As if to confirm it someone shouted: 'Over this way – the skipper's here!' I changed direction, swam towards the sound and came upon a well-laden Carley float with the second-in-command, Skipper Cyril White, there among the survivors (our commanding officer, Skipper Draper, had been lost in the first few seconds of the action). But there was no more room on the life raft and I could do no more than grab a loop of rope and continue to dangle in the freezing water. After some time it became obvious that I couldn't hold on to the thin line much longer, so with struggling effort and rocking change of position, everyone sitting straddle fashion, a small space was made on the raft and I was lugged aboard.

After what seemed like an interminable wait in the churning conditions, help was finally in sight:

In the early dawn, just as two or three men were beginning to give way to the effects of exposure, we heard again the throb of engines, and into view loomed the craft we had seen before, now about half a mile away. We shouted and waved, at the same time holding aloft a rather dim Carley light on a lanyard. The boat carried on, and for a moment our hearts sank as we felt that our last chance before our energy and will faded had deserted us; then to the amazement of us all she heeled and turned. This time there was no doubt – she was making for us straight as a homing pigeon. As she drew near we managed a feeble cheer. She was an RAF rescue launch and we were soon being dragged aboard. The RAF crew were the Samaritans that night, giving us their last smokes and brandy; even their personal and precious stored caches were brought out of hiding. They said they had been almost to Rotterdam seeking a ditched bomber and failed to locate it, but none the less their journey had been necessary – sentiments we were quick, to echo. We reached Harwich about 6 am, and fixed up with some temporary gear we eventually returned to the base at Ipswich which some of us had given up hope of ever seeing again.

Only eleven of the thirty-two crew had survived the ordeal. Six of the crew had been in the service for eight weeks, their first trip out; they had not even had their eighteenth birthdays. Destroyers belonging to the Harwich Flotilla launched a revenge raid the following day against the E-boats in their home base of Rotterdam. After putting the base out of commission they had the sad duty of picking up the bodies of some of the *Adonis* crew.

At the end of April 1943 no fewer than nine German U-boats were ordered to form a line close to Cape Finisterre. The expectation was that some prize merchant victims would soon be arriving. The U-boats were in position by 1 May and two days later one of the submarines, *U-439*, commanded by Oberleutnant zur See von Tippelskirch, was appraised by a German reconnaissance aircraft that fifteen vessels were close by, escorted by a pair of trawlers. The *U-439* was accompanied by the *U-659*, commanded by Captain-Lieutenant Hans Stock, who had already sunk over 30,000 tons of allied shipping. The pair of them made towards the last known position of the allied vessels.

They were in fact closing in on two southbound convoys. The first was escorted by the trawlers *Bream* and *Coverley* and the second convoy was even larger. It was mainly landing craft and they were being escorted by the trawler *Huddersfield Town* and the Norwegian trawler *Molde*.

Just before midnight on 3 May the *U-439* spotted the smaller convoy first. They were coastal force craft and the submarine got into a position ready to attack. The submarine moved ahead of the convoy; the commander's aim was to pass through the convoy and smash them to pieces with his deck guns and torpedoes. The *U-439* surfaced as planned and sped towards the convoy. All of a sudden the *U-659* appeared alongside. The *U-439* could not avoid collision and it struck the other submarine. Both submarines were badly damaged. The *U-659*'s pressure hull had been ripped open and the vessel was filling with oil and seawater. It sank within minutes. Meanwhile the *U-439*, crippled, also began to sink.

The small convoy was closing on the position and the trawler *Coverley* hit an obstruction in the water and shone lights. The crew could see the wreckage of the *U-439* just disappearing below the water. They were able to pick up just thirteen survivors from the submarine.

The trawler *Northern Spray* was involved in a major engagement in the Atlantic in May 1943. In just four days some thirty U-boats managed to destroy ten merchant vessels *en route* to the United States. In return, the convoy escorts claimed at least five U-boats, two of which had been rammed. The *Northern Spray* was operating in amongst the chaos, picking up survivors from the merchantmen until the trawler picked up a U-boat contact on her asdic. It was a difficult situation: there were still men in the water and by dropping depth charges serious injuries if not deaths would result. Nonetheless she did drop depth charges and then turned to pick up more survivors, by which time she had 145 on board. As *Northern Spray* steamed towards Newfoundland she narrowly missed being sunk by an American destroyer, such was the confusion in the area at the time.

In the same vicinity *Northern Foam* was operating, commanded by Lieutenant Bryn Harris, RNVR. She too was on escort duty and there were two inbound convoys on their way. It was known that at least one U-boat was in the area. It was decided to bring both of the convoys together and put them under the protection of the combined escorts. Despite this the U-boat (almost certainly *U-305*) managed to torpedo and sink HMCS *St Croix* at 21.51 on 20 September 1943. There also another U-boat operating in the area, the *U-952*, and just after midnight she claimed the corvette HMS *Polyanthus*. Fog then prevented any further attacks.

The fog was still thick the following day, but *Northern Foam* managed to spot a U-boat just 300m away. She increased speed to ram the submarine but it just managed to get out of the way in time. The trawler opened up with her 4-inch gun and hit the target near the conning tower. She then manoeuvred to try and ram the submarine again. By now the U-boat had dived, so the trawler dropped ten depth charges. The submarine was forced to surface close by and made off with the trawler in pursuit.

Some hours later the *Northern Foam* spotted another U-boat 1,500m away. She fired a star shell just as the U-boat was submerging. The trawler went into the attack with depth charges and there was a loud, bubbling noise before the trawler stopped engines. The bubbling grew fainter and then a large oil slick was visible. In all probability the U-boat had been destroyed.

The trawler then steamed back towards the convoy and arrived just as more German submarines launched an attack, torpedoing three merchant ships. The trawler's asdic was out of action by this time and she began to pick up survivors. By the time she had finished she had seventy-five extra men on board. The fog closed in again and the trawler prudently took the decision to make for St John's Harbour.

The Selby-built trawler *Daneman* had been repaired in Belfast after she had run aground near Archangel in September 1942. She had completed basic repairs in Russia before heading for Belfast. Work was finally finished on her in April 1943 and she was ordered to join a North Atlantic convoy, under the command of Lieutenant Stanley Lock, RNVR. The shipyard workers were still on board when she was given the order to sail. It was clear to Lock that the vessel lacked the storage space for the coal required for such a voyage. Consequently, tons of coal were put onto her deck.

She sailed from Londonderry and only about four days out there was flooding in the engine room. The crew formed a chain, passing buckets backwards and forwards to bale her out. As a consequence she began to fall behind the convoy. Two of the escorts turned back to come to her aid, but by now they were in an ice zone and there were icebergs all around. The little trawler was listing heavily to starboard when the ocean rescue tug *Bulldog* arrived to help. A pump was taken on board the trawler to deal with the flooding. The sea got rougher and the wind increased and by now the *Daneman* was half full of water and listing severely. She was under tow as well and as the hours passed the listing increased.

Close by was a French corvette that had also come to assist. It was finally decided that the trawler should be abandoned. Fifteen of the men got on board the Carley float and the rest of the crew had to jump onto the *Bulldog*. At times there was up to twenty feet between the hulls, so the men had to jump at the right moment. Two of the men got it wrong and fell between the ships. As soon as the crew was off, the *Bulldog* fired at the *Daneman* to finish her off. She caught fire and began to settle in the water. In all, the episode had cost six lives.

Meanwhile, in the Mediterranean, Royal Naval Patrol Service vessels were now to be involved in the allied landings in Sicily and subsequently on the Italian mainland. One of the trawlers, *King Sol*, had been operating from Gibraltar for some time in anti-U-boat sweeps in the Atlantic. Her first trip out of Gibraltar had seen her rendezvous with a convoy coming from the United States around 250 miles to the west. The convoys heading in this direction were all part of the build up for the allied offensive around the Mediterranean. Algeria was, by this stage, in allied hands.

Another trawler operating in the Mediterranean was *Foxtrot*, under the command of Lieutenant John Bald, RNVR. She was operating out of Algiers. On one occasion she steamed to the assistance of a number of convoy vessels that had been attacked by a German U-boat. The submarine had destroyed a tanker carrying high-octane fuel. It had then sunk the French ship *Siddi Bel Abbes* that was carrying 1,500 Senegalese. This vessel sank in three minutes. The third ship hit was the City of Michigan, an American vessel that sunk in around fifteen minutes. *Foxtrot* managed to pick up 400 men and get them safely to Oran.

Shortly before Italy's surrender, Lieutenant Dormer commanding the trawler *Hornpipe* was also on patrol near Algiers. There was a loud noise around midnight and Dormer saw an aircraft crash into the sea. All of a sudden a second aircraft appeared and *Hornpipe*'s crew opened fire, driving it away. There was some confusion after this event, as the trawler was commended for its action and everyone believed that the crashed aircraft, which turned out to be Italian, had actually been shot down by Dormer's crew, rather than just crashed into the sea.

In 1943 the Royal Naval Patrol Service had lost seven trawlers in the Mediterranean alone: two to German submarines, two to Italian submarines and three to mines.

The tide had also turned in the Far East, or at least it was beginning to. Royal Naval Patrol Service trawlers in the minesweeping role were now arriving in force for operations in the Far East. However to get there it was a long and perilous journey.

One such vessel was *Lord Grey*; she had served with the 130th Minesweeping Group in Falmouth and was then converted to tropical service and ordered to proceed to Ceylon (Sri Lanka). In command was Lieutenant Austin, RNVR, and the bulk of the crew were direct from Lowestoft. The first stage of the journey took her from Greenock to the Azores.

On the morning of 22 November 1941, in dreadful seas, Austin had been forced to turn around and make for Campbeltown. Austin was subsequently posted elsewhere and command was taken over by Sub-Lieutenant John Challis. The trawler tried again on 19 December, but once again had to return to harbour, as the new captain had been badly injured. Command now fell on Lieutenant Maurice Hampson, who was told that his vessel was desperately needed. Hampson was a 'hostilities only' man and prior to 1939 had no experience of the sea. He was, however, enthusiastic.

They made the perilous journey to the Azores and then on to Gibraltar. The next stage of the journey was to be even more perilous: a 2,000-mile trip to Freetown. They sailed on 29 January 1942 and spent a week at the staging port then made for Lagos, nearly 1,200 miles away. The next stage of the journey was Walvis Bay, 2,000 miles away. After that was 750 miles to Cape Town and by the time they got there the crew had realised that they were still only halfway to their final destination. The trawler left Cape Town and made for Durban at the beginning of April 1942. They then sailed, on 9 April, for Mombasa; this would be their last major stop before travelling 2,300 miles to Ceylon. They would only make one stop in between, in the Seychelles.

The trawler eventually arrived at Colombo on 25 May 1942. It had been an epic journey and one that had been taken without any asdic on board. The men had suffered broken bones, dysentery and a host of other tropical illnesses.

Another such journey was taken by *Lord Grey*'s sister ship, *Lord Irwin*. She had been sent round the Cape to become the first Royal Naval Patrol Service minesweeper in the Mediterranean. The trip had taken six months and five days. Although the crew suffered enormously during the voyage, it was clear that they were still more than able to carry out their duties when they arrived in the Mediterranean. In their first sweep they destroyed eight enemy mines.

Back in the Mediterranean, it was abundantly clear to the Germans that despite attempts by the allies to persuade them that the offensive would fall on southern France, or even Greece, the big blow would come against Sicily and the Italian mainland. The vast numbers of allied vessels operating in the Mediterranean offered something of a bonanza for German submarines if they could be deployed into the Mediterranean quickly enough. Getting there, however, was a major problem, as the allies had begun to perfect anti-submarine warfare. Vessels of the Royal Naval Patrol Service were a vital part of this perfection.

One such U-boat that aimed to get into the Mediterranean was the *U-732*, commanded by Oberleutnant zur See Klaus Peter Carlsen. The *U-732* slipped out of Brest on 17 October 1943. She was to sail towards the Portuguese coast and then slip through the Straits of Gibraltar and into the Mediterranean. This last part of the journey had to be carried out underwater and at around 13.00 on 31 October, at the entrance to the Straits, the submarine picked up propeller noises on her hydrophones.

Almost directly above the submarine were six merchantmen, heading from Lisbon to Gibraltar. Unfortunately for Carlsen they were accompanied by a pair of trawlers. The first was *Imperialist*, commanded by Lieutenant-Commander Bryan Rodgers, RNVR, and the second was *Loch Oskaig*, commanded by Lieutenant George Clampitt, RNR.

At precisely 13.16 the *Imperialist* picked up a submarine contact. Rodgers checked and it was confirmed that the contact was no more than 1000m away. Action stations were called. *Imperialist* was well armed: she had a 4-inch gun, a Bofors, two machine guns near the funnel, another pair amidships and depth charges. Rodgers ordered Clampitt to continue to guard the convoy whilst he investigated the contact. Four minutes after the initial contact *Imperialist* fired her first of ten depth charges.

The U-boat was around 200ft below them. As the depth charges exploded the U-boat was rocked and choking fumes filled every compartment within the submarine. Moments later the badly mauled U-boat surfaced; the crew on board *Imperialist* could see that the conning tower was buckled and the barrel of one of her guns was bent. She lay in the water inert.

Already *Imperialist*'s Bofors gun was firing at the submarine. As the trawler came about the starboard Oerlikon came into action, as did the 4-inch gun. For ten minutes the trawler fired at the submarine. *Imperialist* was then joined by the steamer *Fylingdale*, who fired machine guns at the U-boat. Then there was an explosion from the submarine and a green-yellow gas started to emerge, just as the submarine began to sink. In moments the U-boat had disappeared under the water. Rodgers decided to make sure that it was finished off and fired ten more depth charges. He felt confident when he could get no contact that the U-boat had been finally destroyed.

Incredibly, the *U-732* had not been destroyed. She had hit the bottom some 585ft below the surface. Carlsen had then ordered the submarine's motors to be turned off. By 21.00 Carlsen had to try to get to the surface as the air had become so foul, and when the U-boat did emerge the scene was deserted. The *U-732* was right in the middle of the Gibraltar Straits and began moving towards the Atlantic. It needed to find somewhere for emergency repairs, but thirty-four minutes later a search beam caught her. It was from an anti-submarine patrol operating out of Gibraltar. HMS *Douglas* had found the submarine and she opened fire. Through his binoculars the destroyer captain could see that the submarine's crew were signalling to surrender. He ordered the destroyer around to ram the U-boat. Just as he got to the point of contact the U-boat turned away and the destroyer dropped a pattern of depth charges. This time the *U-732* could not escape. The captain and twenty-one other survivors were picked up.

CHAPTER EIGHT

Up to Full Strength

On 6 January 1944 the Leith-built Royal Naval Patrol Service trawler, *Wallasea*, was escorting a convoy from the Bristol Channel to Plymouth. She was attacked by a group of E-boats in Mounts Bay, Cornwall. The E-boats sank her, along with two of the convoy.

Three days earlier, on 3 January, the Aberdeen-built trawler *Pine* was also on escort duty, this time off Selsey Bill. She was attacked by three separate E-boat flotillas. The *Pine* had her bows blown off by a torpedo but she remained afloat, trying to fend off the E-boats. Despite her efforts two of the merchant ships were sunk. Help finally arrived, but the courageous little trawler sank whilst in tow *en route* to Portsmouth.

Another near miss in January was the former Belgian trawler that had been converted to a French minesweeper and then had become part of the Royal Naval Patrol Service, *Cap d'Antifer*. She was working off the Humber when she was attacked by four E-boats. She managed to drive them off but in the following month, on February 13, she was not so lucky. A flotilla of E-boats attacked her whilst she was minesweeping, again off the Humber. A torpedo sent her to the bottom in a matter of minutes.

By the spring of 1944 the Royal Naval Patrol Service was up to full strength, with 57,000 officers and men. The vast majority were 'hostilities only' men. There was still an enormous amount of work to be done in the build up to the liberation of Europe and, ultimately, the defeat of Japan. The duties were still as varied as ever: there were convoys in ever-increasing size to be protected; thousands of mines still to be swept; and the ever-present danger of U-boats.

A relatively small convoy, consisting of three merchantmen, had left Loch Ewe on the northwest of Scotland heading for Iceland. Their escorts were the trawlers *Northern Spray* and *Veleta*. Also attached to the convoy was the 1913 Aberdeen-built *Strathella*. She had been carrying out duties as a harbour defence patrol craft off Iceland and had two 6-pdr guns and a pair of Browning machine guns for anti-aircraft work. She also carried an asdic set and depth charges. The trawler, which had been taken over by the Royal Navy in 1940, was commanded by Temporary Lieutenant Osmund Lee, RNVR. He had had no nautical experience before joining the reserve in 1941. The trawler carried a crew of twenty, most of whom were seasoned fishermen. They had spent several months working out of Iceland and had then been sent to North Shields for a refit. From there she had gone to Tobermory, where she had developed some engine problems and consequently she had gone to a repair yard at Oban. She was ready to join up with the convoy, where she took up station on the port beam. *Veleta* covered the starboard beam and *Northern Spray* led the procession.

The weather conditions were relatively good until dusk on 12 January. Shortly after midnight Lee's first lieutenant, Temporary Sub-Lieutenant Alan Bateman, lost sight of the other ships in the convoy. In the heavy seas the trawler was beginning to experience engine problems and there was a gale developing. With the wind blowing at near hurricane strength and the waves 30ft high, Lieutenant Bryant, on board *Veleta*, spotted *Strathella* and then she disappeared.

The gale continued for forty-eight hours. Once it had blown itself out, Lieutenant Downer, the senior officer on board *Northern Spray*, realised that *Strathella* was no longer with them. Now that the weather had improved there was a danger that U-boats might be operating in the area, but the two remaining trawlers set out to search for *Strathella*. They dared not leave the convoy unguarded and after a cursory search they made for Reykjavik, arriving there on 19 January.

A search was instituted and on 23 January the Admiral commanding in Iceland informed the Admiralty that *Strathella* must be presumed lost. So certain were they that she had either sunk or a U-boat had got her that telegrams were sent to relatives. They could not have been more wrong: she was still afloat.

She had heaved to on 12 January in the dreadful conditions. Her machine guns had been washed overboard, her signalling searchlight smashed and some of her depth charges had also gone overboard. Water had got into the wireless cabin and burned out the transmitter, hence she could not respond to the searching vessels' calls. By 21 January, with leaking boiler tubes and falling steam pressure, the decision had been made to hold back what little coal she had left for heating and cooking to try to ensure that the crew survived in the freezing conditions. The crew had managed to rig up a crude sail, but this had little effect and she was barely moving. They began rationing the food and fired off distress signals. They cannibalised the asdic to try to get the wireless set working again, but all they could come up with was a very weak signal.

By now she was being swept west at a rate of five to ten miles a day and the currents had taken her well off course and out of the search area. Lieutenant Lee tried his best to keep up the men's spirits.

On the morning of 27 January they spotted land about thirty miles to the northwest. At a guess it was Greenland. Lee decided to risk all and strip all the wooden fittings and the remaining coal to get her underway again. She was underway by 10.00 hours on 28 January but they found themselves entering an area covered in icebergs. There were only two hours of steam left in the boiler and, finally, the engines gave up. They fired off more distress rockets. The vessel was now well within the Arctic Circle and everything was covered with a thick layer of ice. The men spent their time chipping off the ice, just to keep themselves warm. At least they now had fresh water, which was a scant reward for their predicament. The crew's greatest fear was that they would either freeze or starve to death before they could be found.

Against all hope they spotted land again on 8 February. Once again they tried to make a sail out of bed sheets and blackout screens. It took four days for them to complete this work. All around them were icebergs. It was obvious that when they hoisted the sail on the morning of 12 February it would fall to pieces in anything other than a moderate breeze.

Incredibly, as they were hoisting the sail they spotted an aircraft. It was the only ray of hope that they had had for nearly a month. They fired off flares and rockets and flashed their Aldis lamp, but the aircraft did not see them. Their spirits dropped, but by 13 February the trawler was just four miles from land.

At around 17.00 they heard another aircraft: it was a US Navy Catalina. They fired off more signals and even fired one of the 6-pdr guns to attract attention. The aircraft spotted them and came in low. The Catalina signalled to them and told them that help was on its way from Greenland. Just before dawn the following day the US coastguard cutter, *Madoc*, arrived to end their ordeal.

In the early hours of 22 January 1944 American troops of the US Fifth Army established a beachhead on the Italian coast, below Rome, at Anzio. Royal Naval Patrol Service vessels were heavily involved in minesweeping operations, particularly against Italian minefields around Pantelleria, Sicily, Sardinia, Elba and the coast of mainland Italy. One of the trawlers involved was *Hornpipe*. She was involved in these Anzio landings and we are fortunate that Lieutenant Dormer, the skipper of the vessel, kept a diary:

The typhus has spread, and we are not allowed ashore at all. Nor can laundry be sent. We have all been issued with anti-louse powder. Some 'enterprise of great pith and moment' is in the offing. The port is crowded, heavy air attacks are expected, and we close up at dawn and dusk. The burning question is, are *we going*? Will the steering be repaired in time? We coaled today, a hopeful sign, since there had even been talk of digging our coal out. They brought a coal barge to *us*... never before.

Confinement on board is no joke. Some of the sailors have even taken to writing letters to each other for the benefit of the censor... me.

Tuesday. We are very likely to go on the party now, so there is a crescendo of excitement, and grim jokes. The whole area is in a fever of preparation. German reconnaissance planes have been over, so they'll probably be waiting on the beaches. The only question is, where? Funny to think that some unsuspecting little town or village will, in a few days, be world famous.

Wednesday. The steering is mended, and excitement increased so much that people worked overtime without even remembering to grumble. At last, extricating ourselves with great difficult from the mass of ships and landing craft, we sailed to Castelamare for the night, with best wishes from the stay-at-home. There, as soon as dusk fell, every sort of flap arose... human torpedoes, E-boats.... But nothing happened, though we spent the evening at action stations with a boat full of bombs patrolling round the ship.

Thursday. Checked up on everyone's lifebelts and tin hat. Issued field dressings and checked every detail of organisation and equipment. The CO went to a Most Secret conference of which no details are to be released until actually under way. Let's get cracking, waiting is a strain. Only four trawlers are concerned, we are lucky this time I wonder if we shall be 'lucky' later?

Friday. 'Never sail on a Friday', but we did, about noon, behind a big convoy of landing craft. The officers were only told of the plan in the evening, though Sparks, a leading telegraphist has known all along. So far, at 20.00 hours, all is well. We can see gun flashes, as usual, from the Minturno area, and various aircraft are about.

Saturday. 11.00. The night passed quietly, but the Landing craft were hard to see, and by 03.00 the convoys were in a fair state of confusion. At 05.00 the course seemed wrong, and the speed too slow. I asked the nearest LCI... we were with the wrong convoy. Cracking on we found our flotilla of fleet sweepers at daybreak, and spent a hectic day picking up dan buoys. We had hardly ever done this before, and found it difficult. I spent much of the day in the sea, swimming to shackle on wires.

D-Day. A lovely, calm, sunny day, almost cloudless blue skies. The multitude of ships off the beaches look more like a review than an invasion. The sweepers cut several mines, one of which damaged the A/A cruiser *Palomares*. We are now about to escort her back to Naples, in tow of tugs. There are a few columns of smoke rising from the shore, and every now and then a dull thud. Sometimes a cruiser does a bit of bombarding or a few enemy planes approach. There are constant red warnings, but no attacks yet.

D-Day PLUS 2. Escorted the tug *Evenshaw*, towing two lighters, to Anzio, but had to sink one of them by gunfire as it broke adrift and the sea was too rough to recover it, in spite of using oil. Arrived off the American beaches at 15.00. The town was being heavily shelled, and shells were bursting on the beaches and in the sea. Return fire from US warships was landing quite, close inland. At 16.00 three dive bombers attacked the HQ ship without result, but one American vessel was sunk, with its bows sticking out of the water. At dusk, just as we were setting off with a Naples bound convoy, the Luftwaffe arrived in force, and the next two hours were a terrific muddle of flares and tracer and bombs in all directions. We hardly fired at all ourselves, but I saw four aircraft go down in flames and the destroyer *Janus*, badly hit and burning. We had a nasty half hour later, well out on our own, having lost the convoy in the confusion. Enemy planes dropped dozens of flares in a circle round us, but we made smoke and were not attacked.

Hornpipe arrived off Anzio four days after the landing:

Just at dusk, the worst possible time, with the convoy of LSTs disorganised by a gale, there was a heavy air attack which lasted three hours. A Heinkel attacked us with a torpedo, which I saw drop. We had a go at him but missed, as the ship was rolling in a heavy sea. There were attacks about every half hour all next day as we hung about in the anchorage. I attempted to have a wash but a stick of bombs came down just ahead as soon as I got my shirt off. At 15.00 the BBC boasted about 'our complete mastery of the air over the beach-head'. There were two formations, each of twelve aircraft, cruising overhead, all silvery in the sunshine. We felt nice and safe, until they peeled off and attacked, one after the other. One of them dived straight into the sea: it all looked too like the films to be real. We were very worried about the evening, but the sun went down in a glory of crimson and gold and it got dark without anything happening. No one dared to be the first to say 'I don't think they're coming.' And so it went on.

The trawler was then sent on anti-submarine patrols between the Pontine Islands. The plan was to create a safe zone for inshore shipping. It did not work straight away, as the cruiser HMS *Penelope* was lost to a U-boat. Dormer continued his diary:

One could see for miles, all the beachhead, and the Alban hills, the poplars of the Pontine Marshes, and the great snow capped mountains beyond. All around the perimeter little white puffs appeared, grew into tall columns, and faded away. Against the dark of a leafless wood, we could see the flashes of our own artillery. The afternoon was quiet until the Jerries noticed an LST that had anchored away from the rest. They started shelling it with a most enormous great gun whose shell sent waterspouts up some 150 feet. After the fifth shell, at exactly three minute intervals, the LST was seen to be moving. The sixth shell was close astern of her, but after the seventh they gave up. We, and the *merchant* shipping, remained several miles off shore, the latter unloading into DUKWs.

Mines were still a major problem as Dormer explained:

> One day we were looking forward to provisions from a *fleet*
> sweeper, but they unfortunately hauled up a mine in their
> sweep which killed their first lieutenant. 'Oh dear,' said my
> CO, 'we can hardly ask them for 40 pounds of fresh meat now.'
> Near the end we arrived in the smoke screen one morning,
> simultaneously with several German midget submarines. They
> hadn't a chance, being clearly visible in a glassy calm. Finally,
> just before the breakout from the beach-head, we had to get our
> own sweeps out, to sweep a convoy into Anzio. All the
> sweeping gear was stowed away, and we had forgotten how to
> use it. Surprisingly we got it running, but most of the sweep
> was done in a thick smoke screen, where none of us could see
> each other, and the convoy did not follow in the 'swept' water
> way, so the whole thing was a bit of a farce.

We have already noted that by 1943 to 1944 the bulk of the Royal
Naval Patrol Service personnel were 'hostilities only' men. However
there were also major changes by 1943 in the type of vessels being
used by the service. An enormous number of the original fishing
trawlers had already been lost; a large majority of the vessels now
being used were Admiralty built trawlers. New trawlers were being
commissioned for service on an almost daily basis. The new ones
were far more fit for purpose: they had asdic and radar, they were
faster and had a better endurance. As importantly, they were much
better armed. The vessels were also far more adaptable and could be
used for anti-submarine or for minesweeping duties.

One major innovation was the class known as British Yard
Minesweepers (BYMS). They were wooden, with the idea that they
would not be vulnerable to magnetic mines. Although they were no
bigger than an average fishing trawler they had comparable speeds
and similar range. These vessels were built in US shipyards, under
the lend-lease scheme. Incredibly, they also crossed the Atlantic to
their theatre of operation on their own.

The crews required for these vessels were shipped out to the US,
where they could take over their vessel as soon as it was

commissioned. A prime example was the Seattle-built BYMS *12*. It was taken over by Skipper Lieutenant Cyril Watson, RNR, and his Royal Naval Patrol Service crew. His orders were to proceed to the Mediterranean as soon as the vessel was ready. It was a voyage of 16,000 miles and it would take the vessel five months. They crossed the Gulf of Tehuantepec, off the coast of Mexico in incredibly bad storms. They then worked their way through the Panama Canal, across the Caribbean then made for West Africa. From there the vessel sailed to Gibraltar and into the Mediterranean.

Not all of the vessels were built on the west coast of the United States; the BYMS *39* was built at Beloxi on the Mississippi River. She was commissioned in August 1943 and crewed by Royal Naval Patrol Servicemen. She sailed out of Mobil into the Gulf of Mexico and made for Halifax, Nova Scotia. She then sailed to St John's and begun her Atlantic crossing to Britain. During the voyage she had an unexpected guest one evening, when a U-boat surfaced close beside her. The crew manned their guns and the ship turned to attack. The U-boat crash-dived and made off, but despite the best efforts of the crew they could find no sight of the submarine.

The BYMS vessels were absolute luxury compared to the trawlers and the drifters that many of the men had either trained in or served on. They had all the latest equipment; little wonder as many of the shipyards, particularly around Lake Michigan and the Great Lakes had been used to building expensive pleasure yachts. They were to prove to be incredibly versatile and only six BYMS vessels were lost during the remainder of the war. All of them were lost by mines exploding beside them.

The Germans were losing the battle in attempting to sink allied shipping quicker than it could be built. Of the near 60,000 men directly involved in minesweeping in the run up to Operation Overlord, the Normandy landings in June 1944, 60 per cent of them belonged to the Royal Naval Patrol Service. The sheer numbers of minesweeping vessels was incredible. There were 947 of them operating in British coastal waters, and a further 547 in different locations overseas.

The arrival of the BYMS vessels certainly did not mean the end of trawlers and drifters being deployed in the minesweeping role. It was simply another addition to the enormous menu of different vessels already in use, from motor launches and landing craft, to motor minesweepers and fishing vessels.

A notable casualty in June 1944 was the whaler *Southern Pride*. She had been taken over by the Admiralty before she was completed in 1940. At the time she was the largest whale catcher in the world, along with her sister ship, *Southern Gem*. They were both prototypes of Flower Class corvettes and able to maintain a speed of at least 20 knots. The design had been for her to be capable of reaching South Africa without needing to be refuelled. Now she was armed with a 4-inch gun and depth charges, and by the middle of 1943 *Southern Pride* and *Southern Gem* were operating out of Freetown in West Africa. *Southern Pride* was perfectly capable of crossing the Atlantic, which she did on at least one occasion, when she sailed with a cable ship to Brazil. She escorted vessels across from Brazil to Dakar, via Freetown, on a regular basis.

In June 1944, along with another trawler, *Southern Pride* had been sent to escort a merchant ship to Liberia. She ran onto a shoal thirty miles from Monrovia, off Marshall Port at 1904 on 16 June. The whaler's number one was Lieutenant Allan Waller, who explained what happened next:

> I was sitting with the chief engineer outside the wardroom on the starboard waist when the ship struck. It felt as if she had been mined by an acoustic ground mine. I seized my lifebelt and hurried to my action station on the bridge, while the chief ran aft. There were more shocks as I arrived on the bridge, like exploding depth charges this time. 'We're hit,' said the captain – 'Unprime depth charges.' While we were doing this the ship rocked heavily but was not sinking, and seemed to have stopped. There were more shocks and it now seemed we were striking either rock or hard sand. In four minutes the depth charges had been made safe and I was back on the bridge. A signal was sent to the trawler *Pict* and I tried to fix our exact

position – we were about three miles from shore in shark infested waters – but this was impossible in the failing light.

Despite the best efforts of the crew, as Waller explained, the vessel was doomed:

The cox'n took over the wheel and the captain tried to move the ship at slow ahead, without success. The engines were then tried at slow astern. The wheel would not answer, but the ship appeared to move very slowly. Soundings were taken and two fathoms reported; the bangings and grindings ceased. The captain decided to anchor, as the ship seemed to have cleared the rocks and was riding well, but the chief engineer reported that the pumps were unable to cope with the water and it would soon be necessary to draw the fires. The captain then decided to try to beach the ship, and we began to heave in the anchor, but before this could be done the chief said that the engine room would have to be abandoned. More cable was let out and the anchor secured. The ship was still rising buoyantly and was well out of the water, though she had in fact been holed right under the Scotch boiler. The asdic well had been made watertight. It was now two hours since we had struck the shoal and there was not much more we could do. I helped the captain to decide on the ship's position and compose a signal to senior officer West Africa which we tried to send off over our own set, an attempt which was abandoned when the lights failed and power was low.

The captain and crew could only hope for the best and that help would arrive:

Rum was issued, all hands gathered on the well-deck to hear a reassuring talk by the captain, and a sing-song was organised to help keep up morale. Some men broke into the wardroom spirit locker, and one troublesome seaman had to be shut up in the heads. Watches were organised, those off watch trying to rest. Still the ship showed no signs of sinking, though water was rising slowly in the engine room. Shortly after midnight several shocks were felt and the ship suddenly began to settle port side aft. We had already lost one boat so a few of us now tried to build rafts by lashing together empty oil drums. There were four of us, Sub Lieutenant Dunn, Lieutenant (E) Johansen, the chief engineer, Telegraphist Roberts and myself. But there was a heavy swell running, and just as we had completed one raft the ship lurched heavily to port and lay over at an angle, a huge sea came over and carried away our raft and all other floatable gear on the boat deck. We ourselves escaped, by each selecting a funnel guy and, when the sea came over, swarming up it, though I suffered a badly lacerated leg. A Carley float with three native stokers on it was also swept away, but kept afloat.

It was now becoming clear that the vessel would not last much longer:

I went down to the main deck to see if everyone there was all right. The ship was now listing to an angle of about 30 degrees; most of the hands were sitting on the starboard rail which was clear of the water. I remembered the seaman we had shut up, and making my way forward with difficulty because of the angle of the ship, found him lying completely unconscious outside the heads, the tapes of his lifebelt wound round his neck. Shaking him did no good so in desperation I kicked and punched him. At last he came round a little and started raving. With the help of two men, I sat him up with his lifebelt well inflated and fastened securely fastened round his chest, then got him to the rail, where he seemed to realise to some extent his danger. I left him hanging over a rail with a rating on either side, satisfied that if he kept only slight control he would easily save himself, for at that end the ship was only about four feet under water. Scrambling back along the ship I then tried with Signalman Stone to get a message to a boat from *Pict*, which seemed to be having difficulty in finding us, and in the process was nearly washed over the side. *Pride* was righting herself quickly and the rising waters forced us to climb upwards to the lower bridge veranda and the Oerlikon and four-inch platforms. *Pict's* boat finally took off the first load, and as the lower bridge was crowded I climbed to the upper bridge and from there on to the searchlight platform on top. There was nothing to do now but wait to be taken off. *Pict's* boat came over four or five times for new loads, during which time the swell moderated and it grew lighter.

Waller looked at his watch just before he jumped overboard; it was 05.17 and ten hours since they had struck the shoal. Only one man had been lost and even the ship's dog had swum the three miles to the beach. The three stokers that had been washed overboard with the Carney float managed to make it ashore. The crew had one bright moment: all of their money was sitting in the safe underwater. Waller returned with the salvage crew and he went down to rescue the cash and managed to dry it all out.

There was another loss that same week, on 13 June 1944, when *Birdlip* was torpedoed and sunk by the *U-547*. Fifteen men managed to survive and get ashore in two life rafts when the boat went down off Lagos, Nigeria.

Another major exploit by a Royal Naval Patrol Service vessel, somewhat reminiscent of the trials and tribulations suffered by the crew of *Strathella*, but in altogether more warm conditions, was *Duncton*. She was an Admiralty-built trawler launched in September 1941. She was based at Freetown on the West African coast and in April 1944 she had gone down to Cape Town for a three month refit. The work was completed by the July, but on her way back to Lagos her engine broke down, as her number one, Lieutenant Arthur Miles, recalled:

A few days out of Walvis Bay, where we called for repairs to our W/T transmitter, the engines were stopped owing to leaking boiler tubes. Spare tubes were fitted, but more leaks developed. Our transmitter remained out of order so we couldn't wireless for help, and it was a case of improvising as best we could to stop the leaks, which now affected a great number of the tubes. Several times the boilers were refilled by hand pump, all hands from the captain to the cook taking a spell, but steam was raised only to produce further leaks, and repairs had to be started all over again. Fortunately the weather was perfect, whales and sharks playing around our silent ship. One evening a sing-song on deck came to an abrupt end when the lookout sighted mysterious green flares, and action-stations was sounded. Nothing happened but we felt like sitting ducks, remembering the fate of *Birdlip*. Food and water were now rationed, no fresh water at all for washing, and everyone grew beards. Somebody joked 'Why don't we sail her?' and very soon the idea was being taken seriously. The big foredeck awning made a good mainsail, and every bit of canvas aboard, together with some pretty odd bits of bunting, was hoisted until the ship was festooned with 'sails'. As one of the crew described it, we looked like the washing on the Siegfried Line. There was a steady wind on the beam and the quartermaster steered from the auxiliary wheel aft. By Dutchman's log *Duncton's* speed under sail was a good one knot! The wind blew steadily off the coast so that we could not, with our unwieldy rig, even tack towards it, and the best we could manage was to continue heading north. Every day our dinghy put off on a practice cruise in preparation for sending a volunteer crew hundreds of miles north to the Portuguese island of Sao Tome, to fetch help. This would have been very much a last resort, and luckily the most they did was take snapshots of us – the last sailing man-o'-war, for at last steam was raised. Our engineers' makeshift repairs enabled us to limp slowly into Lagos after about a fortnight without engines. We learned that aircraft had made several fruitless searches for us and our next-of-kin cards had already been taken out at base. We were back from the dead.

CHAPTER NINE

New Men,
New Experiences

For the past four years or more it had been trawlers, drifters and a host of other different vessels that had kept the convoy channels around the British Isles swept and the east coast harbours open for shipping. As the war continued, as we have seen, the majority of the Royal Naval Patrol Service personnel were 'hostilities only' men. However, the supply of men with seagoing experience had been all-but dried up. Amongst the ranks of the patrol service were now farm labourers, navvies, office workers, taxi drivers and men from a host of other different occupations across the British Isles.

The men that had formed the Anti-Invasion Auxiliary Patrol and the River Emergency Service had been completely absorbed into the Royal Naval Patrol Service. The River Emergency Service was made up of Londoners and boat owners who had used their own vessels to help deal with fires and mines around the Thames. The patrol service also had its fair share of conscientious objectors, many of them choosing to join the service in the belief that they would primarily be dealing with minesweeping. The majority discovered that they would in fact be involved in offensive actions against the enemy.

As the influxes of radically different men came into the service there was always the problem of balance. Whilst the officers may have had some ocean-going experience, it was also vital for the 'hostilities only' crews to be supplemented by those whose life was related to the sea. In one example of five BYMS vessels only one of the commanding officers was a Royal Naval Reserve skipper. All of the other skippers were Royal Naval Volunteer Reserve officers with a variety of civilian occupations. Nonetheless, the majority of the crews were moulded into effective units.

This was even possible when some of the crews were in fact foreign nationals, including Belgians, Danes, Dutch, French, Greeks, Poles, Norwegians and Yugoslavs. Many of these foreign nationals had been serving in one way or another for some years. The vast majority of the experienced Belgian fishermen had escaped to Britain after the fall of their country and they had been formed up into a naval force of their own: Section Belge. They had their own motor minesweepers, trawlers, boom defence craft and other vessels. At its peak there were 500 officers and other ratings operating ships from the south coast of England up to Iceland.

There were also large numbers of Norwegians. The first of the Norwegians that had arrived were from the whaling fleets, which had been at sea when the Germans had invaded their country. Appraised of the situation and without hesitation they sailed directly to Britain and offered their services. The Norwegians in particular were a hardy lot: one Norwegian fisherman, so determined that he would not spend the war under German occupation, clambered aboard a rowing boat with just a bottle of water and two loaves of bread and rowed across the North Sea to freedom. Other Norwegians made it to Britain via the most circuitous of routes. Some had escaped or had been in India, or Persia and under their own steam had made it to Britain to volunteer to become part of the Royal Naval Patrol Service. In fact by the middle of the war an entire minesweeping flotilla, operating off the Scottish coast, was Norwegian. By D-Day in 1944 the Norwegians were manning 120 vessels.

There were a number of motor minesweepers manned by Danish fishermen. The only way of telling that they were Danes, as they wore British uniforms, was a red and white shoulder flash. Some French that had not joined the Free French Navy joined the Royal Naval Patrol Service. At Malta there were Yugoslavian naval officers and ratings involved in minesweeping. They operated in the Adriatic, as members of the Royal Naval Patrol Service. Some BYMSs and motor minesweepers were loaned to Greece and manned by Greek sailors.

This all meant that as the war continued the scope of the Royal Naval Patrol Service increased. At Port Edgar in Scotland there was a minesweeping training school and this was used as a centre for many of the RNVR officers that had been promoted and were originally 'hostilities only' men. Throughout the war HMS *Lochinvar*, as the training school was known, catered for 4,050 officers and 13,000 ratings. These men were the lucky ones; at least they had received some training. The men who had been sent via Lowestoft in the early months of the war had gone direct to operational vessels. Everything they knew was on-the-job training.

The training itself had to continually keep up with the latest developments and threats in German mine warfare. As the war progressed minefields became even more dangerous, as it was no longer the case that a minefield would be laid with all the same type of mine. This made minesweeping even more hazardous.

One of the Germans' particular techniques was to fire an acoustic homing torpedo from a submarine. It was known as the 'gnat' and would home in on propeller noises. The anti-submarine trawlers and drifters were subsequently fitted with a device that they could tow which made a noise like a propeller and was known as 'foxer'.

In the period between 1914 and 1917 some 5,000 mines were swept up by British naval forces. The scope of the job in the Second World War was vast by comparison. By September 1941 some 3,360 predominantly magnetic mines had been swept. But this was at a massive cost; not only had the mines managed to sink over 450 vessels, but they had also claimed fifty-six minesweepers within that total. In addition to this the Royal Naval Patrol Service had lost another fifty-three vessels. Nore Command took the brunt of the losses and the work against mines. By June 1942 they had swept 2,000 alone.

At Christmas 1941 the Royal Naval Patrol Service trawler *Rolls Royce* became the first minesweeper in history to have swept 100 mines. The vessel had been built in 1906 and she was attached to the 110th Minesweeping Group, operating out of Grimsby. On her very first day she had detonated three mines and on one day alone, 30 November 1941, in less than eighty minutes she swept thirteen mines. The skipper was Lieutenant L D Romyn, RNR. He was an experienced trawler man from Bridlington and had joined the RNR as a temporary skipper in November 1939. During the war he was awarded the Distinguished Service Cross and Bar for his work. By the end of the war Romyn had achieved the highest patrol service officer rank, of Skipper Lieutenant, and his mine total had reached 197.

Elsewhere the race to clear mines had also led to some remarkable feats. Royal Naval Patrol Vessels attached to the Mediterranean Fleet had assisted in clearing at least 360 mines by May 1942. Equally remarkable was the clearance of the channel between Sicily and North Africa, which had been cleared in just a week up to 15 May 1943. This meant that convoys were able to freely move between Gibraltar and Alexandria.

As the war inexorably went against Germany and her allies, there were not only German and Italian mines to deal with, but also minefields laid by the allies themselves, in an attempt to blockade enemy vessels and their ports. A prime example was the harbour of the Greek island of Leros. A flotilla of BYMS vessels, over the space of twenty-one days, cleared ninety-one mines. They were ably assisted by a pair of minesweeping motor launches who dealt with ninety more mines themselves.

As the time approached for the invasion of Normandy on 6 June 1944, even greater efforts were needed by the Royal Naval Patrol Service. A prime example was the trawler *Ijuin*. She had been completed as a fishing vessel back in 1920 and requisitioned in August 1939. She had been primarily based at Portland and by June 1944 she was a DAN layer with the 9th Minesweeping Flotilla. She would operate off Juno Beach. Her job was to mark the clear channel through the minefields, stretching from St Catherine's Point on the Isle of Wight all the way to Normandy. She would then have to clear an anchorage close inshore.

Onboard the trawler was Signalman Leonard Stent. They had left St Helen's Bay at dusk on 5 June and they worked until the tide changed. They had a short rest and a motor launch came alongside. The crew of the launch told them that they were being followed. The crew of the trawler looked over the side and saw that there was a mine only 2ft from contact with their hull. With considerable coolness and presence of mind they held off the mine with a deck scrubber and then put the trawler ahead and saw the mine drift slowly away.

There was a near miss on D-Day itself for *Grenadier*, which had been built in Beverley and launched in 1907. She had served throughout the First World War and her luck almost ran out when off the D-Day beaches she fired at a German aircraft. The crew of the German plane panicked and jettisoned their bombs. One of them hit the trawler and tore a huge hole in her side. She managed to get back to Portsmouth, where the hole was filled with a concrete patch.

There were other notable exploits that day. The trawler *Clythness* had left Poole during the night of 5 June bound for Normandy with a cargo of oil and petrol. By dawn the following day she found herself isolated, having lost her convoy. One of the crew, Seaman Thomas, recalled the situation:

By nightfall [June 6] we anchored in a small cove under the cliffs somewhere on the French coast. We were alone except for a barge which we had found broken down and taken in tow. The young sub-lieutenant RNVR commanding the barge had gratefully accepted the skipper's offer of the tow in spite of the dire warning he received from our chief engineman, who spent more time on deck than in the engine room, that our Old Man had lost the convoy and would get us all blown up. Next day we found the invasion beaches proper at Arromanches, and the sub overjoyed at his safe arrival, invited us all across to slice the main brace, a rather peculiar little party on the edge of battle.

But not for long, for very soon we received orders to proceed to Omaha Beach, where the fighting had been fiercest.

Another trawler carrying a dangerous load of oil was *Cevic*. She had been built in Aberdeen in 1908 as *Pelican* and had also operated as a minesweeper during the First World War. Since 1943 she had operated in the Mediterranean and had returned to Britain in March 1944 for conversion. Her commanding officer was Skipper Thorpe:

We arrived in Portsmouth harbour on D-Day plus one. We had to pick up 120 drums of oil as deck cargo, distributing them evenly each side of the ship. When loaded, however, I found we had 60 drums on the port side but only 56 on the starboard side, and demanded to know where the other four had gone. It turned out that the lorry driver had been trying to keep them for himself. It stuck in my mind for days, how could he come to do such a thing, when so many men were being killed on the beaches?

During the early stages of the Normandy landings only one trawler was lost, *Lord Austin*. She had been on Russian convoy duty for some time and she was brought down to Falmouth to be refitted for the Normandy landings. She had survived some fairly hairy times with Iceland Command and had been part of the escort for PQ17 in June and July 1942. She had arrived in Falmouth towing a barge and then she was sent on to Southampton. Her skipper was Lieutenant E S Terence Robinson, RNVR. She was absolutely in the thick of it during the Normandy landings. On several occasions bombs had been dropped close to her and she had narrowly missed destruction. It was all to come to a very abrupt and tragic end on Saturday 24 June 1944 when she was at anchor at 05.30 in the Seine Bay. She weighed anchor and began to cover the ten miles to take over on patrol duty. The Germans had dropped parachute mines during the night and it was clear that the area was riddled with mines. At precisely 05.55 a mine went off right below her. Lieutenant Robinson recalled:

Because of the distance we had to go to take up our patrol I had been hurrying; had we been making 7 knots or less we might not have triggered off the acoustic mine. When the explosion came we were thrown about heavily on the bridge, the ship's siren was jammed wide open and making a terrible din, and the engines stopped dead. I rushed to the voice pipe but there was only a roaring sound of steam from the engine room.

In fact the mine had gone off right beside the engine room. The trawler listed to port and Robinson ordered the boat away, but both of the boats had been damaged in the explosion. The crew threw life rafts overboard and dropped down scrambling nets. One last duty was to remove primers from depth charges in case these went off. Robinson was the last man to leave the ship. He dived in and began swimming towards the life raft and was just in time. The trawler righted itself, slumped to starboard, straightened up and then sank stern first. There were two explosions as she went down. The trawler had gone down in just ten minutes, claiming seven of the crew. Within minutes an American coastguard cutter picked up the survivors and they were transferred to another trawler, *Northern Reward*. She did what she could for them and then made for a liner, which was operating as an accommodation ship.

Robinson was keen to keep the crew together, hoping that they would be allocated *en bloc* to another trawler. Consequently, he convinced the naval lieutenant commander to put him and his crew onto the beaches so that they could find their own way home. Robinson described what he saw:

I walked along the beach until I saw an American tank landing ship with her ramp down, and asked the captain if he could give us a lift home. They were a very hospitable lot. We had one or two scares on the way back, and one in particular I wasn't likely to forget. Among my survivor's clothes I had been given a pair of combinations. These had a trap door in the stern which was very difficult to operate. At quite the wrong moment a mine went off rather close, and my nerves not being very steady I leapt out of the heads and arrived on deck in a considerable state of disarray. On a more serious note, the ship was carrying some German prisoners from the 1st Panzer Division, and during the night one of my petty officers came to me and suggested, quite soberly, that we should dispose of the prisoners. He was not alone in his bitter feelings, which took some calming down. When your ship is sunk, and your shipmates with her, it can prove too much.

Robinson and the remainder of the crew were landed at Southampton. The crewmen went off to Lowestoft and the officers reported to Portsmouth.

We left the old trawler *Ijuin* off Juno Beach, but later she found herself off Cherbourg, watching British and American vessels bombarding the German-held port. The old trawler and other vessels were used as bait to encourage the German shore batteries to reveal themselves. They were told to head for Cherbourg and wait until they were fired upon, at which point they could then retire. The *Ijuin* soon came under enemy fire and she turned about and sped away at 12 knots, with British, American and German shells flying overhead. She then stood off and watched the allied fleet smash the shore defences to pieces.

There were other Royal Naval Patrol Service trawlers in operation around Cherbourg at the time. One particularly terrible and dangerous job fell to *Fisher Boy*. A barge load of mines had been sunk in the entrance to Cherbourg harbour and with steely nerve the crew anchored right above the barge and recovered all of the mines, allowing the harbour to be reopened.

As the allied armies advanced into Belgium in the run up to Christmas 1944, it was vital to secure the port of Antwerp, in order to allow supply ships to enter and leave the port. In many respects the allied advance across France and now into the Low Countries had been slowed by the need to transport fuel, ammunition and supplies all the way from the Normandy beachheads. This meant that the River Scheldt had to be cleared and Royal Naval Patrol Service vessels were involved in clearing the area around Walcheren Island.

Chief Petty Officer William Davies, RNR, explained the role the BYMS *2188* had to play:

In the early dawn our fleet of sweepers under the guidance of the base ship, *St Tudno*, hove-to and waited for the *Warspite* and *Black Prince* to finish their pounding of the town of Flushing. When they had spent their deadly cargo and came speeding out, their massive black shapes made us feel rather proud and patriotic, and at the same time made our small wooden ships seem very insignificant, until word was spread that *Warspite* had made the signal: 'My part was easy, yours is vital, good luck and God speed.' Our objective was to get to Terneuzen and Breskens, which were in British hands, on the other side of the estuary from Walcheren, but we only managed to stream sweeps and get a couple of mines before it was realised the Germans were far from finished at Flushing – they let us know of their presence in no uncertain manner. Word was sent to Army Headquarters to bring fire to bear on the town to enable our fleet to make a dash for the harbour, such as it was, of Terneuzen. We made it, though not without casualties on some of the ships. Then came a waiting period while the Marine commandos went across and stormed the fortress-like wall of Flushing, and the RAF, with Dutch approval, blasted the dyke and flooded the island. After this our work began without interference and we cleared the Sheldt from Flushing right into Antwerp with the loss of only three ships, a small price to pay when reckoned against the sight of the big merchantmen immediately sailing up with urgent supplies.

One of the other minesweepers involved in the operation was MMS *44*. Once the operation was over they went into Ijmuiden. There were still large numbers of Germans around who had been either captured or cut off during the allied advance. Leading Cook F J Scadeng described the situation:

In a few days Captain Hopper arrived in *St Tudno*, the base vessel, to demonstrate that he, too, could take a leading part in the mopping-up activities. Together with the commander of the Canadians he arranged a drumhead service and the troops of a

Scottish regiment beat a retreat on the jetty. All this was to impress the Germans, who were being marched off in their thousands, disarmed and disillusioned.

After Ijmuiden we were based in Amsterdam. Captain Hopper promised us leave for Christmas, and just before we sailed, our number one, Sub-Lieutenant 'Lucky' French, came to me to discuss Christmas dinner. He had some inside information which resulted in he and I going ashore to bargain with local smallholder for a couple of geese in exchange for carton of duty free cigarettes. Our Sparks and a seaman volunteered to pluck the geese on the way over and stowed themselves away in the ship's small air-raid shelter to do the job.

It was a lovely sight as we made for home, the *St Tudno*, steaming ahead with her two minesweeping flotillas following in two single lines astern, reminding us of a big swan with her cygnets trailing behind. Halfway across the Channel Captain Hopper made the signal 'Leave to one watch from the day before Christmas', and everyone cheered up immensely. It was a bright day but with a stiff breeze blowing. I peeped into the air-raid shelter to see how the two lads were getting on with their plucking and was astonished at the pile of white feathers they'd made, they were standing in them up to their waists. They wouldn't be long, they said. The fleet sailed on for another half an hour, when suddenly the pluckers opened the shelter door. The breeze caught the feathers and soon a whole fleet of sweepers was steaming through what looked like a snowstorm, a beautiful sight. Our skipper nearly blew his top.

The men of the Royal Naval Patrol Service were nothing if not resourceful. It was often difficult to get hold of those little luxuries that made all the difference between a miserable and dull life and diet and an occasional treat. Buying and selling on the black market, particularly from late-1944 was commonplace. Some of the vessels working out of Dover and making routine trips off Dunkirk, Calais or Boulogne, would spend all of their pay on anything they thought they could turn a profit on once they had got into a European port. They would buy cocoa, English tea and other delicacies that troops based on the continent would find incredibly difficult to buy. They could earn several thousand Francs from each set of transactions.

Before the end of 1944 there were other spectacular exploits of vessels belonging to the Royal Naval Patrol Service. There were five trawlers involved in a naval action in December 1944, to the northwest of Spezia in Italy. The engagement has become known as the 'Battle of Mesco Point'. The trawlers involved in the engagement were HMT *Minuet*, commanded by Lieutenant-Commander Thornton Bate, RNVR, the flotilla leader, HMT *Twostep*, commanded by Lieutenant Jack Nye, HMT *Hornpipe*, commanded by Lieutenant-Commander de Legh, RNR, HMT *Gulland*, commanded by Lieutenant G A Anderson, RNVR and HMT *Ailsa Craig*, commanded by Lieutenant T G Hornsby, RNR. The trawlers were all Admiralty built either from the Dance or Isles Class. Also involved in the engagement were sixteen British and US torpedo boats and gunboats.

There are two very good descriptions of the engagement, one by Sub-Lieutenant Bryan Cambray, RNVR, aboard HMT *Twostep* and one by Lieutenant Geoffrey Dormer, RNR, on board HMT *Hornpipe*.

The allied forces had intercepted a signal that an enemy convoy was trying to make its way from Genoa to Spezia. It was the trawlers' job to engage the enemy at long range to attract their attention and then allow the motor torpedo boats to do the real damage. The RAF was also to be involved:

> Just after dark we arrived off the enemy coast, met our coastal forces and stooged slowly in. Suddenly star shell burst just short of us, and we had a nervous half-hour while the German shore batteries searched and searched. It was eerie, shells whistling over us, gun-flashes along the coast, and star shell all over the place. I don't think they saw us... at least, nothing solid came near. We heard asdic transmissions, and thought an enemy force had come out to intercept, but they kept away. We closed the coast to about two miles and stooged around until

02.00 hours. Several times there were false alarms, as our scouting MLs and MTBs made contacts. We had just about given up hope – I had long ago taken the cotton wool out of my ears and let the air out of my lifebelt. We were simply manoeuvring around at 50-yard intervals, everyone rather tired, bad tempered, and longing to go home. Then... 'ALARM GREEN 100'... 'Oh, just another false one.' But no, the range is given over the R/T... 'OPEN FIRE'.

Now everything happened very quickly as Dormer explained:

The first salvoes of star shell, from the 12-pounders of *Ailsa Craig* and *Gulland*, stationed at each end of the line, burst short; nothing to be seen. Then... there they are... several low, beetle-like objects in the glare, with splashes rising among them as the four-inch guns of *Minuet, Twostep* and ourselves open fire. But stuff is coming back, bunches of gentle-looking tracer shell come sailing over to accelerate and pass with a whoosh, or splash in the sea alongside. The fire becomes heavy. One flak-lighter is pouring out so much muck that it looks like a bloody Catherine wheel. Shells of all sizes, 88mm, 40mm, 20mm, even down to .303 or some such are whistling and splashing all around as shore batteries and land ack-ack sites join in. 'FULL AHEAD'.... We had been going dead slow, even astern... then 'turn in succession straight towards the enemy'. I thought it was a mistake – we are third in line and I am praying hard: 'Our Father, which art'... steer two degrees to port... 'Hail Mary'... 45 revs... 'God Almighty'.... Whoosh bang, crackle, splash... the Bofors come in groups of five. One can tell pretty well where they will land. Of one group three went over, two fell short. *Ailsa Craig*, leading, pours a long burst of 20mm into the nearest small craft. The craft, actually an R-boat (German motor launch) burst into flames, whereupon, the Germans started pouring tracer into it also.... We were steaming now at full speed straight for the shore. *Ailsa Craig* yelped something over the R/T about being

800 yards off... 'RED 18'.... Turn about together.... Maximum speed.... Make smoke... off we go. Never have trawlers gone so fast, under a blaze of enemy star shell, with heavy stuff from the shore batteries splashing all around. A storm of red-hot splinters passes my face from a near miss to starboard. The CO had scarcely needed to say a word throughout. Now he ordered me to steer for the shell splashes, to put the enemy gunners off, but I was more worried about finding the gap in the minefield and mutinously clung to the course provided by our DR plot. Commander Allen was checking up.... 'Report state, puppies.' 'Titus OK' 'Harry OK' 'Jack injured, No.1 in command.' 'Andy on fire aft, no casualties.' And so on. At last we were out of range and by a miracle not hit. It only remained to get the force into some sort of order and go home. We thought the affair had been a complete failure, the gunners said they had hardly been able to see their targets for the smoke and glare, and we were tremendously surprised when Commander Allen announced success – 'A gallant and determined fight against heavy odds' he called it in a signal. Apparently there were eight enemy ships in all. Three of our trawlers had fired about 100 four-inch rounds between them, the other two only providing illuminations. Our only casualty was the CO of *Twostep* who had his right arm broken by one of eight rounds which hit their bridge. On *Hornpipe* we merely collected one hunk of metal, just where I'd been standing.

The enemy had lost one R-boat and three merchantmen out of a force of three R-boats and five merchantmen. The trawlers had taken on the role of major battleships and the torpedo boats their escorting destroyers.

Further east, time was almost up for the Germans who had been occupying the Greek island of Crete since 1941. To a large extent what remained of the German garrison had fallen back to the main centres of population, along the north coast.

In late November 1944 the trawler *Staffa*, leading a force of six other trawlers and whalers, a pair of motor launches, two motor minesweepers and a DAN layer entered the harbour of Heraklion. The senior officer, Lieutenant-Commander Geoffrey Syrett, RNVR, along with two other officers, ventured ashore and began negotiations for the surrender of the German garrison.

Meanwhile, the trawler *Moonstone* was sitting in the harbour of the Greek island of Corfu. It was Christmas Eve 1944 and at around 21.00 hours the trawler headed for the Greek mainland. It was a mercy mission, as Royalists and Communists were engaged in a civil war for control of Greece. In the early hours of Christmas Day they came across a pair of Greek ships filled to capacity with civilians in a pitiful state. Many of them were starving or had malaria and others were wounded. The trawler's crew handed out whatever food they had on board and escorted the vessels to Paxos.

Working in the same area *Moonstone* also intercepted a Greek boat smuggling guns to the Communists. Onboard was a notorious Communist leader and *Moonstone*'s crew handed him over to Greek authorities, for which three of the crew received medals from the Greek government.

The civil war and the deprivations that the Greeks had suffered during the Second World War itself provided a bonanza for the crews of the minesweepers that were working off Piraeus. Absolutely anything had a monetary value. The crew of the trawler *Sheppey* sold anything that was not essential to them. They even sold the ropes that held their life rafts and all of their spare clothing for a massive profit.

There were still five or more months of war in Europe to endure and for the members of the Royal Naval Patrol Service operating in the Far East it was to be even longer. There would still be losses and tasks that seemed to be insurmountable to overcome.

CHAPTER TEN

Did Glory Pass Them By?

It was not until 1946 that the Royal Naval Patrol Service was disbanded, but before then the war had still to be won, not just against the Germans and the Japanese, but against the ever-present threat of tens of thousands of mines.

For the Normandy landings more than 250 minesweepers of every type had been in operation, carving out ten lanes to ensure that the shore was kept open. Throughout June 1944 the Germans desperately tried to close those lanes again by dropping parachute mines. But by 4 July, less than a month since the first landing in Normandy, the minesweepers had managed to keep the lanes clear, disposing of nearly 600 mines.

Throughout the war in Europe at least 16,000 German mines had been dealt with but there were still vast areas of ocean covered in mines, from the North Cape at the tip of Norway, all the way to Alexandria in Egypt. As the war entered its final months many of the trawlers and drifters were returned to their civilian owners and tried to resume their lives as peaceful fishing vessels. But even after the last shots had been fired there were still half a million mines to clear across the world's oceans.

As 1945 dawned the Royal Naval Patrol Service still laboured on, taking more than its fair share of casualties as a result. The Grimsby trawler *Northern Isles* was operating out of Durban on 19 January, working with the South African Navy. The trawler struck rocks at 09.45 and tugs could not get her off due to a heavy swell. The captain ordered a partial abandonment of ship, leaving just a dozen men on board. It soon became clear that the trawler was doomed and reluctantly the captain and the remainder of the crew left the vessel and were taken to Durban. They had barely got themselves dry when at about 04.00 on 20 January the captain decided to try to get back on board and to save *Northern Isles*. As it was the attempt failed and the captain was court-martialled. The officer of the watch was also found guilty of negligence.

In early 1945 mines claimed the trawler *Treern* off the Greek coast and *Arley* in the North Sea. U-boats torpedoed *Southern Flower*, a whaler, off Iceland and *Nordhav II* off Dundee and *Ellesmere* and *Haybourne Wyke* in the English Channel. There were accidents too: *High Tide* foundered off the Welsh coast and *Golden West* off Aberdeen. Meanwhile *Computator* sank after a collision off Normandy.

Northern Sun was dispatched to find the U-boat that sunk the *Southern Flower*. It was 3 March 1945 and they knew that the whaler had gone down in a matter of seconds and that there was only one survivor, Skipper Brown. It was rumoured that a pair of U-boats were working together in the same area and there was also news that the Admiralty had intercepted a U-boat transmission to Bremerhaven. The chilling part of the transmission was that the U-boat had spotted the *Northern Sun*.

The last Royal Naval Patrol Service loss during wartime in Europe was the minesweeping trawler *Ebor Wyke*. She was torpedoed by an E-boat off the east coast of Iceland. Only one of the crewmembers survived the attack. This incident took place on 2 May 1945, the very day that Berlin was overrun by the Russians. Hitler was already dead and Germany was on the verge of having to accept unconditional surrender.

Even in the last few days the trawlers continued to fight for their very lives against the U-boats, E-boats and mines that had plagued their lives since 1939. The trawler *Arab* that had served so gallantly during the Norwegian campaign, winning many of its crewmen decorations for outstanding bravery, was operating off the Minch, a strait in northwest Scotland that separates the northern Inner Hebrides and other islands with the northwest highlands. She picked up a U-boat contact and dropped depth charges. One of the depth charges went off prematurely and severely damaged her. She had to be towed into Tobermory by a destroyer.

Arguably the last offensive wartime action taken by a Royal Naval Patrol Service trawler during the war in Europe occurred off Reykjavik in the penultimate day of the European war. The trawler, *Northern Spray*, was attacked by the German submarine *U-979*. The trawler was escorting convoy RU161, which included a tanker, *Empire Unity*. The submarine torpedoed the tanker and the crew abandoned ship. The trawler then spotted a periscope and moved in to attack. The crew dropped depth charges, which also damaged their own asdic. The asdic dome was then ripped off when the trawler rammed the submarine. The crew never discovered what became of the submarine, as the following day peace was declared. This was in fact the very same U-boat, commanded by Captain-Lieutenant Johannes Meermeier, which had sunk the steam trawler *Ebor Wyke*. The *Empire Unity* had been struck when the submarine had fired a spread of three torpedoes at 01.05 on 5 May 1945. The tanker was actually struck by two of the torpedoes. Initially the tanker was abandoned but *Northern Spray* managed to nurse her back to port. Twelve survivors were also picked up *Northern Sky* and taken into Belfast.

There was another strange encounter for *Stella Canopus*. On the last day of the war the skipper, Billy Mullender, DSC, was off Loch Eriboll on the north coast of Scotland. The crew was as alert as ever but shocked when they spotted a surfaced U-boat ahead of them. Mullender ordered the trawler to attack and the crew manned the guns ready to open fire. Through his binoculars Mullender saw a black flag being hoisted. The U-boat commander was surrendering and as Mullender's trawler came alongside the U-boat commander was ordered to hand over his chronometer and sextant. Unfortunately Mullender could not finish his war with a flourish by escorting the captured U-boat into harbour, as shortly afterwards an armed yacht with a more senior officer took control of the situation.

The trawlers of the Royal Naval Patrol Service were also on hand to see the U-boats begin to come into surrender. One such trawler was *Guardsman*, which brought in a U-boat to Wallasey Dock. As for the *U-979*, she did not surrender but instead she was scuttled at Amrum on 24 May 1945, after she had deliberately run herself aground.

The trawlers were also present to see the surrender of the German minesweepers. A number of German armed trawlers, based at Jersey, came under the protection of the Royal Naval Patrol Service trawler *Skomer*. She escorted them from Jersey into Plymouth. All along the cliffs and on the quays there were thousands of people cheering her as she made her approach, followed by the German armed trawlers, each of which had a precautionary Royal Marine escort on board. *Skomer* would also bring in many hundreds of Germans' prisoners of war from Jersey. Amongst the passengers that she brought back from Jersey was a woman who had been sent to Belsen concentration camp and the crew were delighted to reunite her with her husband.

In the Far East, just forty-eight hours before the planned liberation of Malaya, the war against the Japanese had come to an end. One of the vessels that would have taken part in the operation was BYMS *2006*. Even after the Japanese surrender there was still an enormous amount of work to do, dealing with the Japanese mines that were scattered all along the Malayan coast. There would be months of hard work ahead.

October 1945 saw the last three Royal Naval Patrol Service trawlers lost in the Second World War. In all, over 400 whalers, drifters and trawlers had been lost by the Royal Naval Patrol Service. However, other vessels crewed by men of the service, from armed yachts to BYMSs and motor minesweepers added nearly another 100 to this total. The Royal Naval Patrol Service had lost more vessels than the combined loss of the Royal Navy.

Although the war was now coming to an end for the 'hostilities only' men, and many of the minesweepers that had been peacetime fishing vessels were returning to their civilian role, for many of the vessels their naval working life was not yet over. Many of the vessels, particularly the Admiralty-built trawlers, found their way into foreign navies. As soon as hostilities had ended in Europe the International Mine Clearance Board, consisting of thirteen countries, was created. Each nation had a responsibility to deal with mines in their immediate area and, more broadly, in the Atlantic and the Mediterranean. They would have to tackle every single type of mine and by July 1946 some 2,000 vessels were involved in minesweeping. A year later, in July 1947, 140,000sq miles of European waters had been cleared of mines. To put this into perspective, just in the Kattegat area, the strait between Denmark and Sweden, there were 17,000 German mines and up to 5,000 mines that had been dropped by the Royal Air Force. The area consisted of 2,000sq miles of water. The operation was not without dangers and particularly not for the merchant ships that were still being sunk in considerable numbers. In the period 1946 to 1947 130 merchant ships were sunk and sixty were badly damaged.

Eventually the white ensign was lowered for the last time over the Sparrow's Nest. The municipal garden began to return to its civilian guise, as wartime buildings were torn down. Across Lowestoft, bowls clubs and cricketers got their recreational areas returned to them and slowly but surely the Royal Naval Patrol Service disappeared from the town.

In October 1953 a permanent memorial was created at Belle Vue Park, above the Sparrow's Nest and looking out towards the North Sea. This was seven years after HMS *Europa* had been formally closed down. The newly erected monument was a tall column with a bronze ship on top and around it were seventeen bronze panels set into the base. Around the sides of the base hung seventeen white ensigns. Admiral of the Fleet, Sir Rhoderick McGrigor, the First Sea Lord and Chief of Naval Staff, spoke a few words and then pressed a button and the seventeen white ensigns fell away to reveal the names of the officers and men of the Royal Naval Patrol Service who had died during the Second World War, who have no known grave other than the sea. The First Sea Lord had said:

> In two world wars Lowestoft became the centre of the Patrol Service, who manned the small ships which played an invaluable part in the struggle for victory. The world will little note nor long remember what we say here, but it will never forget what they did in the cause of freedom that ships might pass on the seas upon their lawful occasions as they do today.

For six years the men of the Royal Naval Patrol Service, short on resources but replete with courage, tackled any task that had been assigned to them. They had protected merchantmen, they had dealt with every conceivable type of mine, they had hunted and destroyed enemy U-boats and E-boats and they had been present at every significant operation in the war. Not all the men were ex-fishermen; many of them were land lubbers. The fighting force of trawlers and drifters had helped to best the enemy and had proved to be of incalculable value in the war at sea. They had done it without a great fanfare, with little public recognition and often without glory.

Although the authors' connection with the Royal Naval Patrol Service is not a close one, there are strong links that tie us to the exploits of these men. Our families both have a fishing heritage, from northeast Scotland all the way down to Norfolk and many of the ports in between. Successive generations have spent their lives and earned their livelihoods from the sea. Nonetheless, our knowledge of the Royal Naval Patrol Service was as scant as that of most people. One of the author's late fathers worked closely with the Royal Naval Patrol Service during the Second World War, but more recently, in researching *Air War Over the Nore*, we were contacted by the descendents of Seaman Charles H Brown. He was serving on board the Admiralty built trawler *Their Merit*. It had been constructed in Canada in 1917 and had operated out of Milford Haven. On 25 January 1941 the vessel was moored on the quayside at Great Yarmouth, close to the Town Hall. A German aircraft on a bombing run across Great Yarmouth skimmed over the rooftops and was brought under fire by the anti-aircraft guns on board the trawler. One of the bombs narrowly missed the vessel, but the blast killed Seaman Brown and Seaman William Jackson. Charles Henry Brown was given a full military funeral and is buried in Caister Village Cemetery. His grave, just like the memorial to the men in Belle Vue Park, is in the perpetual care of the Commonwealth War Graves Commission.

APPENDIX ONE

Trawler Losses 1939–1945

Admiralty and Requisitioned

Additional information on the vessel is given where known

Adonis (1,004t, 1915), sunk by E-boat torpedo off Lowestoft, 15 April 1943

Actually a Norwegian fishing vessel launched in 1915 originally named *Norhav I* and hired from the owners after the fall of Norway in June 1940. First named *Avalon* and then *Adonis*, she was based at Ipswich in 1943, then at Immingham for refit. Returned to Ipswich on 13 April and sunk two days later, there were eleven survivors.

Agate (627t, 1934), grounded off Cromer Norfolk, total loss, 6 August 1941

Built in 1934 at Southbank on Tees and bought in November 1935 then converted into an anti-submarine trawler.

Akranes (R, 358t, 1929), sunk by aircraft Bridlington Bay, Yorkshire, 4 July 1941

Launched in 1929 and built at Selby and fitted out as a minesweeper after being requisitioned in August 1939. Attached to the 40th Mine Sweeping Group based at Grimsby.

Alberic (R, 286t, 1910), sunk in collision off Scapa, Orkneys, 3 May 1941

Built at Selby in 1910 and originally named *Alberia*. She was requisitioned in December 1914 and converted to a minesweeper.

She was then returned to the owners in 1919 and requisitioned in April 1940 and renamed *Alberic*. She was converted once more to a minesweeper.

Alder (560t, 1929), grounded E Scotland, total loss, 22 October 1941

Built at Selby in 1929, she was bought by the Admiralty in February 1939 and converted to a minesweeper based at Grimsby.

Almond (505t, 1940), mined off Falmouth, 2 February 1941

A Tree class trawler, launched on 22 May 1940, she was designed to be a minesweeper and was an Admiralty-built trawler.

Alouette (R, 520t, 1939), sunk by U-boat torpedo off Portugal, 19 September 1942

Launched in 1939 and built at Southbank on Tees and converted as an anti-submarine vessel, having been requisitioned in August 1939. She was sunk by the *U-552*.

Amethyst (627t, 1928), sunk by mine, Thames Estuary, 24 November 1940

Purchased in November 1935 and converted to an anti-submarine trawler. She was hit by a mine in the Barrow Deep and took ten minutes to sink. The survivors were arrested on Southend Pier by local police who thought they were Germans.

Aracari (R, 245t, 1908), grounded, total loss, Filicudi island, North of Sicily, 13 October 1943

This vessel was built in Beverley and launched in 1908. She had been converted as a minesweeper after being requisitioned during the First World War in September 1914. She was returned to her owners in 1919. Requisitioned again in 1939 and converted to minesweeping duties. Returned to owners once again in 1940 and then requisitioned for the last time in 1943 to act as a fuel carrier (designated 'Esso') and operated in the Mediterranean until lost

Aragonite (R, 315t, 1934), mined off Deal, 22 November 1939

Built at Beverley in 1934 and requisitioned in August 1939, to be converted to a minesweeper. She was based at Dover. When she was mined off Deal she broke in two and sank.

Arctic Trapper (R, 352t, 1928), sunk by aircraft off Ramsgate, 3 February 1941

Built at Selby in 1928 and requisitioned in May 1940 to operate as a auxiliary patrol vessel. She was based at Grimsby but sunk by enemy aircraft off Ramsgate.

Argyllshire (R, 540t, 1938), sunk by E-boat during evacuation from Dunkirk, 1 June 1940

Built at Southbank on Tees in 1938 and requisitioned in September 1939, she joined the 11th Anti-Submarine Striking Group. She was involved in the Norwegian campaign during April and May 1940. She was sunk during Operation Dynamo, after being torpedoed by an E-boat off Dunkirk.

Arley (R, 304t, 1914), damaged by mine, sank in tow, North Sea, 3 February 1945

Built at Middlesbrough and launched in 1914, she was requisitioned in October 1914 and became a minesweeper. In 1919 she was returned to her owners and twenty years later requisitioned again in August and converted once more to a minesweeper. In 1943 she was attached to the 51st Minesweeper Group based at Grimsby. She was hit by a mine and sank whilst being towed in 1945.

Arsenal (530t, 1933), sunk in collision off Clyde, Scotland, 16 November 1940

Built at Middlesbrough and launched in 1933 and requisitioned in August 1939, she was converted for anti-submarine warfare. She sank off the Clyde when she collided with the Polish destroyer, *Burza*.

Asama (R, 303t, 1929), sunk by aircraft in Plymouth, 21 March 1941

Built at Southbank on Tees in 1929, she was requisitioned in September 1939 and became a minesweeper. She was sunk by German aircraft off Plymouth.

Ash (505t, 1939), mined, Thames Estuary, June 5, 1941

Built at Selby and launched in 1939 as a Tree class Admiralty built minesweeping trawler.

Aston Villa (R, 546t, 1937), sunk by aircraft off Norway, 3 May 1940

Built at Southbank on Tees and launched in 1937, she was requisitioned and converted to an anti-submarine trawler. Based at Aberdeen, she was the group leader of 16th Anti-Submarine Strike Force. She was involved in operations around northern Scotland and was hit by an enemy bomb off Norway but survived this attack, only to be sunk during another Luftwaffe attack shortly afterwards.

Avanturine (R, 296t, 1930), sunk by E-boats off Beachy Head, 1 December 1943

Built at Beverley and launched in 1930, she was requisitioned in February 1940 and became an auxiliary patrol vessel. She was converted to a minesweeper in 1942. All hands were lost when she was hit by a torpedo fired from an E-boat whilst she was under tow.

Bandolero (913t, 1935), sunk in collision, Gulf of Sollum Egypt, 30 December 1940

Built at Southbank on Tees and launched in 1935, she was purchased in August 1939 and converted to an anti-submarine trawler. She was sunk when she collided with the destroyer, *Waterhen*.

Barbara Robertson (R, 325t, 1919), German U-boat gunfire, North of Hebrides, W Scotland, 23 December 1939

Built at Selby and launched in 1919 as the *James McDonald*, she subsequently became *The Grand Fleet* and then the *Barbara Robertson*. She was requisitioned in 1939 and converted to a minesweeper and sunk by gunfire from a U-boat to the north of the Hebrides.

Bedfordshire (on loan to USN, 913t, 1935), sunk by U-boat off Cape Lookout, N Carolina, USA, 11 May 1942

Built at Southbank on Tees and launched in August 1935, she was bought by the Royal Navy in August 1939 and converted to anti-submarine work. She joined the 17th Anti-Submarine Group at Swansea and operated in the Bristol Channel. In 1942 she operated to protect convoys in the Bristol Channel and the English Channel. The *Bedfordshire* and her crew were loaned to the United States

Navy in March 1942. She escorted the damaged AMC *Queen of Bermuda* from Halifax to New York. She was then employed on convoy escorts off the east coast of Canada and the United States. She was hit by two torpedoes fired by *U-558* and literally disintegrated. Only one of the thirty-four members of her crew survived.

Beech (540t, 1929), sunk by aircraft in Scrabster, N Scotland, 22 June 1941

Another Tree class trawler, built at Selby and launched in 1929, she was purchased by the Royal Navy in February 1939 and became a minesweeper. She was lost whilst attached to the 18th Minesweeping Group based at Grimsby.

Ben Ardna (R, 226t, 1917), collision, Tyne area, 12 May 1942

Built at Aberdeen and launched in July 1917, as the *John Bradford*, she was renamed *Dorileen* in 1920 and subsequently renamed *Ben Ardna*. She was requisitioned in August 1939 and converted for the examination service.

Ben Gairn (R, 234t, 1916), sunk by parachute mine, Lowestoft, 4 May 1941

Built in Aberdeen and launched in 1916, she was requisitioned in November 1916 and became a minesweeper. In 1919 she was returned to her owners and requisitioned again in June 1940 to become a minesweeper once again.

Ben Rossal (R, 260t, 1929), sank at moorings and later salvaged, 29 November 1941, 1942

Built at Aberdeen in 1929, she was requisitioned in September 1939 as a boom defence vessel. She was based at Scapa Flow and although she sank at her moorings she was salvaged and returned to her owners in March 1946.

Bengali (880t, 1937), explosion, Lagos, Nigeria, 5 December 1942

Built at Southbank on Tees and launched in 1937, she was bought by the Royal Navy in August 1939 for anti-submarine duties. She was operating off West Africa on escort duty. The tanker *Athel Victor* accidentally discharged petrol into Lagos Harbour, which then ignited. *Bengali, Canna,* and *Spaniard* were destroyed and *Kelt* badly damaged.

Benvolio (R, 352t, 1930), mined off Humber, 23 February 1940

Built at Selby and launched in 1930, she was requisitioned in September 1939 as a minesweeper.

Birdlip (750t, 1941), sunk by U-boat torpedo off W Africa, 13 June 1944

A Hills class Admiralty trawler, ordered in November 1940 and launched in July 1941, being built at Beverley as an anti-submarine trawler. She was commissioned at Birkenhead in May and was one of the first trawlers to have radar. She was transferred to the Mediterranean in time for Operation Torch in November 1943 and then transferred to the West African Escort Force at Freetown. Whilst escorting the French vessel *St Bastile* off Lagos, along with the trawlers *Inkpen* and *Turcoman,* she was torpedoed by the U-547. Fifteen of the crew survived. The surviving officer trekked through the jungle in order to get help for the men.

Blackburn Rovers (R, 422t, 1934), sunk by U-boat or mine, North Sea, 2 June 1940

Built at Southbank on Tees and launched in 1934, she was requisitioned in August 1939 to become an anti-submarine trawler. She was based at Dover and whilst on patrol off the Goodwin Sands in heavy weather a cable wrapped around the screws. She drifted into a minefield. The Dover lifeboat managed to take off the crew and equipment. The coxswain of the lifeboat was awarded for his gallantry. Orders were given to sink her, but she was still afloat a couple of days later, off the Kentish Knock Sand. The trawlers *Westella* and *Saon* tried to get close to her and detected a U-boat close by. An officer got on board *Blackburn Rovers* and sailed her into a known British minefield, where she hit a mine and sank.

Botanic (670t, 1928), sunk by aircraft bombs, North Sea, 18 February 1942

Built at Selby and launched in 1928, she was requisitioned in August 1939 and converted into a minesweeper.

Bradman (R, 452t, 1937), sunk by aircraft, West Coast of Norway, 25 April 1940
Built at Selby and launched in 1937, she was requisitioned in August 1939 and became an anti-submarine trawler with the 22nd Anti-Submarine Group. She was involved in the Norwegian campaign in April 1940 and sunk by German aircraft off Norway, but she was salvaged by the Germans, recommissioned and renamed *Freise*.

Bredon (750t, 1941), sunk by U-boat torpedo, North Atlantic, 8 February 1943
A Hills class Royal Navy trawler ordered in March 1941 and launched in November at Beverley as an escort. She joined the 2nd Anti-Submarine Group based at Freetown in West Africa. She was sunk in the North Atlantic by *U-521*.

Brora (530t, 1941), grounded Hebrides, W Scotland; total loss, 6 September 1941
Ordered in April 1940 and completed at Beverley in December as an anti-submarine trawler, she was wrecked in the Hebrides.

Calverton (R, 214t, 1913), mined, entrance to Humber, 29 November 1940

Calvi (R, 363t, 1930), sunk by aircraft bombs, off Dunkirk, 29 May 1940
Built at Beverley and launched in 1930, she was originally *Galleon* but was renamed *Calvi* in 1938. She was requisitioned in September 1939 and converted to a minesweeper, based at Dover. She was lost during Operation Dynamo whilst evacuating troops from Dunkirk.

Campina (R, 289t, 1913), mined off Holyhead, 22 July 1940

Campobello (545t, 1942), badly damaged at Quebec, Canada and foundered on passage to UK, 16 March 1943
Built in Ontario, Canada in 1942 as an anti-submarine trawler she sank in the North Atlantic.

Canna (545t, 1940), explosion, Lagos, Nigeria, 5 December 1942
Built at Selby and launched in November 1940 she was destroyed by an accidental explosion at Lagos Harbour. See also: *Bengali*

Cap D'Antifer (R, 294t, 1920), sunk by E-boat off Humber, 13 February 1944

A Belgian trawler, launched in 1920, and converted to a French minesweeper in 1940. She was seized by the Royal Navy in Southampton during Operation Grab on 3 July 1940 and became an auxiliary patrol vessel. In 1941 she was converted to a minesweeper and sent to the Humber. In 1943 she was part of 19th Minesweeping Group based at Grimsby. In January 1944, whilst minesweeping off the Humber she was attacked by four German E-boats, but they were driven off. On 13 February another flotilla of E-boats attacked and this time she was struck by a torpedo and sunk.

Cape Chelyuskin (550t, 1936), sunk by aircraft bombs, off Norway, 29 April 1940

Built at Selby and launched in 1936, she was bought by the Royal Navy in August 1939 and joined the 12th Anti-Submarine Strike Force in Belfast. She was lost whilst taking part in the Norwegian campaign in April 1940.

Cape Finisterre (R, 590t, 1939), sunk by aircraft off Harwich, 2 August 1940

Built at Selby and launched in 1939, she was requisitioned in February 1940 and converted to anti-submarine warfare. On 2 August she was attacked by four enemy aircraft off Harwich. She shot one down and damaged at least one other before being sunk.

Cape Passaro (R, 590t, 1939), sunk by aircraft, Narvik area, Norway, 21 May 1940

Built at Selby and launched in 1939, she was requisitioned in September to become an anti-submarine trawler. She was based at Aberdeen and was leader of the 15th Anti-Submarine Strike Force. She was inspected by HM Queen in Aberdeen but she was lost off Narvik during the Norwegian campaign.

Cape Siretoko (R, 590t, 1939), sunk by aircraft, West Coast of Norway, 29 April 1940

Built at Selby and launched in 1939 she was purchased by the Royal Navy in the September and became an anti-submarine trawler. She joined the 11th Anti-Submarine Strike Force and she was sunk by enemy aircraft off Norway on 29 April 1940. The Germans salvaged her and renamed her *Gote*, but she was sunk for the second time near Makkaur, off Norway, on 11 May 1944.

Cape Spartel (R, 346t, 1929), sunk by aircraft, Humber Area, 2 February 1942

Built at Selby and launched in 1929, she was requisitioned in August 1939 and became a minesweeper.

Capricornus (R, 219t, 1917), sunk by mine off S E England, 7 December 1940

Built at Goole and launched in 1917, she was requisitioned in April 1917 and became a minesweeper, being returned to her owners in 1919. Twenty years later she was again requisitioned in November and became an auxiliary patrol vessel. In 1940 she was converted into a minesweeper.

Caroline (R, 253t, 1930), mined off Milford Haven, 28 April 1941

A Dutch vessel launched in 1930 and hired from the Dutch owners in 1940, along with the Dutch crew, as a minesweeper. She was lost off Milford Haven.

Caulonia (R, 296t, 1912), ran aground and foundered, Rye Bay, Sussex, 31 March 1943

Built at Selby and launched in 1912, she was requisitioned in May 1915 and became a minesweeper. She was returned to her owners in 1919 but in 1940 she was again requisitioned and became an auxiliary patrol vessel. She was then converted into a minesweeper in 1942 and ran aground in Rye Bay the following year.

Cayton Wyke (550t, 1932), sunk by torpedo off Dover, 8 July 1940

Built at Selby and launched in 1932, she was bought by the Royal Navy in August 1939. After being converted to an anti-submarine trawler she was based at Dover, along with the *Puffin* and *Saon* she attacked the German submarine U-16 on 23 October 1939. They forced the submarine onto the Goodwin Sands, where she was destroyed. *Cayton Wyke* was lost to an E-boat torpedo off Dover.

Charles Boyes (R, 290t, 1918), sunk by mine, East Coast of England, 25 May 1940

Built at Beverley and launched in 1918, she was fitted with listening hydrophones. After the First World War she was acquired by Lady Beardmore of Glasgow but was requisitioned in September 1939 and became a minesweeper. She was attached to 40th Minesweeping Group at Great Yarmouth when she was lost to a mine of 25 May and only three of her twenty-two man crew survived.

Chestnut (505t, 1940), sunk by mine off N Foreland, Kent, 30 November 1940

Built at Goole and launched in February 1940 as an Admiralty minesweeping trawler.

Choice (R, 197t, 1899), wrecked, Arromanches, Normandy, 25 August 1944

Built in Hull in 1899 as *Jeria*, she changed hands in 1913 and became *Stalker*. She was requisitioned in July 1915 and converted into a minesweeper. She was returned to her owners in 1919. As a civilian craft she was hit by a bomb from a German aircraft in the Humber on 1 April 1944. She was requisitioned in April 1944 and converted into a fuel tanker. She collided with the tug *Empire Samson* off the Normandy coast in late August 1944.

Cloughton Wyke (R, 324t, 1918), sunk by aircraft, Humber Area, 2 February 1942

Built at Selby and launched in 1918 as the *John Johnson*, she was renamed in 1922. The Royal Navy purchased her in May 1940 and converted her into a minesweeper.

Colsay (554t, 1944), sunk by human torpedo off Ostend, Belgium, 2 November 1944

Built at Beverley as an Admiralty trawler and completed in March 1944, she was involved in Operation Neptune in June as a DAN layer with the 1st Minesweeping Flotilla off Sword Beach. She was sunk when she was attacked by a German human torpedo off Ostend.

Comet (R, 301t, 1924), sunk by mine off Falmouth, 30 September 1940

Built at Southbank on Tees and launched in 1924, she was requisitioned in September 1939 and converted into a decoy vessel.

Computator (R, 286t, 1919), sunk in collision, Seine Bay, Normandy, 21 January 1945

Built at Beverley and launched in March 1919 as a fishing vessel named *Egilias Akerman*. She was sold and renamed *Kesteven* and bought by French owners in 1926 when she was renamed *Imprevu*. She was sold again in 1930 and renamed *Daily Mirror* and once again in 1935 and renamed *Computator*. She was requisitioned in 1939 and converted into a minesweeper. She was sunk after a collision with the destroyer *Vanoc* off Normandy in January 1945.

Conquistador (R, 224t, 1915), sunk in collision Thames Estuary, 25 November 1940

Built at Aberdeen and launched in 1915, she became an auxiliary patrol vessel after being requisitioned in November 1939. In June 1940 she was converted into a minesweeper and was sunk after a collision in the Thames Estuary.

Coral (705t, 1935), sunk by aircraft during raid on Malta, 13 April 1942

A Gem type trawler built at Selby in 1935, she was purchased by the Royal Navy in 1939 and converted for anti-submarine warfare. She joined the 4th Anti-Submarine and Minesweeping Group and was transferred to the Mediterranean fleet. In 1942 she was sunk by enemy aircraft at Malta.

Cortina (R, 213t, 1913), sunk in collision off Humber, 7 December 1940

Built at Beverley and launched in 1913, she was requisitioned in April 1915 and converted into a minesweeper. She was returned to her owners in 1919 and requisitioned again in November 1939 to become an auxiliary patrol vessel. She was initially based at Grimsby and was converted into a minesweeper in June 1940 and subsequently joined the 111th Minesweeping Group based at Grimsby. She was lost after a collision in the Humber.

Cramond Island (R, 180t, 1910), sunk by aircraft off St Abb's Head, E Scotland, 2 April 1941

Built at Govan and launched in 1910, she was requisitioned in May 1915 and became a minesweeper before being returned to her owners in 1919. She was requisitioned again in November 1939 and converted to become a boom defence vessel. She was sunk by enemy aircraft at the beginning of April 1941.

Crestflower (550t, 1930), foundered after damage by aircraft off Portsmouth, 19 July 1940

Built at Selby and launched in 1930, she was bought by the Royal Navy in August 1939 and converted to a minesweeper in Grimsby. She was lost to enemy aircraft in July 1940.

Daneman (1050t, 1937), believed to have struck submerged ice. Abandoned after being taken in tow, N Atlantic, 8 May 1943

Built at Selby and launched in 1937 she was bought by the Royal Navy in August 1939 and converted into an anti-submarine trawler. She was initially used to protect Atlantic convoys as part of the 21st Anti-Submarine Striking Force. She was involved in the Norwegian campaign in 1940, but as an escort to convoy PQ18, making its way from Iceland to Russia in September 1942, she ran out of fuel 20 miles out of Archangel. She ran aground on 21 September, initially being abandoned. She was then taken in tow into Murmansk. She sailed out of Russia on 30 December to escort a convoy bound for Iceland, arriving there on 5 January 1943 and was then sent to Belfast for repairs. She was once again in the Atlantic by April 1943 but she collided with ice and sank whilst in tow.

Darogah (R, 221t, 1914), mined, Thames Estuary, 27 January 1941

Launched in 1914 and requisitioned in May 1915 to become a minesweeper, she was returned to her owners in 1920 and requisitioned in December 1939 to become an auxiliary patrol vessel. In February 1940 she was converted into a minesweeper and in this role she was lost in the Thames Estuary in January 1941.

Dervish (R, 346t, 1911), mined off Humber, 9 September 1940

Originally built in Beverley in 1911 as *Norman* she was requisitioned in May 1915 to become a minesweeper and renamed *Norman II* in December and used for escort duties. She reverted to her original name when she was returned to her owners in 1919. She was subsequently sold and renamed *Dervish* and requisitioned in June 1940 to become an auxiliary patrol vessel. She hit a mine off the Humber in early September 1940 with three of her crew being killed.

Desiree (R, 213t, 1912), mined, Thames Estuary, 16 January 1941

Built at Beverley and launched in 1912, she was requisitioned in August 1914 and became a minesweeper. She was returned to her owners in 1919 and requisitioned in November 1939, again as a minesweeper. She was lost to a mine in the Thames Estuary in early 1941.

Donna Nook (R, 307t, 1916), sunk in collision, North Sea, 25 September 1943

Built at Selby and launched in 1915, she was requisitioned in February 1916 and became a minesweeper. After being returned to the owners in 1919 she was requisitioned in 1939 and became an auxiliary patrol vessel. In 1941 she was converted into a minesweeper. On September 25 1943 she collided with the *Stella Rigel*, another trawler, off Harwich. They were then attacked by E-boats. Whilst taking evasive action the *Stella Rigel* rammed *Donna Nook* amidships and rolled her over and she sank.

Dox (R, 35t, 1931), sunk by enemy action, Plymouth, SW England, 20 March 1941

Dromio (R, 380t, 1929), collision, N of Whitby, North Sea, 22 December 1939

Built at Beverley in 1929, she was requisitioned in August 1939 to become a minesweeper. She was based at Sheerness and was lost after a collision to the north of Whitby in late December 1939.

Drummer (R, 297t, 1915), mined off Brightlingsea, Essex, 4 August 1940

Purchased by the Royal Navy while she was still being built at Middlesbrough, as *Dragoon*, she was launched in January 1915 and renamed *Drummer* in January 1919. She then was sold to private owners but was requisitioned in August 1939 and converted into a minesweeper. In July 1940 she became an auxiliary patrol vessel and was hit by a mine off Brightlingsea in August 1940.

Dungeness (R, 263t, 1914), bombed and total loss off Happisburgh, Norfolk, 15 November 1940

Built at Selby and launched in 1914 as *Sea Ranger*, she was requisitioned in February 1915 and became a minesweeper. In 1919 she was returned to her owners and renamed *Dungeness*. She was then requisitioned in May 1940 and became an auxiliary patrol vessel. She was wrecked by enemy bombs off Happisburg in mid-November 1940.

Ebor Wyke (R, 348t, 1929), presumed torpedoed by U-boat off E Coast of Iceland, 2 May 1945

Built at Selby and launched in 1929, she was requisitioned in August 1939 and converted into a minesweeper. In 1940 she was based at Iceland but by 1943 she had joined the 134th Minesweeping Group at Grimsby. She was torpedoed on patrol off Iceland. There was only one survivor, the *Ebor Wyke* was the last British warship of the Second World War to be sunk by a U-boat.

Eileen Duncan (R, 223t, 1910), sunk by aircraft, N Shields, 30 September 1941

Built at Selby and launched in 1910, she was requisitioned in January 1915 to become a minesweeper. After being returned to her owners in 1919 she became a minesweeper once again after being requisitioned in January 1940. She was sunk by German aircraft at the end of September 1941.

Elizabeth Angela (R, 253t, 1928), sunk by aircraft in Downs, 13 August 1940

Built at Dalmuir and launched in 1928, she was requisitioned in November 1939 and sunk by enemy aircraft in mid-August 1940.

Elk (R, 181t, 1902), mined at Plymouth, 27 November 1940

Built at Beverley and launched in 1902, she was requisitioned in December 1914 to become a minesweeper. She was transferred to the Fishery Reserve in 1917 and in 1918 was renamed *Elk II*. She was returned to her owners in July 1919 and was then requisitioned in October 1939, becoming a DAN layer. She was lost off east Cornwall with no loss of life.

Emilion (R, 201t, 1914), mined, Thames Estuary, 24 October 1941

Built at Middlesbrough and launched in 1914, she spent four years from 1915 as a minesweeper. She was requisitioned in November 1939, again as a minesweeper based at Grimsby. She was lost in the Thames Estuary to a mine.

Erin (R, 394t, 1933), explosion, Gibraltar harbour, 11 January 1942

Built at Beverley in 1933, she was originally named *Sheffield Wednesday*, but was renamed *Erin* after she had been requisitioned in 1940 to become an anti-submarine trawler. She was attached to the 7th Anti-Submarine Group based at Gibraltar. Whilst in the middle of three trawlers she blew up on January 11 1942. The *Honjo* was also destroyed and *Imperialist* was badly damaged. The probable cause of the explosion was either an Italian frogman or a Spanish saboteur.

Ethel Taylor (R, 276t, 1917), mined off Tyne, 22 November 1940

Built at Southbank on Tees on January 24 1917 as the *James Hunniford*, she was sold in 1919 and renamed *Cremlyn*. Subsequently she was sold again and renamed *Ethel Taylor*. She was requisitioned in 1940 as an auxiliary patrol vessel and was lost to a mine on November 22.

Evalina (R, 202t, 1919), believed mined, Tyne area, North Sea, 16 December 1939

Built at Winenhoe in 1919 as the *John Howard*, she was delivered in 1921 and renamed *Evalina*. She was requisitioned in November 1939 as an auxiliary patrol vessel and was lost to a mine off the Tyne in mid-December.

Evesham (R, 239t, 1925), sunk by aircraft off Great Yarmouth, Norfolk, 27 May 1941

Built at Selby and launched in 1915, she was requisitioned in June and returned to her owners four years later. She became an auxiliary patrol vessel after being requisitioned in December 1939. She was sunk off Great Yarmouth in late May 1941. The wreck was subsequently salvaged but she was broken up at Troon in April 1946.

Fifeshire (R, 540t, 1938), aircraft east of Copinsay, Orkneys, 20 February 1940

Built at Southbank on Tees and launched in 1938, she was requisitioned in September 1939 for anti-submarine work. She was based at Rosyth as part of the 11th Anti-Submarine Striking Force. She was some 70 miles to the east of Copinsay on February 20 1940, along with her sister ship, *Ayreshire*, when they were attacked by two Heinkel 111s. *Fifeshire* only had two Lewis guns to protect herself and consequently she was hit by two bombs; there was only one survivor. *Ayreshire* was luckier as she had been given her 4-inch gun and fended off the enemy aircraft.

Fleming (R, 356t, 1929), sunk by aircraft, Thames Estuary, 24 June 1940

Built at Beverley and launched in 1929, she was converted into a minesweeper after being requisitioned in August 1939. Under a year later she was lost when attacked by enemy aircraft in the Thames Estuary.

Flotta (530t, 1941), grounded on 29 October off Buchan Ness, E Scotland and foundered, 6 November 1941

Built at Selby and launched as a Royal Naval trawler in February 1941, she ran aground off Buchan Ness and finally foundered eight days later.

Fontenoy (R, 376t, 1918), sunk by aircraft off Lowestoft, Suffolk, 19 November 1940

Built at Paisley in 1918, she was temporarily loaned to the United States Navy in 1919. Two years later she returned to the Royal Navy and then was sold and renamed *Edouard Anseele*. She was hired in

February 1940 as the *Fonteno* and sunk by German aircraft off Lowestoft.

Force (R, 324t, 1917), sunk by aircraft off Great Yarmouth, Norfolk, 27 June 1941

Built at Selby and launched in September 1917 as *James Buchanan*, she was an Admiralty trawler fitted with listening hydrophones. In 1922 she was sold into private ownership and renamed *Stoneferry*. She was requisitioned in February 1940 as *Force* and became a minesweeper. She was attached to the Lowestoft Minesweeping Group and responsible for sweeps from Lowestoft to Sheringham in Norfolk. After being attacked by enemy aircraft whilst at anchor off Great Yarmouth she took twenty minutes to sink, but there was no loss of life.

Fort Royal (550t, 1931), aircraft off Aberdeen, 9 February 1940

Launched in 1931, she was requisitioned in August 1939 and then purchased by the Royal Navy to become a minesweeper. She was based at Aberdeen along with other trawlers and whilst sweeping around 20 miles to the northeast of Aberdeen in early February 1940 she was attacked by a pair of Heinkel 111s. During their second sweep the German aircraft hit her with two bombs and she sank in 3 minutes.

Fortuna (R, 259t, 1906), sunk by aircraft off St Abb's Head, E Scotland. 3 April 1941

Built at Beverley and launched in 1906, she became part of the Fishery Reserve in 1917, being returned to her owners two years later. She became an auxiliary patrol vessel after being requisitioned in June 1940 but was sunk by German aircraft in early April 1941.

Franc Tireur (R, 314t, 1916), sunk by E-boat off Harwich, E England, 29 September 1943

Built at Selby and launched in 1916, she was requisitioned in June 1917 to become a minesweeper. After being returned to her owners in 1919 she was requisitioned in May 1940, becoming an auxiliary patrol vessel based at Grimsby. In 1941 she became a minesweeper

HM Minesweeper *Bernard Shaw*.

HMT *Negro*, Italy, June 1944.

Skipper and No 1, HMS *Clotilde*.

HMT *Lord Hotham*, Gibraltar, October 1939 to July 1942, skippered by Lieutenant Morris of Milford Haven.

IMT *Solon*, April 1945.

YMS 2181, off Penang in the Malacca Straits.

Conditions aboard a trawler off Iceland.

Gun turret and deck of trawler off Iceland.

HMT *Kennet*, taken in the Middle East.

A muster of ratings at the Sparrow's Nest, Lowestoft.

The author Alfred Draper, a member of the Royal Naval Patrol Service during World War Two, is on the right of the back row. He served onboard HMT *Tervani*.

HMT *Kintyre* near Malta in 1945 and HMT *Olvina* in Plymouth, 1942.

HMT *Tervani* was sunk on February 2 1943 off Algiers by an Italian submarine.

HMT *Tiree* operated as an anti-submarine vessel from 1942 onwards.

A detail from the painting, Clean Sweep, by Ernie Childs.

A detail from the painting, Clean Sweep, by Ernie Childs.

A detail from the painting, Clean Sweep, by Ernie Childs.

A detail from the painting, Foul Sweep, by Ernie Childs.

The crew of HMT *Negro*, Naples, June 1944.

HMT *Solon*, April 1945.

MMS 192.

The reconstructed bandstand at the Sparrow's Nest, Lowestoft.

HMT *Northern Gem*, which operated off Norway and protected convoys bound for Russia.

MT *Finese*.

he drifter *Young Mun* (LT1147) during the First World War.

The RNPSA memorial at the National Memorial Arboretum.

and was posted to Harwich. A torpedo from an E-boat sunk her, claiming sixteen or her crew, in late September 1943.

Francolin (R, 322t, 1916), sunk by aircraft off Cromer, Norfolk, 12 November 1941

Built at Selby and launched in 1916 as the *Faraday*, she was requisitioned in the November to become a minesweeper for the next three years. In December 1939 she was requisitioned again and became an auxiliary patrol vessel. She was renamed *Francolin* in 1941 and was sunk by German aircraft off Cromer.

Gairsay (545t, 1942), sunk off Normandy, 3 August 1944

Built at Ardrossan, having been ordered by the Royal Navy in June 1941 and launched in May the following year. She was designed for anti-submarine warfare and was operating as an anti-submarine escort during Operation Neptune in June 1944 when a German motorboat sunk her.

Ganilly (545t, 1943), sunk by mine, English Channel, 5 July 1944

Built at Beverley and launched in May 1943, as a Royal Navy anti-submarine trawler, she was lost to a mine in the English Channel during Operation Neptune whilst she was working on escort duty.

Gaul (550t, 1936), sunk by aircraft off Norway, 3 May 1940

Built at Southbank on Tees and launched in 1936, she was bought by the Royal Navy and converted into an anti-submarine trawler in 1939. She was based at Aberdeen as part of the 16th Anti-Submarine Strike Force. She was lost in action to German aircraft during the Norwegian campaign.

Gulfoss (730t, 1929), mined, English Channel, 9 March 1941

Built at Selby and launched in 1929, she was requisitioned ten years later, in the August, to become a minesweeper. She was lost whilst on duty in the English Channel in early March 1941.

Hammond (R, 452T, 1936), sunk by aircraft, Aandalsnes, Norway, 25 April 1940

Built at Selby and launched in 1936, she was requisitioned in August 1939 to become an anti-submarine trawler. She joined the 22nd Anti-

Submarine Group and was sunk by enemy aircraft off Norway in late April 1940. In 1941 she was salvaged by the Germans and commissioned into the German navy in February 1942. In 1945 she was bought by Faroese owners and renamed *Vesturskin*. After this she was bought by Norwegians and renamed *Sletnes*.

Hayburn Wyke (R, 324t, 1917), torpedoed by U-boat at anchor off Ostend, Belgium, 2 January 1945

Built at Selby and launched in August 1917, as *Robert Barton*, she was sold in 1922 and renamed *Hayburn Wyke*. She was requisitioned in May 1940 and became an auxiliary patrol vessel. In the following year she was converted into a minesweeper. She was lost off Ostend in early 1945 to a U-boat torpedo.

Henriette (R, 261t, 1906), mined off Humber, 26 December 1941

Originally a French fishing vessel launched in 1906, by 1940 she was a French minesweeper and was seized in Northampton on July 3 1940, during Operation Grab. In September 1940 she was commissioned with a Free French crew but was lost to a mine in late December 1941 off the Humber.

Herring (590t, 1942), sunk in collision, North Sea, 22 April 1943

A Fish class trawler ordered by the Royal Navy in April 1942 and launched in December as an anti-submarine trawler. She sank in a collision in the North Sea four months later.

Hickory (505t, 1940), sunk by mine, English Channel, 22 October 1940

A Tree class Royal Naval trawler launched in February 1940, as a minesweeper. She was lost in the English Channel to a mine on October 22 1940.

Hildasay (545t, 1941), grounded on reef near Kilindini, E Africa, 21 June 1945

An Isles class Royal Naval vessel ordered in September 1940 and launched in May 1941 at Beverley. She was wrecked off the coast of East Africa in June 1945.

Honjo (R, 308t, 1928), explosion, Gibraltar harbour, 18 January 1942

Built at Southbank on Tees and launched in 1928, she was requisitioned in October 1939 and converted into a minesweeper. She burned at Gibraltar when the *Erin* blew up. *See also: Erin*

Horatio (545t, 1941), sunk by E-boat torpedo, Western Mediterranean, 7 January 1943

An Admiralty built Shakespearean class trawler ordered in December 1939 and launched in August 1940 at Beverley. She was an anti-submarine and minesweeping trawler. Sunk by an Italian motor torpedo boat in the Western Mediterranean in 1943.

Inverclyde (R, 215t, 1914), sank in tow off Beachy Head, 16 October 1942

Built at Goole and launched in 1914 as the *Perihelion*, she was requisitioned in September 1914 and became a minesweeper. After being returned to its owners in 1920 she became *Inverclyde*. She was requisitioned in August 1939 and became a water carrier. She foundered whilst being towed off Beachy Head in October 1942.

Irvana (R, 276t, 1917), sunk by aircraft off Great Yarmouth, Norfolk, 16 January 1942

Built at Southbank on Tees as a Royal Naval escort trawler, *Arthur Lessimore*, and launched in 1917, she was sold in 1919 and renamed *Avanturina*. She was sold again and renamed *Irvana*. She was requisitioned in 1940 and became an auxiliary patrol vessel. Enemy aircraft sunk her in mid-January 1942 off Great Yarmouth.

Jade (630t, 1933), sunk by aircraft during raid on Malta, 21 April 1942

This was a Royal Naval trawler of the Gem group. She was built at Beverley and launched in 1933, originally in private hands, but was bought by the Royal Navy in January 1939 and converted into an anti-submarine trawler. She was sent to the Mediterranean and was based at Malta as part of the 4th Minesweeper Anti-Submarine Group. In June 1941 she was involved in the search for a missing airman off Sicily. She was pounced on by two German E-boats. Over the next ninety minutes she damaged one of the German craft and forced the other to withdraw, all at ranges of 400m or less. Enemy aircraft sank her in the Grand Harbour of Malta in April 1942. She was broken up for scrap *in situ* in December 1943.

James Ludford (506t, 1919), mined off Tyne, North Sea, 14 December 1939

Built at Selby and launched in 1919, she was originally used as a mark buoy vessel. In 1939 she was mined off the Tyne in mid-December and lost.

Jardine (452t, 1936), scuttled after damage by enemy aircraft, West Coast of Norway, 30 April 1940

Built at Selby and launched in 1936, she was bought by the Royal Navy in August 1939 to become an anti-submarine trawler. She was attached to the 22nd Anti-Submarine Group and involved in the Norwegian campaign in April 1940. Having been hit by enemy aircraft she was scuttled, but the Germans salvaged her, repaired her and renamed her *Cherusker*. As a German vessel she was lost on December 6 1942 to a mine.

Jasper (596t, 1932), sunk by E-boat torpedo, English Channel, 1 December 1942

A Gem class vessel built at Beverley and launched in 1932, she was bought by the Royal Navy in November 1935 and was converted into an anti-submarine trawler. In 1939 she joined 2nd Anti-Submarine Group at Plymouth. The German E-boat *S81* torpedoed her in the English Channel on December 1 1942.

Jean Frederic (R, 329t, 1919), sunk by aircraft off Start Point, English Channel, 1 May 1941

Built at Renfrew and launched in 1919 as a fishing vessel called *James Hulbert*, she was subsequently sold and renamed *M J Reid*. In November 1940, as the *Jean Frederic*, she was hired from Dutch owners and converted into a minesweeper. She was sunk by enemy aircraft off Start Point on 1 May 1941.

Joseph Button (R, 290t, 1917), sunk by mine off Aldeburgh, Suffolk, 22 October 1940

Built at Beverley and launched in December 1917, she was originally a Royal Naval trawler but was sold in 1919. She was requisitioned in 1939 and became a minesweeper. She was lost to a mind off Aldeburgh in late October 1940.

Jura (545t, 1942), sunk by U-boat torpedo, Western Mediterranean, 7 January 1943

An Isles class Admiralty trawler, ordered in July 1940 and launched at Ardrossan in November 1941. In 1942 she was sent to the Mediterranean and was sunk in the Western Mediterranean on 7 January 1943, by *U-371*.

Juniper (505t, 1939), sunk by *Admiral Hipper* gunfire off Norway, 8 June 1940

Built at Port Glasgow and launched in December 1939, she was fully commissioned by March 1940 as an anti-submarine trawler with the 19th Anti-Submarine Strike Force in the Orkney Islands. She was involved in escorting a tanker from Tromso on 8 June 1940 when she was spotted by a German squadron consisting of the *Scharnhorst*, *Gneisenau*, *Admiral Hipper* and three escorting destroyers. She was probably sunk by the *Admiral Hipper*, but the crew, realising that there was no escape, hoisted the battle ensign and sailed to meet the German ships. She lasted an hour and a half and sank with only four of the crew surviving.

Kennymore (R, 325t, 1914), mined, Thames Estuary, 25 November 1940

Built at Beverley and launched in 1914, she was requisitioned in April 1915 and became a minesweeper. She was returned to her owners in 1919 and then requisitioned in November 1939 and converted back into a minesweeper. She was lost to a mine in the Thames Estuary in late November 1940.

Keryado (R, 252t, 1920), mined, English Channel, 6 March 1941

Launched in 1920 as a French fishing vessel, she was seized by the Royal Navy in July 1940, by which time she was a French minesweeper. She was sunk by a mine in the English Channel at the beginning of March 1941.

Kingston Alalite (550t, 1933), sunk by mine off Plymouth, 10 November 1940

Built at Beverley and launched in 1933, she was requisitioned in August 1939 and became an anti-submarine trawler with the 9th Anti-Submarine Group at Devonport. She was hit by a mine close to the Plymouth breakwater on November 10 1940.

Kingston Beryl (R, 356t, 1928), mined, NW Approaches, 25 December 1943

Built in Beverley and launched in 1928, she was requisitioned in September 1939 and converted into an armed boarding vessel. In March 1941 she was converted into an anti-submarine trawler. She was to the southwest of Skerrymore on Christmas Day 1943 escorting a small convoy but she ran into a British mine that had broken free from a minefield. All twenty-eight men on board were lost.

Kingston Cairngorm (R, 448t, 1935), sunk by mine, English Channel, 18 October 1940

Built in Beverley and launched in 1935, after being requisitioned in September 1939 she was posted to Portsmouth as part of the 27th Anti-Submarine Group. In June 1940 she ran aground and was towed into Portsmouth for repairs. Her luck ran out on October 18 when she hit a mine in the English Channel.

Kingston Ceylonite (940t, 1935), mined off Chesapeake Bay, USA, 15 June 1942

Built at Beverley and launched in 1935, she was requisitioned in September 1939 and converted into an anti-submarine trawler. She was then purchased by the Royal Navy in the November. In March 1942, along with her crew, she was loaned to the United States Navy. She hit a mine in Chesapeake Bay on June 15. Eighteen of her thirty-two crewmembers were killed. At the same time a destroyer and two tankers were also lost in the same minefield.

Kingston Cornelian (550T, 1934), collision, E of Gibraltar Straits, 5 January 1940

Built in Beverley and launched in 1934, she was bought by the Royal Navy in August 1939 and converted into an anti-submarine trawler. She subsequently joined the 7th Anti-Submarine Group at Gibraltar. On January 5 1940 she collided with the French liner *Cheila* to the east of Gibraltar. *Kingston Cornelian's* depth charges exploded as she began to sink and all of her crew were lost.

Kingston Galena (550t, 1934), sunk by aircraft off Dover, 24 July 1940

Built in Beverley and launched in 1934, she was bought by the Royal Navy in August 1939 to become an anti-submarine trawler with the Dover-based 9th Anti-Submarine Group. Enemy aircraft claimed her off Dover towards the end of July 1940.

Kingston Jacinth (R, 356t, 1929), mined off Portsmouth, 12 January 1943

A Beverley built trawler launched in 1929, she was requisitioned ten years later and converted into an armed boarding vessel. In 1940 she became an anti-submarine trawler and was lost to a mine off Portsmouth in January 1943.

Kingston Sapphire (R, 356t, 1929), sunk by Italian submarine torpedo, Straits of Gibraltar, 5 October 1940

Beverley built trawler launched in 1929 and purchased by the Royal Navy ten years later to become an armed boarding vessel, based at Gibraltar. She was sunk off Gibraltar by the Italian submarine *Nani* on 5 October. Thirteen of her crew were killed. The remaining twenty-eight endured fifteen days in a lifeboat before they were picked up by a Spanish tanker.

Kopanes (R, 351t, 1915), sunk by aircraft off Tyne, 19 April 1941

Built in Beverley and launched in 1914, she remained in private hands until she was requisitioned in June 1940 when she was converted into an auxiliary patrol vessel, based at Grimsby, for fishery protection duties. Enemy aircraft sunk her off the Tyne in April 1941.

Kurd (R, 352t, 1930), sunk by mine off Lizard Head, Cornwall, SE England, 10 July 1945

Built in Selby and launched in 1930, she was requisitioned in 1939 and became a minesweeper based at Grimsby and subsequently in the following year she became part of 17th Minesweeping Group. In 1943 she was transferred to the 40th Minesweeping Group, also based at Grimsby. She was lost off the Lizard on 10 July 1945.

La Nantaise (R, 359, 1934), sunk in collision off SE England, 8 July 1945

Built in Beverley and launched in 1934 as the *St Arcadius* she was bought by the Royal Navy in August 1939 and converted into an anti-submarine trawler. She was then transferred to the French navy where she was used as an auxiliary patrol vessel and renamed *La Nantaise*. She was seized by the Royal Navy in Portsmouth in July 1940 and reverted to her original name. In June 1945 she was due to be returned to the French navy but she sank after a collision with SS *Helencrest* on 8 July.

Lady Lilian (R, 581t, 1939), sunk by aircraft, W of Ireland, 16 March 1941

Built in Beverley and launched in 1939, she was requisitioned in January 1940 and as an anti-submarine trawler was posted to Belfast. She was sunk by German aircraft off the west of Ireland in mid-March 1940.

Lady Shirley (R, 477t, 1937), sunk by U-boat, Gibraltar Straits, 11 December 1941

Built at Beverley and launched in 1937, she was requisitioned in May 1940 to become an auxiliary patrol vessel. In January 1941 she was converted into an anti-submarine trawler and joined the 31st Anti-Submarine Group based at Gibraltar. In September 1941 she experienced engine trouble whilst out to sea and was towed into Madeira by *Lady Hogarth*. After repairs she sank off Tenerife the German submarine *U-111* on October 4. After picking up forty-five German sailors she made it to Gibraltar on October 8. The commanding officer was awarded the Distinguished Service Order;

two lieutenants received the Distinguished Service Cross, a seaman received the Conspicuous Gallantry Medal and five others were awarded the Distinguished Service Medal. Tragically she was torpedoed off Gibraltar on December 11 by the *U-374*; all thirty-three crewmen were lost.

Laertes (530t, 1941), sunk by U-boat torpedo, W Africa, 25 July 1942

A Shakespearean class Admiralty trawler, built at Beverley and launched in October 1940, as an anti-submarine trawler. She was attached to the 1st Minesweeper Anti-Submarine Group at Freetown in West Africa. Whilst on convoy duty in July 1942 she was torpedoed by the German submarine *U-201*.

Larwood (R, 453T, 1936), sunk by aircraft, West Coast of Norway, 25 April 1940

Built at Selby and launched in 1936, she was requisitioned in August 1939 and as an anti-submarine trawler joined the 22nd Anti-Submarine Group. Whilst taking part in the Norwegian campaign in April 1940 she was sunk by German aircraft. The Germans, however, salvaged her and renamed her *Franke*. She was recovered by the Royal Navy in 1945 and sold into private ownership in April 1947.

Leyland (857t, 1936), collision, Gibraltar Bay, 25 November 1942

Built at Selby and launched in 1936, she was purchased by the Royal Navy in September 1939 and converted into an anti-submarine trawler. She collided with a merchantman off Gibraltar in November 1942 and was sunk.

Lincoln City (R, 398t, 1933), sunk by aircraft, Faroe Islands, 21 February 1941

Built at Selby and launched in 1933, she became an anti-submarine trawler having been requisitioned in September 1939. Enemy aircraft sank her off the Faroe Islands in February 1941.

Loch Alsh (R, 358t, 1926), sunk by aircraft, Humber Area, 30 January 1942

Built at Beverley and launched in 1926 as the *Lady Madeleine* she was sold in 1934 and renamed *Cameron*. She was sold again in 1939 and became *Loch Alsh*. After being requisitioned in December 1939 she became a minesweeper and part of the Grimsby-based 17th Minesweeping Group. She was badly damaged by German aircraft off the Humber towards the end of January 1942 and was taken in tow but sank to the northeast of Skegness.

Loch Assater (R, 210t, 1910), British mine, E coast of Scotland, 22 March 1940

Built at Aberdeen and launched in 1910, she served from 1915 to 1919 as a requisitioned minesweeper. She was bought by the Royal Navy in February 1940 and converted into an auxiliary patrol vessel. She was sunk by a Royal Naval mine off the east coast of Scotland towards the end of March 1940.

Loch Doon (R, 534t, 1937), probably mined, off Blyth, North Sea, 25 December 1939

Built at Southbank on Tees and launched in 1937, she was requisitioned in August 1939 to become an anti-submarine trawler. Fifteen of her crew were killed when she probably struck a mine off Blyth on Christmas Day.

Loch Inver (R, 356t, 1930), probably mined, Harwich area, 24 September 1940

Built at Beverley and launched in 1930 and after changing hands three times was requisitioned in October 1939 to become a Harwich-based auxiliary patrol vessel. All hands were lost when she struck a mine off Harwich towards the end of September 1940.

Loch Naver (R, 278t, 1919), sunk in collision off Hartlepool, 6 May 1940

Built at Troon as a fishing vessel and launched in March 1919 as *Edward Cattelly*, she was sold and renamed *Sir John Hotham* before being sold again and renamed *Loch Naver*. The Royal Navy requisitioned her in August 1939, converting her into a minesweeping trawler. She was lost after a collision off Hartlepool in May 1940.

Lord Austin (R, 473t, 1937), mined and sunk, Seine Bay, Normandy, 24 June 1944

Built at Selby and launched in 1937, she was requisitioned in September two years later to join the Northern Patrol as an anti-submarine trawler. In August 1941 she joined the Iceland Command, covering convoys bound for Russia. In April 1942 she escorted PQ14 and in June and July the disastrous PQ17 convoy. Her last convoy mission was in December 1943 and she was refitted and re commissioned in May 1944. She then towed a barge from the Clyde down to Falmouth and then to Southampton. She was involved as an anti-submarine trawler for Operation Neptune and also escorted vessels to Juno Beach. This is where she was hit by a bomb, which blew a hole in her side. On June 24 1944 she triggered off an acoustic mine in the Seine Bay. She sank in ten minutes and seven of her crew were lost.

Lord Hailsham (891t, 1934), sunk by E-boats, probably torpedoed, English Channel, 27 February 1943

Built at Selby and launched in 1934, she was purchased by the Royal Navy in August 1939 to become and anti-submarine trawler. She was lost to a torpedo from a German E-boat in the English Channel in February 1943.

Lord Inchcape (R, 338t, 1924), sunk by mine off Plymouth, later salvaged, 25 October 1940

She was built at Selby and launched in 1924. Fifteen years later, in the August, she was requisitioned to become a minesweeping trawler. She hit a mine in late October 1940 off Plymouth but was salvaged and sold to the Royal Navy. They sold her to private owners in August 1946.

Lord Selborne (R, 247t, 1917), mined, Humber, 31 March 1941

Built at Beverley and launched in 1917, she was requisitioned in October 1917 and spent the next two years as a minesweeper and escort. She was requisitioned again in June 1940 to become an auxiliary patrol vessel. A mine claimed her in the Humber Estuary just three miles off Spurn Head at the end of March 1941.

Lord Snowdon (R, 444t, 1934), collision off Falmouth, 13 April 1942

Built at Selby in 1934 and requisitioned in August 1939 for anti-submarine duties. Sank in a collision off Falmouth in April 1942.

Lord Stamp (R, 448t, 1935), sunk by mine, English Channel, 14 October 1940

She was built at Selby and launched in 1935 and subsequently requisitioned in August 1939 for anti-submarine work. She was lost to a mine in the English Channel in October 1940.

Lord Stonehaven (R, 444t, 1934), sank during E-boat attack off Eddystone, English Channel, 2 October 1942

Built at Selby and launched in 1934, she was requisitioned for anti-submarine duties in August 1939. A German E-boat torpedoed her close to the Eddystone Light near Plymouth in October 1942.

Lord Wakefield (825t deep, 1933), sunk by aircraft off Normandy, 29 July 1944

Built at Selby and launched in 1933, the Royal Navy bought her in August 1939 and converted her to join the 17th Anti-Submarine Group at Swansea. She was transferred to Portsmouth in 1940 to become group leader. She was operating as an anti-submarine escort during Operation Neptune in June 1944 when German aircraft sank, killing twenty-six crewmen.

Lorinda (R, 348t, 1928), engine problems and fire off Freetown, W Africa, 20 August 1941

Built at Beverley and launched in 1928, she was requisitioned in September 1939 and became a minesweeping trawler. After experiencing engine trouble followed by a fire she foundered off Freetown, West Africa, in August 1941.

Luda Lady (R, 234t, 1914), mined, Humber area, 22 January 1941

Originally built at Selby and launched in 1914, she spent 1915 to 1920 under requisition. In 1922 she was sold and renamed *Stelmo*, having been originally christened *Mena*. She was sold again in 1936 to become *Luda Lady*. She was requisitioned in November 1939 and became a minesweeping trawler. But she fell to one in the Humber in late January 1941.

Manor (R, 314t, 1913), sunk during E-boat attack, English Channel, February 1942

Built at Aberdeen and launched in 1913, she spent between 1914 and 1919 as a minesweeper. In August 1939 she was requisitioned and became an anti-submarine trawler. She fell to the torpedo of an E-boat whilst on escort duty in the English Channel in February 1942. Only one of her crew survived the attack. He was picked up by the trawler *Ruby*.

Manx Prince (R, 221t, 1910), mined, entrance to Humber, 28 November 1940

Built at Selby and launched in 1910, she spent from August 1914 to 1919 as a requisitioned minesweeper. She was requisitioned again in December 1939 to become an auxiliary patrol vessel. In June the following year she was converted into a minesweeper but lost toward the end of November 1940 in the entrance to the Humber Estuary.

Marconi (R, 322t, 1916), lost in collision off Harwich, 20 September 1941

Built at Selby and launched in 1916 she was requisitioned in August. On November 14 1916, along with the trawler *Pelican* and the yacht *Lorna* she chased off a German U-boat that was stalking a merchantman. She was returned to her owners in 1919 and requisitioned in March 1940 to become a minesweeper. She was rammed and sunk by a Harwich patrol vessel on 20 September 1941. Whilst the crew were abandoning ship a German aircraft attacked them, but they all managed to evacuate the stricken vessel.

Marsona (R, 276t, 1918), mined off Cromarty, 4 August 1940

Built at South Shields and launched in 1918 as an Admiralty trawler called *James Christopher*, she was sold into private hands and at some point renamed *Marsona*. She was requisitioned in October 1939 to become a minesweeping trawler, but a mine claimed her off Cromarty at the beginning of August 1940.

Mastiff (520t, 1938), mined, Thames Estuary, 20 November 1939
Built as a Basset class Royal Navy minesweeping trawler and launched in February 1938, she hit a mine in the Thames Estuary in late November 1939.

Melbourne (R, 466t, 1936), sunk by aircraft, Narvik area, Norway, 22 May 1940
Built at Southbank on Tees and launched in 1936 she was purchased by the Royal Navy in October 1939 to join 23rd Anti-Submarine Group. She was lost when hit by German aircraft off Norway in May 1940.

Meror (R, 250t, 1905), mined, Humber area, E England, 3 October 1943
Built at Selby and originally launched in 1905, she spent six years from 1914 as a minesweeper. She served the same role after being requisitioned in September 1940. In 1941 she joined the 72nd Minesweeping Group at Grimsby. A mine claimed her off the Humber in early October 1943.

Milford Earl (R, 290t, 1919), sunk by aircraft off E coast of Scotland, 8 December 1941
Originally built as *Andrew Apsley* at Beverley and launched in 1919 as a fishing vessel, in October she was renamed *Callancroft* after being sold on. She was sold again in 1930 and renamed *Duncan Mcrae*. In 1936 she was sold once more and renamed *Milford Earl*. In August 1939 she was requisitioned to become a minesweeping trawler. Five of her crew were lost and five saved when German aircraft sank her off Lunan Bay in early December 1941.

Mirabelle (R, 203t, 1918), rammed and sunk by accident, 17 November 1944
Built at Aberdeen and launched in November 1918 as *Edward Barker*, she became *Mirabelle* in 1921. In 1939 she was requisitioned and became an auxiliary patrol vessel based at Grimsby. She was converted into a fuel tanker in 1944 but was accidentally rammed and sunk on 17 November.

Moravia (R, 306t, 1917), mined, North Sea, 14 March 1943

Built at Beverley and launched in 1917, she was almost immediately requisitioned and spent the next two years as a minesweeper. She sustained heavy damage off Iceland in January 1932, with the skipper and a crewman being swept overboard, as well as suffering structural damage. In August 1940 she was requisitioned to become an auxiliary patrol vessel and later in the year a minesweeping trawler. She was mined off Sheerness in mid-March 1943.

Murmansk (R, 348t, 1929), grounded at Brest and abandoned, 17 June 1940

Built at Beverley in 1929 as *Night Watch*, she was stranded at Stem Island in Norway and abandoned in 1937. A year later she was salvaged and taken to Grimsby. After changing hands in 1939 she was renamed *Murmansk*. In August she was requisitioned to become an auxiliary patrol vessel. She ran aground near Brest on 17 June 1940, but in 1942 the Germans salvaged her and used her as a patrol boat until she was sunk in 1944.

Myrtle (550t, 1928), sunk by mine, Thames Estuary, 14 June 1940

Myrtle was a Tree class trawler originally named *St Irene*. She was built at Beverley and launched in 1928. Eleven years later she was bought by the Royal Navy to become a minesweeper, but was lost to a mine in mid-June 1940 in the Thames Estuary.

Nogi (R, 299t, 1923), sunk off Norfolk, 23 June 1941

Built at Southbank on Tees and launched in 1923, she was requisitioned in August 1939 and became a minesweeping trawler. She was lost to German aircraft off the coast of Norfolk in late June 1941.

Northcoates (R, 277t, 1918), sank in tow, English Channel, 2 December 1944

Built at Falmouth and launched in 1918, she was sold into private ownership in 1921, originally named *George Corton*, she was renamed *Zencon* then *Zircon*. By 1939 when she was requisitioned in the August she was called *Northcoates* and became a minesweeping trawler. Whilst under tow in the English Channel at the beginning of December 1944 she was lost.

Northern Isles (R, 655t, 1936), ran aground off Durban, S Africa total loss, 19 January 1945

A German built Bremerhaven vessel launched in 1936 as part of the German reparation programme relating to the First World War. After private ownership she was requisitioned in August 1939 to become an armed boarding vessel. She was converted to anti-submarine work in 1942 and was temporarily loaned to the US Navy. She was returned to the Royal Navy in October and transferred to South Africa. She became stranded whilst on patrol near Durban in mid-January 1945 and was written off.

Northern Princess (R, 655t, 1936), sunk, W Atlantic, 7 March 1942

Another Bremerhaven built vessel launched in 1936 that was requisitioned as an armed boarding vessel in August 1939. She was originally posted on contraband patrols based at Kirkwall. In 1942 she became an anti-submarine trawler. In February 1942 she was sent from Londonderry to be loaned to the US Navy but she ran into thick fog off the Grand Banks, near Newfoundland. She disappeared and it was believed that the German submarine *U-94* sank her. At the time her loss was a mystery and it was believed that she may have run into an iceberg. After the war German records confirmed that the *U-94* had indeed claimed her.

Northern Rover (R, 655t, 1936), overdue at Kirkwall, Orkneys, 5 November 1939

A third Bremerhaven built and launched in 1936 vessel, she was requisitioned in August 1939 as an armed boarding vessel and posted to Kirkwall to operate with *Northern Isles*. She was lost somewhere between Iceland and the Faroe Islands whilst *en route* to Kirkwall. German records after the war confirmed that the *U-59* had sunk her.

Notts County (R, 541t, 1937), sunk by U-boat, S of Iceland, 8 March 1942

Built at Southbank on Tees and launched in 1938, she became an anti-submarine trawler, having been requisitioned in September 1939. She fell foul of a torpedo fired by the German submarine *U-701*, to the south of Iceland in early March 1942.

Orfasy (545t, 1942), lost, probably by U-boat torpedo off W Africa, 22 October 1943

An Isles class Admiralty built trawler launched at Aberdeen in March 1942, she is believed to have been torpedoed by a German submarine off the coast of West Africa in late October 1943.

Ormonde (R, 250t, 1906), sunk by aircraft off E coast of Scotland, 16 February 1941

Originally launched in 1906 having been built at Selby, she became a minesweeper in 1914 after requisition. In 1917 she became the *Ormonde II* and was returned to her owners in 1919. Twenty years later she became an auxiliary patrol vessel. In November 1940 she was converted to minesweeping duties. The vessel was sunk by German aircraft off the east coast of Scotland in mid-February 1941.

Oswaldian (R, 260t, 1917), mined, Bristol Channel, 4 August 1940

Built at Beverley and launched in 1917, she spent two years from September as a minesweeper. After changing hands in 1940 she was requisitioned in May to become an auxiliary patrol vessel based at Milford Haven. Just seven of her crew survived when she struck a mine in the Bristol Channel at the beginning of August.

Ouse (462t, 1917), mined, Tobruk, Libya, 20 February 1941

Originally the *Andrew King*, built at Selby and launched in 1917 as a minesweeper with listening hydrophones, she was renamed *Ouse* in September 1920. She fell foul of a mine off Tobruk on 20 February 1941.

Pelton (R, 358t, 1925), sunk by E-boat off Yarmouth, 24 December 1940

Built at Beverley and launched in 1925, she was requisitioned in August 1939 and converted for minesweeping duties. In 1940 she was involved in the operations to cut the telephone cables between Germany and Britain in the North Sea. She became the victim of a torpedo fired by an enemy E-boat off Great Yarmouth the day before Christmas in 1940.

Pentland Firth (900t, 1934), collision off New York, USA, 19 September 1942

Built at Beverley and launched in 1934, she was bought by the Royal Navy in August 1939 for anti-submarine duties. In February 1942 she was loaned to the US Navy. On 19 September she sank after colliding with the American minesweeper *Chaffinch* off New York.

Peridot (550t, 1933), mined off Dover, 15 March 1940

Originally built at Southbank on Tees and launched in 1922 as *Barry Castle*, she was renamed in 1934 as *Manchester City*. When she was purchased by the Royal Navy in August 1939 she not only became an anti-submarine trawler, but also acquired her new name, *Peridot*. She was lost to a mine off Dover in mid-March 1940.

Phineas Beard (R, 278t, 1918), sunk by aircraft off E coast of Scotland, 8 December 1941

A Castle class Beverley built trawler launched in 1917, she was sold into private hands in 1919. She was requisitioned and converted for minesweeping duties in August 1939. The vessel was lost to German aircraft off the east coast of Scotland at the beginning of December 1941.

Pine (545t, 1940), sunk by E-boat torpedo off Selsey Bill, Sussex, 3 January 1944

A Tree class Admiralty built trawler constructed in Aberdeen and launched in March 1940 as a minesweeper, she was on convoy duty off Selsey Bill on 3 January 1944 when she was attacked by three E-boat flotillas. Incredibly she stayed afloat despite the fact that her bow had been blown off by a torpedo. She continued firing at the enemy until they made off but she finally rolled over and sank under tow close to Portsmouth.

Polly Johnson (R, 290t, 1918), sunk by aircraft bombs, off Dunkirk, 29 May 1940

An Admiralty built trawler constructed at Beverley and launched in December 1918, she was finished off as a fishing vessel called *John Aikenhead*. After changing hands she became the *Polly Johnson*. She was requisitioned in August 1939 to become a minesweeper. She was lost during the evacuation of Dunkirk, having been straddled by German bombs dropped from an aircraft.

Pyrope (R, 295t, 1932), sunk by aircraft, Thames Estuary, 12 August 1940

Built in Beverley and launched in 1932, she was requisitioned in August 1939 to join the Sheerness based 2nd Minesweeping Group. Enemy aircraft sank her in the Thames Estuary in mid-August 1940.

Recoil (R, 344t, 1938), lost on patrol, presumed mined, English Channel, 28 September 1940

Launched as a German fishing vessel named *Blankenburg* in 1938, she was bought by British owners and renamed *Recoil*. In June 1940 she was requisitioned and became an anti-submarine trawler based in Portland. She was missing in action with all hands lost on 28 September. The only clue to her demise was the recovery of a body a month later.

Red Gauntlet (R, 338t, 1930), sunk by E-boats, North Sea, 5 August 1943

Built in Stockton and launched in 1930, after being requisitioned in August 1939 she joined the minesweeping groups at Harwich. It was in this role, off Harwich, that she was sunk with many casualties by a torpedo fired by a German E-boat.

Refundo (R, 338t, 1917), sunk by mine off Harwich, 18 December 1940

Built at Beverley and launched in 1917, she was requisitioned in July, fitted with listening hydrophones and became a minesweeper for the next two years. She returned to this role after being requisitioned in November 1939 and subsequently joined the Harwich based 117th Minesweeping Group. In 1940 she was fitted with an electronic hammer device that had been designed to detonate acoustic mines at a range of a mile. Whilst testing the equipment off Harwich in mid-December 1940 she set off a mine under her bow, which killed two of the crew. The vessel subsequently sank as it was being towed to safety.

Relonzo (R, 245t, 1914), mined, Crosby Channel, Liverpool, 20 January 1941

Built at Beverley and launched in 1914, she was requisitioned in April 1915 and returned to her owners five years later. She was again requisitioned in April 1939 and converted into an auxiliary patrol vessel. Thirteen months later she was converted to a minesweeper and joined the Birkenhead based 136th Minesweeping Group. She was lost towards the end of January 1941 when she hit a mine in the Crosby Channel.

Remillo (R, 266t, 1917), mined, Humber, 27 February 1941

Built at Beverley and launched in April 1917, she was originally to be called *Remillo* but was purchased by the Royal Navy and called *Robert Betson*. In 1919 she returned to private ownership and to her original name. In April 1940 she was requisitioned and became a DAN layer and then into an auxiliary patrol vessel in September, where she was based at Grimsby. She fell foul of a mine off the Humber at the end of February 1941.

Resmilo (R, 258t, 1917), sunk by aircraft at Peterhead, E Scotland, 20 June 1941

Built at Beverley and launched in 1917, she spent her first three years as a minesweeper fitted with listening hydrophones. In September 1940 she was requisitioned again and became a minesweeper and part of the 70th Minesweeping Group at Aberdeen. None of her crew was lost when she was sunk by German aircraft at Peterhead in late June 1941.

Resolvo (R, 231t, 1913), sunk by mine, Thames Estuary, 12 October 1940

A Beverley built vessel launched in 1913, she was not requisitioned until February 1915, but she spent the next five years as a minesweeper. She returned to this role after being requisitioned in November 1939. She was lost to a mine in the Thames Estuary on 12 October, but she was beached near Sheerness and subsequently broken up.

Resparko (R, 248t, 1916), sunk by aircraft at Falmouth, 20 August 1940

Another Beverley built 1916 launched vessel that spent until 1919 as a minesweeper; she became an auxiliary patrol vessel after being requisitioned in November 1939. Subsequently, in April 1940, she took on a minesweeping role, being based at Portsmouth. Enemy aircraft sank her off Falmouth in late August 1940 and all the crew survived.

Rifsnes (R, 431t, 1932), sunk by aircraft off Ostend, 20 May 1940

A Beverley built vessel launched in 1932, she was requisitioned in August 1939 and became a minesweeper operating out of Great Yarmouth. Enemy aircraft sank her, killing three crew, off Ostend towards the end of May 1940.

Rinovia (R, 499t, 1931), sunk by mine off Falmouth, 2 November 1940

Originally built as *Blakkur* at Beverley and launched in 1931, she was renamed *Renovia* in 1938 and requisitioned in August the following year to become a minesweeper. She ran aground at Dartmouth in September but was refloated but was sunk after striking a mine some two miles from St Antony Light near Falmouth on 2 November 1940.

River Clyde (R, 276t, 1919), sunk by mine off Aldeburgh, Suffolk, 5 August 1940

Originally commissioned as an Admiralty trawler, she was launched in August 1919, so was finished off as a fishing vessel called *Richard Cundy*. She was sold in 1920 and renamed *River Clyde*. She became a minesweeper after being requisitioned in August 1939. A year later she was lost, having struck a mine off Aldeburgh.

Robert Bowen (R, 290t, 1918), aircraft off Aberdeen, 9 February 1940

Built in Beverley and launched in March 1918, she went into private hands in 1919 and after changing ownership she was requisitioned in August 1939 and took up her role as a minesweeping group leader based in Aberdeen. She was attacked by a pair of Heinkel 111s on 9 February. Two bombs that were intended to hit *Fort Royal* hit *Robert Bowen* instead, blowing her to pieces and killing all of her crew.

Roche Bonne (R, 258t, 1913), aircraft off the Lizard, Cornwall, 7 April 1941

Built in Middlesbrough and launched in 1913, she was requisitioned in February 1940 for minesweeping duties. German aircraft claimed her off the Cornish coast at the beginning of April 1941.

Rodino (R, 230t, 1913), aircraft off Dover, 24 July 1940

Built in Beverley and launched in 1913, she was requisitioned in June 1915 and spent the next five years on minesweeping duties. In November 1939 she returned to this role, being based at Grimsby, but it was off Dover towards the end of July 1940 that German aircraft claimed her.

Rosemonde (R, 364t, 1910), probably torpedoed by U-boat, Atlantic, 22 January 1942

Originally a French fishing vessel that had been launched in 1910 and seized at Southampton in July 1940, by which time she was a French minesweeper, she was sunk by the *U-203* in the Atlantic towards the end of January 1942.

Royalo (R, 248t, 1916), sunk by mine off S Cornwall, 1 September 1940

Built at Beverley and launched in 1915, for her first three years she was a minesweeper. After being requisitioned in November 1939 she became an auxiliary patrol vessel. By January 1940 she was a minesweeper again and in this role she was lost in Mounts Bay on 1 September 1940.

Rubens (R, 320t, 1937), sunk by aircraft, Western Approaches, 13 February 1941

Originally a Belgian fishing vessel launched in 1937, in August 1940 she was hired and converted to anti-submarine duties. She was lost to German aircraft in mid-February 1941.

Rutlandshire (R, 458t, 1936), attacked by aircraft and grounded, Namsos, Norway, 20 April 1940

Built at Southbank on Tees and launched in September 1936. Requisitioned in October 1939 she joined the 23rd Anti-Submarine Group. She was hit by German aircraft at Namsos in 1940 and ran aground. In August 1941 she was salvaged by the Germans and renamed *Ubier*. She was lost to a mine on December 6 1942.

Rysa (545t, 1941), sunk by mine off Maddalena, Sardinia, 8 December 1943

Built at Selby and launched in March 1941, she fell victim to a mine off the Sardinian coast during Operation Husky, the invasion of Sicily, at the beginning of December 1943.

Sea King (R, 321t, 1916), sunk by underwater explosion in Grimsby Roads, 9 October 1940

Built at Selby and launched in 1916, between 1917 and 1919 she was a minesweeper and then a Q ship (a vessel that appeared to be unarmed but in fact had hidden weapons). She was requisitioned in August 1939 to become a minesweeper, joining the Grimsby based 40th Minesweeping Group. She was lost near Grimsby when in all likelihood a mine exploded underneath her.

Sedgefly (R, 520t, 1939), believed mined, Tyne area, North Sea, 16 December 1939

Launched in 1939 she was requisitioned in September for anti-submarine duties. Her life was incredibly short as she fell foul of a mine off the Tyne in mid-December.

Senateur Duhamel (R, 913t, 1927), collision off Wilmington, USA, 6 May 1942

A former French fishing vessel launched in 1927, she was seized in the Atlantic on December 28 1940. In January 1941 she joined the Royal Navy as an anti-submarine trawler. In 1942, whilst on loan to the US Navy, she sank after a collision off the North Carolina coast.

Silicia (R, 250t, 1912), mined off Humber, 8 May 1941

Built in Beverley and launched in 1912, she spent between

September 1914 and 1919 as a requisitioned minesweeper. She returned to this role after being requisitioned in August 1939, joining the 72nd Minesweeping Group based at Grimsby. She was lost a mine off the Humber at the beginning of May 1941.

Sindonis (913t, 1934), sunk by aircraft at Tobruk, Libya, 29 May 1941

Built at Southbank on Tees and launched as *Soudanese* she was requisitioned in August 1939 and became an anti-submarine trawler. In 1941 she was sent to join the inshore iquadron operating off Tobruk in the Mediterranean. It was here in late May that German aircraft sunk her.

Sisapon (R, 326t, 1928), mined off Harwich, 12 June 1940

Built at Beverley and launched in 1928, she was requisitioned eleven years later for minesweeping duties. By 1940 she was at Grimsby and was lost off Harwich in mid-June.

Solomon (R, 357t, 1928), mined, N of Cromer, 1 April 1942

Built at Beverley and launched in 1928, originally as the *Lady Rachael*, she changed hands and received her new name in 1937. She was requisitioned in August 1939 to become a minesweeper based at Grimsby. She joined the 17th Minesweeping Group there in 1940 and two years later she fell victim to a mine to the north of Cromer on April 1.

Spaniard (880t, 1937), explosion, Lagos, Nigeria, 5 December 1942

Launched in 1937 the Royal Navy bought her two years later. She was one of the vessels lost in an explosion in Lagos Harbour in early December 1941. *See also Kelt.*

St Achilleus (R, 484t, 1934), sunk by mine, Dunkirk area, 31 May 1940

Built at Beverley and launched in 1934, she was requisitioned in August 1939 to join the 12th Anti-Submarine Group based in Grimsby. She was transferred to the 11th Anti-Submarine Group at Harwich in 1940. She fell victim to a mine off Dunkirk on the last day of May 1940 whilst engaged in Operation Dynamo.

St Apollo (R, 580t, 1940), collision off Hebrides, W Scotland, 22 November 1941

Built at Beverley and launched in 1940, she was bought by the Royal Navy in February for anti-submarine work. In 1941 she joined the 3rd Escort Group at Greenock. She worked on convoy escort duty in the Atlantic but she was lost towards the end of November when she was involved in a collision with HMS *Sardonyx* off the Hebrides.

St Cathan (R, 565t, 1936), collision off S Carolina, USA, 11 April 1942

Built in Beverley and launched in 1936, she was requisitioned in September 1939 as an anti-submarine trawler. During the Norwegian campaign in 1940 she was attacked on twenty-nine occasions by German aircraft, but came through unscathed. In February 1942 she was loaned to the US Navy and it was on 11 April that she collided with the Dutch merchant ship SS *Hebe* off South Carolina. Both vessels were lost.

St Donats (R, 349t, 1924), collision off Humber, 1 March 1941

Built in Beverley and launched in 1924, she was requisitioned in August 1939 to join minesweepers based at Grimsby. In the following year she joined the 17th Minesweeping Group there but was lost on the first day of March in the Humber when she collided with HMS *Cotswold*.

St Goran (R, 565t, 1936), sunk by aircraft, Namsos, Norway, 3 May 1940

Built at Beverley and launched in 1936, after being requisitioned in September 1939 she joined the Aberdeen based 15th Anti-Submarine Strike Force. During the Norwegian campaign she was badly damaged by German aircraft at Namsos and had to be scuttled.

Star Of Devoran (R, 220t, 1915), sunk by aircraft, N Shields, 30 September 1941

Originally built at Aberdeen and launched in 1915 as *Star Of Peace*, she spent until 1919 as a minesweeper. At some point she was renamed *Star Of Devoran*, probably in 1939 when she was requisitioned once again. Enemy aircraft claimed her off North Shields at the end of September 1941.

Staunton (R, 283t, 1907), mine, Thames Estuary, 28 July 1940

Built in Beverley and launched in 1907, she spent between 1914 and 1920 as an auxiliary patrol vessel. She once again assumed this role after being requisitioned in June 1940, but she was returned to her owners in the July. Technically she was therefore not a naval loss when she struck a magnetic mine near Knoll Buoy on 28 July. She was in the process of being returned to her owners. All of the thirteen crewmembers were killed.

Stella Capella (815t, 1937), missing, Iceland area, 11 March 1942

A Beverley built vessel launched in 1937 as *Admiral Hawke*, she was sold in 1938 and renamed *Stella Capella*. The Royal Navy bought her in August 1939 to join the Belfast based 12th Anti-Submarine Strike Force. She survived the Norwegian campaign of 1940 and in the following year was transferred to the 41st Anti-Submarine Group in Iceland. On 11 March 1942 she was torpedoed and sunk by *U-701*.

Stella Dorado (550t, 1935), sunk by E-boat Dunkirk, 1 June 1940

Launched in 1935 she was bought by the Royal Navy four years later. She was lost to a German U-boat off Dunkirk on 1 June 1940, during Operation Dynamo.

Stella Orion (R, 417t, 1935), mined, Thames Estuary, 11 November 1940

Built at Selby and launched in 1935 she was requisitioned for use as a minesweeper in September 1939. Just over a year later she struck a mine and was sunk in the Thames Estuary.

Stella Sirius (550t, 1934), sunk by bombs during air raid on Gibraltar, 25 September 1940

Built at Southbank on Tees and launched in 1934, she became an anti-submarine trawler after she was requisitioned in September 1939. A year later, whilst in Gibraltar, she was sunk by French aircraft.

Strathborve (R, 216t, 1930), mined off Humber, 6 September 1941
Built in Aberdeen and launched in 1930, she was requisitioned ten
years later to join the 152nd Minesweeping Group based at Grimsby.
She is listed also as a mercantile loss, *Strathborne*, having been
mined in the Humber in early September 1941.

Stronsay (545t, 1942), sunk by Italian submarine, Western
Mediterranean, 5 February 1943
Built in Glasgow and launched in 1942 as a minesweeper and anti-
submarine vessel, she was sent to the Mediterranean and lost when
she was torpedoed by the Italian submarine *Avorio* on 5 February
1943.

Susarion (R, 260t, 1917), sunk by aircraft off Humber, 7 May
1941
Built in Beverley and launched in 1917, its first two years were as a
minesweeping trawler. She was requisitioned in June 1940 to become
an auxiliary patrol vessel based at Grimsby. She fell victim to
German aircraft off the Humber at the beginning of May 1941.

Sword Dance (530t, 1940), Collision, Moray Firth, E Scotland, 5
July 1942
Built at Leith and launched in September 1940, as an anti-submarine
trawler destined for coastal convoy duties. She was moored in Hull
harbour when she was hit in an air raid and two of her crew were lost.
However she was sunk when she was rammed by a merchantman in
thick fog. There was no loss of life.

Tervani (409t, 1930), probably sunk by U-boat off Cape
Bougaroni, Algeria, 7 February 1943
Built in Beverley and launched in 1930, originally as *Rylston*, she
was renamed *Tervani* in 1939 and requisitioned in October for
conversion to a auxiliary patrol vessel. She became a minesweeper in
1941. She was claimed by the Italian submarine *Acciaio* off Algiers
on 7 February 1943.

Texas (301t, 1919), sunk in collision, Jamaica Area, 19 July 1944
Built in Ontario and launched in 1919, in 1920 she was sold and

renamed *Colonel Roosevelt*. By 1940 she was an American pilot vessel and bought by the Royal Navy to be renamed *Texas*. She became an auxiliary patrol vessel and was lost in a collision off Jamaica in mid-July 1944.

Thomas Bartlett (R, 290t, 1918), sunk by British mine off Calais, 28 May 1940

Built in Beverley and launched in 1918, in 1920 she was sold to private owners and changed hands several times, being renamed *Hordern*. She was requisitioned in November 1939 and converted into a minesweeper named the *Thomas Bartlett*. She fell victim to a British mine off Calais at the end of May 1940.

Tilbury Ness (R, 279t, 1917), sunk by aircraft, Thames Estuary, 1 November 1940

Built at Beverley and launched in November 1917 as the *Joseph Barrett*, she was sold on and renamed *Loch Morar* in 1919. By 1933, having changed hands at least once more, she was then bought by a Bordeaux based company and renamed *St Barnaby*. In the following year she was sold on again and renamed *Harry Hawke*. In 1935 there was another sale and she was now called *Loch Kinnord*. In 1939 she was bought again and renamed *Tilbury Ness*. By September she had been requisitioned and converted into a minesweeping trawler. Just over a year later enemy aircraft sunk her in the Thames Estuary.

Topaz (251t, 1916), sunk by aircraft off Cromer, 12 January 1940

Built at Selby and launched in 1916, she spent until 1919 as a minesweeper. She was then sold on and renamed *Valdora* and converted into an auxiliary patrol vessel. She was sunk off Cromer by German aircraft in mid-January 1940.

Topaz (142t, 1895), sunk by enemy aircraft off Norway, 15 December 1941

Built in Hull and launched in 1895, she was an unlucky ship as she was sunk in the Humber after a collision with another trawler in 1908. She was salvaged and sold on in 1910. She was requisitioned for a short period of time in 1916. By 1931 she had Norwegian owners and she is technically a mercantile loss as she was sunk by enemy aircraft off Norway in mid-December 1941.

Topaze (608t, 1935), collision off Clyde, 20 April 1941

Built at Southbank on Tees and launched in 1935, it was bought by the Royal Navy in November 1935 for use in anti-submarine warfare. It was based at Portland and was involved in Operation Dynamo in 1940. She was lost when it collided with HMS *Rodney* in the Clyde on 20 April 1941.

Tourmaline (641t, 1935), sunk by aircraft, off N Foreland, Kent, 5 February 1941

Built at Southbank on Tees and launched in 1935, after just eight months as a peaceful fishing vessel she was bought by the Royal Navy and converted for anti-submarine duties. She was escorting a convoy in the English Channel in 1940 when she was attacked by a pair of E-boats; she sank one and damaged the other. Unfortunately enemy aircraft got her off the North Foreland on 5 February 1941, killing three of her crew.

Tranio (R, 275t, 1918) in tow and sunk by aircraft bombs, North Sea, 26 June 1941

Built at South Shields and launched in 1918, she was requisitioned twenty-one years later for minesweeping duties. She was under tow in the North Sea when she was attacked and sunk by enemy aircraft in late June 1941.

Tranquil (R, 294t, 1912), collision off Deal, 16 June 1942

Originally launched in 1912, she was requisitioned in April 1915 for conversion to a minesweeper. Two years later she was an escort and in 1919 she was returned to her owners. By 1940 when she was requisitioned in the April she was called the *Tranquil*, her original name having been *Good Luck*. Her former name meant nothing, unfortunately, as she was sunk in a collision off Deal in mid-June 1942.

Transvaal (R, 250t, 1916), foundered in gale, English Channel, 18 November 1944

Built at Selby and launched in 1916, she spent her first three years as a minesweeper. She was requisitioned again in December 1939 for work as an auxiliary patrol vessel. In 1942 she was converted for work as a fuel tanker in the Mediterranean. By 1943 she joined what was nicknamed Walt Disney's Navy, a motley group of different vessels supplying invasion forces throughout the Mediterranean. She left the Mediterranean in 1944 and on her way home she foundered in a gale in the English Channel and sank in the mid-November.

Valdora (R, 251t, 1916), believed sunk by German aircraft, Cromer area, 12 January 1940

See *Topaz* (251t 1916).

Van Orley (R, 352t, 1927), sunk by air attack, Liverpool, 4 May 1941

Built in Beverley and launched in 1927, as *Kingston Garnet*, she was bought by Belgian owners, but in 1940 made it to Fleetwood in May 1940. In June she was hired and converted into an auxiliary patrol vessel, operating out of Liverpool. She was sunk by German aircraft on 4 May 1941. She was raised in November then broken up.

Velia (R, 290T, 1914), sunk, presumed mined, Harwich, 19 October 1940

Originally launched in 1914, having been built at Selby, she was requisitioned for the next five years as a minesweeper, under the name of *Sitvel*. In 1919 she was renamed *Velia* and requisitioned twenty years later as an auxiliary patrol vessel. She was probably sunk by a mine in the Harwich area in mid-October 1940.

Vidonia (R, 276t, 1907), sunk in collision, English Channel, 6 October 1944

Built in Selby and launched in 1907, she was requisitioned in December 1914 and operated as a minesweeper until 1919. Twenty-one years later, in the June, she was requisitioned and became an auxiliary patrol vessel. In April 1943 she became a fuel tanker but she was lost after a collision in the English Channel.

Wallasea (545t, 1943), torpedoed off Mounts Bay, Cornwall, 6 January 1944

Built at Leith and launched in April 1943, she was guarding a small convoy making its way from the Bristol Channel to Plymouth when she was attacked by E-boats in Mounts Bay, Cornwall. She was torpedoed and sank on 6 January.

Warland (214t, 1912), sunk by aircraft bombs, North Sea, 18 February 1942

Built in Beverley and launched in 1912, she spent between 1916 and 1919 as a requisitioned minesweeper. The Royal Navy bought her in May 1940 for conversion to anti-submarine duties. She was sunk in the North Sea in mid-February 1942.

Warwick Deeping (350t, 1934), sunk by torpedo, English Channel, 12 October 1940

Built in Selby and launched in 1934, she was requisitioned in August 1939 for anti-submarine work. She was sunk by German destroyers in the English Channel, some 25 miles southwest of St Catherine's Point in mid-October 1940, probably by torpedoes.

Warwickshire (R, 466t, 1936), sunk by aircraft, Trondheim area, Norway, 30 April 1940

Built at Southbank on Tees and launched in 1936, she was requisitioned in August 1939 and joined the 22nd Anti-Submarine Group. She was sunk off Trondheim in Norway by German aircraft on 30 April 1940. But exactly two years later, after being salvaged, she was commissioned as the *Alane*. She was sunk and lost for the final time as a German vessel by the Russian submarine *S51* on 19 July 1943.

Washington (R, 209t, 1909), mined in North Sea, 6 December 1939

Built at Selby and launched in 1909, she was not requisitioned until 1914 but spent the next five years as a minesweeper. She did the same job having been requisitioned again in November 1939. However she was being sent to Great Yarmouth to be fitted out when she was sunk with all hands on 6 December. She had hit a mine that had only been laid the previous night by the German submarine U-59.

Waterfly (R, 387t, 1931), sunk by aircraft off Dungeness, 17 September 1942

Built in Beverley and launched in 1931, as *Walpole*, she was renamed after she was requisitioned in September 1939. She operated as a minesweeper out of Kirkwall, with duties in the Scapa Flow area. In 1941 she was transferred to the Dover patrol, joining the 46th Minesweeping Group. Enemy aircraft targeted her off Dungeness in mid-September 1942. A bomb hit the magazine and only one crewman survived the blast.

Waveflower (550t, 1929), sunk by mine off Aldeburgh, Suffolk, 21 October 1940

Built in Selby and launched in 1929, she was bought ten years later by the Royal Navy as a minesweeper, but a mine got her off Aldeburgh towards the end of October 1940.

Westella (550t, 1934), torpedoed or mined off Dunkirk, 2 June 1940

Built at Selby and launched in 1934, five years later she was bought by the Royal Navy for anti-submarine work. She was lost during Operation Dynamo and she may either have been torpedoed or mined.

William Hallett (R, 202t, 1919), mined, Tyne area, North Sea, 13 December 1939

Built at Wivenhoe and launched in 1919, she passed into private hands in 1921, keeping the same name. She was requisitioned in November 1939 and converted into a auxiliary patrol vessel, but she was lost to a mine off the Tyne in mid-December 1939.

William Stephen (R, 935t, 1917), sunk by E-boat off Cromer, E England, 25 October 1943

Built in Aberdeen and launched in September 1917, as the *Joseph Annison*, she was eventually acquired by new owners and renamed *William Stephen*. She was requisitioned in November 1939 and converted into a minesweeper. She was targeted and sunk by an E-boat off Cromer in late October 1943.

William Wesney (R, 364t, 1930), sunk by mine off Orfordness, 7 November 1940

Built in Beverley and launched in 1930, she was requisitioned in 1939 for minesweeping duties but fell to a mine off Orfordness at the beginning of November 1940.

Wyoming (R, 302t, 1915), mined and sunk off Harwich, 20 May 1944

Built at Selby and launched in 1915 as *Veresis*, she was requisitioned for the first five years. In 1920 after a change of ownership she was renamed *Wyoming*. The Navy requisitioned her in November 1939 as an auxiliary patrol vessel and she was based at Grimsby and engaged in fishery protection. In 1941 she became a minesweeper and survived the next three years, until she was mined off Harwich in late May 1944.

APPENDIX TWO

Report of Lt. Stannard to the Admiralty on the events at Namsos and VC Citation
(Copy to A.C.O.S.)

To: Naval Officer-in-Charge
ABERDEEN.
 H.M.S. Arab
ABERDEEN.
May 10th, 1940

A Report on the Namsen Fjord actions, the embarking and disembarking of Troops at Namsos, the manning of a shore defense position and experience gained against aircraft.

———

H.M.S. Arab arrived and anchored off Namsos town in company with the 15th A/S Striking Forces at 02.00 Sunday 28th April, 1940. At 02.45, 'Arab' was ordered alongside H.M.S. 'Carlisle' (C.S.20) to take off the remaining stores that the latter ship had brought from Scapa for the French.

At 04.00 - cast off owing to air-raid.
04.50 - Returned alongside and completed taking off stores.
06.00 - Proceeded and made fast to Namsos wharf astern of French ammunition ship S/S 'Saumur'.
   07.30 – As noone appeared to discharge these 40 tons of stores, I collected some British and French soldiers, who assisted my crew to

discharge. At 11.45 high bomber dropped 500lb. bomb which exploded 50 yards from us abreast of S.S. 'Saumur' on wharf, setting stores and ammunition on fire.

Cast off from wharf at low water. At 13,00 was ordered by 'Carlisle' to take S/S 'Saumur' in tow with H.M.S. 'Angle' – the former had a wire around propeller and was aground. Before I got there, 'Angle' had towed her off and did not need my help. Proceeded to run my bows into burning wharf, left engines going slow ahead and ran two hoses over forecastle head to try and put out Ammunition Dump Fire. I signalled 'Carlisle' that as 'Angle' could manage the towing I would try and put out fire as 'Arab' has good water pressure and no water was obtainable from the shore. 'Carlisle' answered 'Carry on'.

14.00. Heavy high bombing attack, 16 planes. 15.00. No hope of putting out fire. I proceeded down fjord, put 'Arab' alongside S/S 'Saumur' as 'Angle' had parted towing rope. Kept her in position while propeller was cleared. 17.00 – 'Brestois' (French destroyer) asked how long would 'Saumur' be clearing propeller. 17.15. Slipped 'Saumur' when propeller was cleared. 18.00. Another high bombing attack. Proceeded patrol in fjord. Reverberations from our A/S were coming back from the cliff side like shots from a gun.

Signalman Wiggins who was left on H.M.S. 'Bittern' charging our Aldis batteries, returned via H.M.S. 'Gaul'. Returned Seaman Towers and Stratton to H.M.S. 'St. Keenan'. (These two men had been left on shore earlier on). Received message from H.M.S. 'Carlisle' to put myself under French Destroyer 'Brestois' orders. Order by latter vessel to embark French 'Chasseurs Alpins' and put them on transport S/S 'Aminois'.

29th Monday 03.00 – Finished embarking troops 03.30 – Proceeded to find place under cliff at Hamnesshuken Mountain. (By this time my crew were exhausted through lack of sleep). H.M.S. 'Aston Villa' was on patrol at Ornskaget, H.M.S. 'Gaul' at Finsneset. 04.30 – Heard German planes, got under way. 05.00 – Attacked by high and dive bombers. 16 bombs were dropped, all near misses, mostly ahead and astern. Kept bombers on beam (this would be done as a rough idea could be obtained by watching the dive bombers diving from 10,000 ft. They usually flattened out at 3,000 ft., and wheel was put hard over just before. Consider it was through only giving them the beam of the ship to aim at that saved 'Arab'. This attack damaged fan casting in engineroom, and also damaged rudder and propellor.

07.00 - rejoined H.M.S. 'Angle' and 'Aston Villa' at Ormshaget. Attacked again. Ordered by Commander Congreve to relieve H.M.S. 'Gaul' next morning. 13.00 – Attacked again by divebombers. Proceeded up to Namsos. Sighted H.M.S. 'Aston Villa' alongside wharf behind Hoo island, closed her and found most of her castings in the engineroom had been fractured by near misses.

Commander Congreve was busy, with the help of some Norwegians, in disguising 'Aston Villa' with fir trees. Was ordered to proceed and find sheltered spot in the shadow of a cliff to give my men a rest as they had been on continuous watch for the last two days. Made fast alongside Kvarsodden cliff. 16.00 – received message by launch from Army G.H.Q. that submarine had been sighted proceeding up Namsen Fjord towards Namsos. 'Gaul' was bombed and a 15 ft. hole was blown in her bows, although her forward bulkhead was still holding. She had made fast in Kroken Bay. Cannot keep track of the number of air attacks made. They were coming over in flights of 6 to 9 every hour.

1700 – Bittern arrived. 20.00 – 'Bittern' cruising around Namsos Bay, joined her. Reported on board to her commander and placed myself under his orders. He suggested that 'Arab' should lie off Maevraneset Point which is the west point of Namsos Bay, keeping a steady bearing with A/S Transmission. This day we had repeated attacks by high bombers and dive bombers as no other ships except trawlers were in Namsen Fjord until 'Bittern' arrived at 20.00. Was told by 'Bittern' that in the morning when bombing commenced I should place 'Arab' about 400 yards to the west of Bittern to get the best angle of fire for Lewis guns and Oerlikon as the dive bombers flattened out over 'Bittern'.

30th, Tuesday 0700 – Heavy dive bombing raid, 16 planes mostly attacking 'Bittern'. We were in a very good position to give them all our guns after they had dropped their bombs at 'Bittern'. These close and assist her. Asked permission from 'Bittern' who told me to carry on. 0915 – Close 'Aston Villa' and embarked Commander Cogreve, who wanted to look at 'Gaul'. Proceeded down fjord. 1130 – Sighted 'St. Goran' alongside cliff at Hamneshuken Mountain. Bomb had exploded on bridge killing Captain, Coxswain and two ratings. Crew had taken to boats.

Proceeded alongside her lifeboat in which were her wounded, her Carley floats contained the rest of her crew. Picked up wounded while heavy bombing was going on. Sergeant of the Royal Marines (who was only on board to supervise the transferring of Medical supplies from storeship to shore) badly wounded, shrapnel in back and losing blood and two ratings with slight wounds. Attempted to do as much as possible to dress the seriously wounded man with the limited supply from our medical chest. Proceeded and lay alongside 200 ft. cliff at the south side of Kroken bay. 13.00 – Signalled destroyer 'Janus' as she entered that urgent medical aid was required. Surgeon and Sick Berth Attendant arrived. Sent back two slightly wounded men. Commander Congreve also joined Janus for passage back to 'Aston Villa'. Surgeon remained in 'Arab' with badly wounded Royal marine.

1500 – 'Carlisle' arrived, signalled for boat to transfer Surgeon and royal Marine. Sent message to Admiral C.S.20 stating 'Aston Villa' and 'Gaul' disabled. 'Arab''s castings broken and propellor damaged. Would send my men to assist in shoring up 'Gaul's' forward bulkhead. Received V/S message stating: 'Enemy ships and submarines expected, keep a good look out day and night, and prepare to engage enemy'.

1600 - Heavy bombing raids. Commenced to take Lewis guns up to top of cliff, land food, blankets etc. by boat to Kroken Bay, where a large cave was found. Decided to make this cave the lower base. Machine gunposts were built at cliff head, which commanded the entrance to Namsen Fjord and also Kroken bay, where 'Gaul' was lying. Further machine gun positions were made 100 yards further in and up, overlooking the cliff. This is where I had the crew. As I still had some French stores on deck which were never landed, I took the liberty of opening same, finding automatic rifles and ammunition, a 60 m/m bomb-throwing mortar with bombs and detonators complete.

When posts were finished, I had 6 Lewis guns, 2 Automatic Rifles and one bomb-thrower, the latter capable of throwing bombs 1500 yards. Also the 4 inch gun was loaded and put on a bearing covering the fjord entrance, the Oerlikon likewise. 2000 – Carlisle and 'Janus' left Namsen Fjord. Signalled former and reported, stating what a strong position I had ashore. Reply came back from Admiral C.S.20 – 'Well done. Carry on'. Set A/S Watch and W/T Watch on 1579 KCs as ordered by 'Carlisle'. Crew slept at machine gun posts, look-outs on duty.

Wednesday 1st May – 'Bittern' passed and asked if we were keeping A/S watch. Answered yes. 0500 'Angle' passed and gave verbal orders to destroy all A/S gear, dome and oscillator and land all on deck ready to be destroyed. Commander Congreve and his crew from 'Aston Villa' had changed over to 'Angle' to give the latter a rest (not much of a rest, as it turned out later.). 'Angle' proceeded to sink 'St. Goran' by gunfire [Forbes: According to Lieutenant Alan Reid R.N.V.R. this was done by the 'Cape Passaro'] and then carried on with patrol outside fjord. 05.30 – 'Aston Villa' made fast about 100 yards south of 'Arab'. (The former had now the 'Angle's' crew). Continuous bombing and machine gunning by High and Dive bombers who came over in flights of 6, 9 and 12 planes – 12.00 – Bombs dropping all around. 'Gaul' commenced to sink. The planes were now machine gunning our position and the valley. 13.30 – 'Gaul' sank. 16.00 Called conference with Captains of 'Gaul' and 'Aston Villa'.

Decided that the three crews would man 'Arab's' position ashore. 17.00 – 'Aston Villa' set on fire by direct hit from dive bomber. Luckily only a few of her crew were aboard. (H.M.S. 'Bittern' hit by bomb and set on fire after being attacked all day). Rescued the wounded and transferred them to top of cliffs by means of stretchers made out of fir trees. Sub-Lieut. Burt, R.N.V.R. and three ratings wounded. 20.00 – Jettisoned all A/S gear in 250 fathoms. 'Aston Villa' on fire still, considered her magazine might blow up and damage 'Arab'. Requested permission from Commander Congreve to board but answer was: 'Keep away, it is too dangerous'. Decided to take Sub-Lieut. Lees, R.N.V.R., J. Nicholson and myself and try to save 'Arab'. Cut lines and proceeded to move. Had moved 100 yards when 'Aston Villa' blew up. Proceeded alongside Kroken Bay. Destroyer 'Griffin had landed Surgeon to attend wounded. 23.00 – Commenced embarking wounded, stores, guns and the three crews on board 'Arab'. Was told to do same with all despatch.

Thursday 2nd May 02.00 – proceeded up Fjord, met fleet leaving, transported wounded, Aston Villa's and Gaul's crews, to H.M.S. 'Griffin' proceeded down fjord, ordered to proceed to England. Decided I would keep well north as I was on my own and my speed was about 5/6 knots. 05.00 – Clear of Namsen Fjord. 1000 – Speed 3 knots. Attacked by Heinkel 115 who signalled by V/S in plain language 'Go east or be sunk'. (Had sent out W/T message half an hour before reporting a friendly or captured cargo ship about 8 miles north was being escorted by sea plane, heading S.E.) Could not intercept her owing to lack of speed. A suitable answer was sent in reply. The pilot of this machine seemed a novice or else thought we had no ammunition left as he circled us closing towards us each time. He was keeping up a continuous fire with his two guns but I decided to hold my fire until he was closer. He banked at 800 yards just forward of the beam so opened fire with all Lewis guns and Oerlikon. Could see the H.E. Oerliken shells bursting on him. The Heinkel 115 came down about 2 miles astern of us but I did not attempt to save the crew. Proceeded well north, then south and west of Shetlands, arriving Scapa 17.00 May 6th, Monday. Reported to Chief of Staff, watered and stored – 19.30 – left Scapa.

Tuesday, May 7th 08.00 arrived Aberdeen.

Report on A/S.
It was very difficult for efficient A/S work to be carried out in Fjords. (1) The reverberations come back very strong from cliff side: (2)

Numerous false echoes owing to quick change in depth of water: (3) The best way to maintain a watch was by keeping the ship in a fixed position, the oscillator on a steady bearing, recorder running, and this gave steady lines of non-subs; as soon as anything else crossed, it could be easily seen amongst the false echoes. This was proved by the use of service launches.

Aircraft

The old idea of only attacking from the stern is completely misleading. They attack from any direction, preferably from the sun. The High Bombers did not even bother about that: they dropped the bombs at 10,000 ft. The Dive Bombers made all their attacks from the sun, generally coming over at 12/15000 ft., passing away as if they had not seen us, and then coming down in a dive of about 800 to a height of about 3000 ft. dropping their bombs just before flattening out. These are the most difficult attacks to fend off, giving a very small target, and after flattening out they are over and past like a flash. The best position in a Fjord to withstand an attack by air is the shadow of a steep cliff, preferably at right angles to the sun, keeping the ship moving. 80% of the attacks were made from ahead and 20% from the stern: they never attacked from the beam, which I assume is because there is only the width of the ship to aim at.

A mistaken idea is that zig-zagging is of no use with a speed below 13 knots. I consider that it was the saving of the 'Arab'. By carefully watching the dive bombers and putting the wheel hard over after they had commenced to dive, it is very hard for them to hit a small ship even at a height of 2000 ft. After the first plane has dropped her bombs (generally 2 only) which can be seen leaving the plane, bring the wheel hard over the other way. Bringing them on the beam also gives the chance of all guns to bear.

Another way is to make fast in the shadow of a cliff so that no water is showing between ship and shore. This is a good hide out for the ship, and attacks can be made on planes before they suspect you are there. I found that the best thing to do in Namsen Fjord was to lie under the shadow of the cliffs on the east side in the morning and the west side in the evening, remaining on the latter side till the daily reconnaissance plane had been over at about 03.00 and viewed everything: then we knew we had one hour before the bombers arrived, steamed across to the east side and remained under way there.

The planes never attacked over high cliffs, generally down a valley or over the water. I noticed that the dive bombers were very poor shots, they seemed to pull out of their dive far too quickly, as if the A/A fire was too hot for them and their bombs were sometimes falling 50 to 100 yards away. This was especially noticed during attacks on the Bittern. About 25% of the attacking planes seemed to be old hands at the game as after pulling out from their dive they banked and varied height a great deal while the other 75% kept flying straight. I noticed it was the 25% who had the nearest misses. The bullets from their machine guns (Heinkel 115) are S.A.P. steel nosed capped, copper elsewhere with a slug inside.

The Arab was moored alongside cliffs frequently without danger of hitting rocks. The large 2? diameter hazel feet fenders were used about 3 feet below water line, ropes fast fore and aft to trees. The ship lay like this perfectly, no surging or bumping taking place.

Damage.
Superficial deck work by machine gunning, mainmast rigging shot away, a few rivets leaking. The near misses that dropped astern about 6 feet have damaged either the propellor or stern posts, as speed was very much reduced after that.

Armament and Defence.
The Pill Box fitted to the Bridge is useless, impossible to see when the planes commenced to dive bomb. Also when shrapnel hits against the pill box, it acts as a sound box and deafens anyone in it. Ships that are fitted with a 12-pounder protection on the aft side of Gun platform with the opening ahead. Anyone sheltering in this would be wiped out by attacks anywhere for'd of the beam. This box would collect any ricochets.

The Steel Box fitted in the wheelhouse for protection of helmsman is very good. The helmsman has complete control over the wheel from this position.

Lewis Guns.

The 18' circular pillars are protection enough and fitted on top bridge as in Arab cover both sides at the same time, only one place where they are blanketed and that is an arc of 15 each quarter but one mounting always covers each side that double Lewis gun aft covers all except 10 ahead where funnel and mainmast are.

After the first attacks I had Lewis Gun pans loaded with 1 tracer to 2 ordinary. Hose pipe firing as sights could not be maintained on target. No stoppages occurred while firing 3,000 rounds.Guns were stripped and cleaned during darkness.

Oerlikon.

This gun is the most effective weapon against low flying. Hose pipe firing was used. Pans loaded 1 tracer, 1 H.E. These shells could been seen exploding on aircraft. Would like to see two more Oerlikons fitted. Would then keep one ready to fire while pans were changed.

1,100 rounds fitted and no stoppages. Spring tension released at dark and gun cleaned. Consider a 3' protection screen could be fitted around Oerlikon more for the protection of men reloading pans. This reloading was carried out under protected For'cals Head which is too far away.

Suggest that no more funk holes etc., except the Oerlikon protection, should be fitted in my ship as they interfere with the fighting efficiency. Consider that too much attention is being paid to shelters etc. which tend to induce the feeling in everyone that the only thing to do when attacked from the air is to get inside or behind something instead of fighting it out.

Two Officers always manned Oerlikon and Double Lewis Guns. The third officer was supervising reloading pans under protection and was therefore ready to take over in case of accident to C/O and other two officers.

Attacks made in 4 days – 31
- 24 by dive bombers (2000/3000 ft.)
- 7 'High' (8000/10,000 ft.)

Consider that the ideal craft for A/S work in Fjords would be the new cutters. They have the speed to reach all small fjords, small enough to get under shelter and hidden, do not through up a lot of smoke. Bases could be made in any secluded spot to refuel from. Disadvantages of 'Arab' class, no speed, too large, can be seen by planes before getting into HA range owing to the enormous amount of smoke from funnels. Advantages of Arab Class – can stand a lot of near miss bombs without serious damage. The Arab was often lifted 6 ft. by explosions. The first attacks were made by delayed action bombs which exploded about 5 seconds after hitting water and acted like a depth charge (believe these bombs were never meant to hit). These did all the damage in engine room. The other attacks were made with direct action bombs which did very little damage on exploding when hitting water.

Morale.

Most of my crew have been with me since the beginning of the war, therefore I was in a better position than other ships. It was the continuous stand to at 'Action Stations' during daylight hours and the embarking and disembarking troops and stores during darkness (which meant they had no rest whatsoever) that rather got the crew down. Except for three ratings I can say they stood it very well. Would like to see trawler crews sent to barracks for a few weeks to stiffen them up. Practically all crews have never seen what a parade ground is like.

Conditions while maintaining machine gun posts ashore.

This was very trying as only once could we have a fire. During the day it was quite warm but from 19.00 onwards, very cold. Men suffered from a kind of trench feet caused by wearing rubber sea boots in the snow which seemed to make the boots continually wet inside through condensation.

Clothing.

We were very well off as we had the original issue of clothes which were issued to us for the Petsamo affair. Lammy coats, woollen helmets and wind proof coats. After 'Aston Villa' and 'Gaul' had been sunk we were not so well off as I shared everything with these two crews. Special attention had to be given to the wounded. As no hot water bottles were available we built a small red ash fire and heated stones which acted very well. This fire was put out 4 times before we finally had the stones heated (machine gunning).

Medical Stores.

The medical stores fitted to the Arab were totally inadequate; they consisted of one imitation No. 5, holding 6 bottles, Cascara, Black Draught, sweating mixture, castor Oil, Liniment, Condy's fluid, in fact everything which was of no use. I had to dress 20 wounded (4) with one bottle of iodine (small) and 12 small bandages. (Used Officers' sheets for this purpose). Small pieces of shrapnel were removed with a small pair of long pliers and canvas sewing needle. I had one box containing 16 pieces of morphia which were dissolved under the tongue (this was on board by a lucky error). Whisky was used for cleaning purposes. Rum watered to 6 parts was very useful and seemed to put spirit into the crews. The 'Gaul' had one case of Ryvita biscuits which made a welcome change from bully beef and hard biscuits. Tinned milk and tinned soup drunk cold were good. The few Norwegians we met did what they could to help us. One small house supplied us with enough fresh milk for a cup all round.

Bombing and machine gunning ashore.

It is dangerous to take shelter under cliffs as bombs dropped near set massive boulders rolling down. The side of a sloped hillock on top of the cliffs was the best place, under trees and in large 15 to 25 ft. holes of which there were many, the east side in the morning and west side in the afternoon, planes always attacked from the sun. Only one man was hit during all the attacks while ashore. Attempted to keep men from walking in snow as tracks were easily visible.

Losses.

A certain amount of stores were destroyed by bombs, these were for use in emergency and were landed to assist in case of having to take to the lifeboats.

Two pairs of binoculars.
1 Sextant.
1 chronometer watch.

2 Norway pilots, part 1 & 2.

108 lbs of preserved meat.

48 tins of milk.

56 lbs of biscuits.

1 Lewis Gun.

300 rounds of ammunition.

1 bayonet.

1 Aldis Lamp.

2 torches.

48 lbs of tinned sausages.

Stores condemned and thrown overboard.

5 Mattresses and 6 blankets (unfit after being used for wounded).

4 Officers' sheets used for bandages.

Personal effects of a number of Arab's crew which were given to 'Aston Villa' and 'Gaul's' crews (list separate).

Gain.

2 Lewis Guns.

1 complete lifeboat, sails, etc.

1 Carley float.

4 Rifles.

1 Aldis lamp.

Number of blankets.

Saved from H.M.S. 'Gaul' and brought to Aberdeen.

I am, Sir, Your obedient Servant

R. B. Stannard

Lieut. in Command

H.M.S. 'Arab'

Lt. R. Stannard - VC Citation

RNPS VC – Lieut R. Stannard

From the London Gazette of 16 August 1940:

Admiralty, Whitehall, 16th August, 1940.

The KING has been graciously pleased to approve the grant of the Victoria Cross to Lieutenant Richard Been Stannard, R.N.R., H.M.S. Arab, for outstanding valour and signal devotion to duty at Namsos. When enemy bombing attacks had set on fire many tons of hand grenades on Namsos wharf, with no shore water supply available, Lieutenant Stannard ran Arab's bows against the wharf and held her there. Sending all but two of his crew aft, he then endeavoured for two hours to extinguish the fire with hoses from the forecastle. He persisted in this work till the attempt had to be given up as hopeless.

After helping other ships against air attacks, he placed his own damaged vessel under shelter of a cliff, landed his crew and those of two other trawlers, and established an armed camp. Here those off duty could rest while he attacked enemy aircraft which approached by day, and kept anti-submarine watch during the night.

When another trawler near-by was hit and set on fire by a bomb, he, with two others, boarded Arab and moved her 100 yards before the other vessel blew up. Finally, when leaving the fjord, he was attacked by a German bomber which ordered him to steer East or be sunk. He held on his course, reserved his fire till the enemy was within 800 yards, and then brought the aircraft down.

Throughout a period of five days Arab was subjected to 31 bombing attacks and the camp and Lewis gun positions ashore were repeatedly machine-gunned and bombed; yet the defensive position was so well planned that only one man was wounded.

Lieutenant Stannard ultimately brought his damaged ship back to an English port. His continuous gallantry in the presence of the enemy was magnificent, and his enterprise and resource not only caused losses to the Germans but saved his ship and many lives.'

Selected RNPS Second World War Awards for Minesweeping

Source: Royal Navy

1 Killed on duty	VC: Victoria Cross	B&MD: Bomb & Mine Disposal
2 Award not for Minesweeping	GC: George Cross	BD: Bomb Disposal
3 Reason for award unknown	CBE: Commander of the Order of the British Empire	BSO: Bomb Safety Officer
	DSO: Distinguished Service Order	
	OBE: Officer of the Order of the British Empire	HMD: His Majesty's Drifter
	MBE: Member of the Order of the British Empire DSC: Distinguished Service Cross	HMT: His Majesty's Trawler
	MC: Military Cross	M/S: Minesweeper
	CGM: Conspicuous Gallantry Medal	
	GM: George Medal	
	DSM: Distinguished Service Medal	
	BEM: British Empire Medal (now superseded by MBE)	
	MID: Mention in Despatches	
	Commend'n: King's Commendation for Brave Conduct	

NAME	RANK/RATE	UNIT	DATE GAZETTED	AWARD	NOTES
ALCOCK James Wakelin	Engineman	HMT *Clythness* (M/S)	29 Sep 42	DSM	Minesweeping – DSM awarded for bravery and skill while minesweeping (Dover Jun–Jul 1942)
ALDAN George William	A/Skipper Lt RNR	HMT *John Cattling* HMT *Gwenllian* HMT *Gwenllian*	7 Jun 40 11 Jun 42 6 Jun 44	DSC2 MID Bar to DSC	Minesweeping – DSC awarded for Dunkirk evacuation. MID awarded Birthday Honours 1942. Bar to DSC awarded for leadership, skill and devotion to duty in an important minesweeping operation (Humber area 28 Jan 44).
ALEXAN-DER Albert Edward	A/Lt Cdr RNVR	HMT *Proof* (M/S)	3 Jul 45	DSC	Minesweeping – DSC awarded for consistent zeal, courage and good seamanship whilst serving in HM 104th and 31st Minesweeper Flotilla and the 159th Trawler Group and in HMCS Blairmore in arduous operations along the coasts of Southern England and Northern France. (Opening port of Le Havre and Seine)
ALLAN George Robert Coull	LS	HMT *Their Merit* (M/S)	11 Apr 44	DSM	Minesweeping – DSM awarded for courage and skill in a successful mine clearance operation. (Swept QZX 120B)
ALLEN Albert Sydney	LS	HMT *Elbury* (M/S)	5 Oct 43	DSM	Minesweeping – DSM awarded for courage and skill in many successful minesweeping operations in Mediterranean waters Jan–May 1943.

Name	Rank/Rate	Ship	Date	Award	Citation
ASHLEY Patrick Hamilton	Leading Cook RNPS	HMT *William Bell* (M/S)	13 Apr 43	MID	Minesweeping – MID awarded for bravery and skill while employed on the hazardous duties of keeping the seas clear of mines 18 Jun 1943.
ASHTON George	Lt RNVR A/Lt Cdr RNVR	HMT *Courtier* HMS *Ambitious* (M/S Depot Ship)	1 Jan 41 23 Jan 45	DSC MID	Minesweeping – DSC awarded New Year honours 1941. MID awarded for courage and skill in minesweeping operations in the approaches to Le Havre.
AUSTIN George William	Signalman	BYMS 2252	28 Nov 44 3 Apr 45	MID DSM	Minesweeping –MID awarded for Op Neptune (Normandy landings Jun 1944) DSM awarded for great gallantry and endurance in clearing Scheldt estuary of mines Sep–Nov 1944.
BARKER William John	Seaman	HMT *Triton* (M/S)	5 Oct 43	MID	Minesweeping – MID awarded for courage and skill in many successful minesweeping operations in Mediterranean waters.
BARTHRAM Peter Andrew	Signalman	HMT *Prophet*	4 Sep 45	MID	Minesweeping – MID awarded for courage, resolution and skill in minesweeping operations clearing a channel from the Humber to Heligoland and thence along the North German Coast to Cuxhaven, Hamburg and Bremerhaven during May 1945.
BATEY Robert Alan	Leading Wireman	BYMS 2040	4 Sep 45	MID	As Above
BAXTER Gordon	Lt RNVR	HMT *Welsbach*	13 Apr 43	MID	Minesweeping – MID awarded for bravery and skill while employed on the hazardous duties of keeping the seas clear of mines. (Minesweeping ops 18 Jan 1943)

BEESLEY Ronald Fitzgerald Barton	A/Lt Cdr RNVR	BYMS 2189	14 Jun 45 4 Sep 45 13 Jun 46	MID MID OBE	Minesweeping – First MID awarded Birthday Honours 1945. Second MID awarded for courage, resolution and skill in minesweeping operations clearing a channel from the Humber to Heligoland and thence along the North German Coast to Cuxhaven, Hamburg and Bremerhaven during May 1945. Appointed OBE Birthday Honours 1946.
BELLMAN Cyril Ernest	Lt RNVR	HMT Prope	3 Jul 45	MID	Minesweeping – MID awarded for consistent zeal, courage and good seamanship whilst serving in HM 104th and 31st Minesweeper Flotilla and the 159th Trawler Group and in HMCS Blairmore in arduous operations along the coasts of Southern England and Northern France. (Opening port of Le Havre and Seine)
ENSON John Cecil	Lt Cdr RNVR Lt Cdr RNVR A/Cdr VD RNVR	HMT Darthema (M/S) HMS Bramble (Halcyon Class M/S) HMS Lyme Regis (Bangor Class M/S)	6 Dec 41 1 Jan 43 3 Apr 45	DSC MID Bar to DSC	Minesweeping – DSC awarded for minesweeping ops QZX 314. MID awarded New Year Honours 1943. Bar to DSC awarded for great gallantry and endurance in clearing the Scheldt estuary of mines Sep–Nov 1944.
BEST Peter Frank Matthew	Signalman	HMT Filey Bay (M/S)	7 Dec 43	MID	Minesweeping – MID awarded for steadfast courage and skill in a dangerous and important minesweeping operation. (Op Antidote – Galita, Algeria to Sousse, Tunisia)

Name	Rank	Ship	Date	Award	Citation
BETT Joseph	Chief Engineman	HMT *Alafoss* (M/S)	6 Jun 44	DSM	Minesweeping – DSM awarded for leadership, skill and devotion to duty in an important minesweeping operation. (Humber 28 Jan 1944)
BETTISON Ronald Henry	Chief Engineman	BYMS *2189*	4 Sep 45	MID	Minesweeping – MID awarded for courage, resolution and skill in minesweeping operations clearing a channel from the Humber to Heligoland and thence along the North German Coast to Cuxhaven, Hamburg and Bremerhaven during May 1945.
BLACK-BURN Albert Edward	T/Lt RNR	HMT King *Emperor* (M/S)	1 Jul 41	DSC	Minesweeping – DSC awarded for outstanding zeal, patience and cheerfulness, and for never failing to set an example of wholehearted devotion to duty, without which the high tradition of the Royal Navy could not have been upheld.
BOOTH John Albert	A/Lt Cdr RNR	BYMS *2155*	13 Feb 45	DSC	Minesweeping – DSC awarded for courage and skill in minesweeping operations during the landing of Allied Forces in Normandy Jun–Sep 1944.
BOYD Robert James	Seaman	HMT *Sarpedon* (M/S)	31 Dec 40 8 Jun 44	MID MID	Minesweeping – First MID awarded for good services in HM Minesweeping Trawlers and Drifters. Second MID awarded Birthday Honours 1944.

Name	Rank	Ship	Award	Date	Citation
BRADLEY Herbert Emmanuel	AB	HMT *Dhoon* (M/S) (Renamed HMT *Dhoon Glen* in 1943)	MID	1 Jul 41	Minesweeping – Awarded for outstanding zeal, patience and cheerfulness, and for never failing to set an example of wholehearted devotion to duty, without which the high tradition of the Royal Navy could not have been upheld.
BRAMM-ALL Harry Whittaker	Lt Cdr RNR	HMT *Kurd* (M/S) HMS *St Angelo* (Malta)	DSC DSO	11 Jul 40 29 Sep 42	Minesweeping – DSC awarded Birthday Honours 1940. DSO awarded for bravery and sustained devotion to duty in keeping the Approaches to the Harbours of Malta clear of mines May–Jun 1942.
BRANNAN Hugh	Stoker	HMT *Elbury* (M/S)	MID	5 Oct 43	Minesweeping – MID awarded for courage and skill in many successful minesweeping operations in Mediterranean waters Jan–May 1942.
BREAREY Reginald	Wireman	HMT *War Duke* (M/S)	MID	1 Jan 43	Minesweeping – MID awarded for bravery in face of the enemy or in dangerous waters, or for zeal and devotion to duty.
BROWN Frederick Charles	AB	HMT *Beryl* (M/S)	MID	29 Sep 42	Minesweeping – MID awarded for bravery and sustained devotion to duty in keeping the Approaches to the Harbours of Malta clear of mines May–Jun 1942.
BROWN Norman Owen	Ty Skipper RNR	HMT *Reboundo* (M/S)	MID	6 Jun 41	Minesweeping – MID awarded for courage and endurance while minesweeping.
BROWNING Henry John	Signalman	BYMS 2189	MID	3 Apr 45	Minesweeping – MID awarded for great gallantry and endurance in clearing the estuary of the Scheldt of mines during the period of October to November 1944.

Name	Rank	Ship	Date	Award	Citation
BULLOCK Joseph William	T/Lt RNVR	HMT *Jude* (M/S)	20 Feb 45	MID	Minesweeping – MID awarded for minesweeping and enemy human torpedo attacks.
BURGOYNE Hector Douglas	Seaman	HMT *Elbury* (M/S)	5 Oct 43	DSM	Minesweeping – DSM awarded for courage and skill in many successful minesweeping operations in Mediterranean waters.
BURR-OUGHS James Henry Lindin	Sub Lt RNVR	HMT *Stella Orion* (M/S)	31 Dec 40	MID	Minesweeping – MID awarded for good services in HM Minesweeping Trawlers and Drifters.
BURTON Noel	Second Hand RNR	HMT *Oku* (M/S)	8 Feb 44	DSM	Minesweeping – DSM awarded for bravery and skill in minesweeping in Nore Command.
BUTLER Albert Thomas	Signalman	HMT *Valesca* (M/S)	3 Apr 45	MID	Minesweeping – MID awarded for great gallantry and endurance in clearing the estuary of the Scheldt of mines during the period of October to November 1944.
CAMERON John Ewan	T/A/Lt Cdr RNVR	BYMS 2068	14 Jun 45	DSC	Minesweeping – DSC awarded Birthday Honours 1945.
CAMPBELL Donald	PO RNR PO RNR	BYMS 2048 BYMS 2048	3 Apr 45 4 Sep 45	MID MID	Minesweeping – First MID awarded for great gallantry and endurance in clearing the estuary of the Scheldt of mines during the period of October to November 1944. Second MID awarded for courage, resolution and skill in minesweeping operations clearing a channel from the Humber to Heligoland and thence along the North German Coast to Cuxhaven, Hamburg and Bremerhaven during May 1945.

207

CAMPBELL Herbert Arthur	A/Chief Engineman RNR	HMT *Wellsbach* (M/S)	13 Apr 43	DSM	Minesweeping – DSM awarded for bravery and skill while employed on the hazardous duties of keeping the seas clear of mines 18 January 1943.
CARR Arthur John	Lt RNVR	HMT *Valesca* (M/S)	3 Apr 45	DSC	Minesweeping – DSC awarded for great gallantry and endurance in clearing the estuary of the Scheldt of mines during the period of October to November 1944.
CHILVERS Charles William	Skipper RNR	HMT *St Kilda* (M/S)	12 Jun 45	DSC	Minesweeping – DSC awarded for skill, perseverance and great devotion to duty in arduous minesweeping operations along the West Coast of Italy.
CHILVERS Percy James	Leading Wireman	BYMS 2173	16 Jan 45	DSM	Minesweeping – DSM awarded for gallantry and skill in minesweeping operations off the coast of France. Cherbourg Approaches.
CHRIST-IANS Gerard	Chief Engineman	BYMS 2188 BYMS 2188	16 Jan 45 3 Apr 45	MID DSM	Minesweeping – MID awarded for gallantry and skill in minesweeping operations off the coast of France. Cherbourg approaches. DSM awarded for great gallantry and endurance in clearing the estuary of the Scheldt of mines during the period of October to November 1944.
CLARK John Richard	A/Skipper Lt RNR	BYMS 2028	12 Jun 45	MID	Minesweeping – MID awarded for gallantry, outstanding skill and devotion to duty in minesweeping operations over dense and shallow minefields in the opening up of Greek ports of Patras and Itea in the Gulf of Corinth.

CLARK Reginald	Signalman	HMT *Bracondene* (M/S)	6 Jun 44	DSM	Minesweeping – DSM awarded for leadership, skill and devotion to duty in an important minesweeping operation. Humber 28 January 1944.
CLARKE Robert Gerald Stephen	Lt RNVR	HMT *Dhoon* (M/S)	13 Apr 43	DSC	Minesweeping – DSC awarded for bravery and skill while employed on the hazardous duties of keeping the seas clear of mines. North Sea August 1942.
COLLIER John Henry Campbell	T/Lt RNVR	HMT *Gunner* MMS *79* MMS *79*	9 Aug 40 29 Sep 42 11 Dec 42	MID MID DSC	Minesweeping – First MID awarded for rescue of enemy airmen. Second MID awarded for bravery and skill while minesweeping. DSC awarded for wind-up ops Europe 1945.
COLQUH-OUN Robert	Signalman	BYMS *2173*	16 Jan 45	MID	Minesweeping – MID awarded for gallantry and skill in minesweeping operations off the coast of France. Cherbourg approaches and harbour.
COOK Richard Johnston	PO Wireman	BYMS *2076*	3 Apr 45	DSM	Minesweeping – DSM awarded for great gallantry and endurance in clearing the estuary of the Scheldt of mines during the period of October to November 1944.
COOMBS Douglas Arthur	Leading Wireman	BYMS *2157*	16 Jan 45	MID	Minesweeping – MID awarded for gallantry and skill in minesweeping operations off the coast of France. Cherbourg approaches and harbour.

COPPOCK Arthur James	T/Lt RNVR	HMT *Harris* (M/S) HMT *Harris* (M/S)	3 Apr 45 1 Jun 46	MID MID	Minesweeping – First MID awarded for great gallantry and endurance in clearing the estuary of the Scheldt of mines during the period of October to November 1944. Second MID awarded New Year honours 1946.
CORAM John Henry	PO	BYMS 2071	16 Jan 45	DSM	Minesweeping – DSM awarded for gallantry and skill in minesweeping operations off the coast of France. Cherbourg harbour.
COSSAR John Alexander	T/Lt RNR	BYMS 2023	15 May 45	MID	Minesweeping – MID awarded for gallantry, perseverance and devotion to duty in minesweeping operations under enemy fire in the Adriatic August to October 1944.
COURSE Ernest James	Leading Wireman	BYMS 2020	12 Jun 45	MID	Minesweeping – MID awarded for gallantry, outstanding skill and devotion to duty in minesweeping operations over dense and shallow minefields in the opening up of Greek ports in the Gulf of Corinth.
COX Edward David James	Lt RNR	HMT *Cava* (M/S)	9 Jun 42	MID	Minesweeping – MID awarded for bravery, determination and fortitude in important minesweeping operations. Orkneys and Shetland October 1941.
CREIGH-TON Arthur Henry	Second Hand	BYMS 2213	30 May 44	MID	Minesweeping – MID awarded for enterprise and devotion to duty in minesweeping.

Name	Rank	Ship	Date	Award	Citation
CRELLIN Alfred Clucas	Signalman RNPS	HMT *Cape Nyemetski* (M/S)	5 Jun 42	MID	Minesweeping – MID awarded for bravery, determination and fortitude in important minesweeping operations. Orkneys and Shetland 1941.
CRESSEY Herbert	CPO	HMT *Achroite* (M/S)	5 Oct 43	MID	Minesweeping – MID awarded for courage and skill in many successful minesweeping operations in Mediterranean waters. December 1942 to January 1943.
CURRIE Peter Paterson	PO Wireman	BYMS 2204	20 Nov 45	DSM	Minesweeping – DSM awarded for courage, efficiency and devotion to duty in the establishment of navigational aids in the approaches to the Rangoon river, in minesweeping and in the survey of the river prior to the assault on the city, May 1945. Irrawaddy.
DANDO Frederick Leslie	Leading Wireman	BYMS 2039	4 Sep 45	DSM	Minesweeping – DSM awarded for courage, resolution and skill in minesweeping operations clearing a channel from the Humber to Heligoland and thence along the North German Coast to Cuxhaven, Hamburg and Bremerhaven during May 1945.
DAVIES Peter Errington	Lt RNVR	BYMS 2053	15 May 45	DSC	Minesweeping – DSC awarded for gallantry, perseverance and devotion to duty in minesweeping operations under enemy fire in the Adriatic August to October 1944.

| DAVIES Stanley Ewart | A/Lt Cdr RNR (later Cdr RNR) | HMT *War Duke* (M/S) BYMS 2211 as SO 159th MSF BYMS 2211 as SO 159th MSF BYMS 2211 as SO 159th MSF BYMS 2211 as SO 159th MSF | 1 Jan 42 9 May 44 6 Jun 44 21 Nov 44 3 Apr 45 | DSC Bar to DSC MID Bar to DSC MID | Minesweeping – DSC awarded for meritorious work in minesweeping in the North Sea. New Year honours 1942. First Bar to DSC awarded for enterprise and skill minesweeping around Orkney and Shetland July 1943 (Op SN 123). First MID awarded for leadership, skill and devotion to duty in an important minesweeping operation (Humber 28 January 1944). Second Bar to DSC awarded for gallantry, skill, determination and undaunted devotion to duty during the landing of Allied Forces on the coast of Normandy Second MID awarded for great gallantry and endurance in clearing the estuary of the Scheldt of mines during the period of October to November 1944. |
| DELMAR-MORGAN Curtis | T/A/Lt Cdr RNVR | BYMS 2076 BYMS 2076 BYMS 2076 | 11 Apr 44 3 Apr 45 4 Sep 45 | DSC MID MID | Minesweeping – DSC awarded for courage and skill in a successful mine clearance operation. First MID awarded for great gallantry and endurance in clearing the estuary of the Scheldt of mines during the period of October to November 1944. Second MID awarded for courage and determination while serving in HM Minesweepers in clearing a passage into Rotterdam, Yjmuiden and Den Helder thereby making possible the swift relief of Holland (Op Fireball). |

Name	Rank	Ship	Date	Award	Citation
DEMPSEY Frank	A/Cook	HMT *Joseph Button* (M/S)	4 Oct 40	MID	Minesweeping – MID awarded for zeal and devotion to duty in minesweeping operations.
EACOTT Francis James	PO Wireman	HMT *St Tudno* (M/S)	3 Apr 45	DSM	Minesweeping – DSM awarded for great gallantry and endurance in clearing the estuary of the Scheldt of mines during the period of October to November 1944.
EALEY Edward Charles	Lt RNVR	HMT *Adam* (M/S)	14 Sep 43	MID	Minesweeping – MID awarded for skill and daring in successful minesweeping operations. Dover Strait Apr – Jun 1943.
EDWARDS Eric John Campbell	T/Lt RNVR T/Lt RNVR T/A/Cdr RNVR T/A/Cdr RNVR	HM *Trawler* HM *Trawler* Cdr M/S BYMS 2204	4 Oct 40 1 Jan 41 10 Jul 45 16 Nov 45	DSC2 Bar to DSC2 MID 2nd Bar to DSC	Minesweeping – DSC awarded for beating off air attacks. First bar to DSC awarded New Year Honours 1941. MID awarded for operation off Arakan Coast Nov 44 – Mar 45. Second bar to DSC awarded for courage, efficiency and devotion to duty in the establishment of navigational aids in the approaches to the Rangoon river, in minesweeping and in the survey of the river prior to the assault on the city, May 1945.
ELLIS Thomas	Signalman	BYMS 2041	3 Apr 45	MID	Minesweeping – MID awarded for great gallantry and endurance in clearing the estuary of the Scheldt of mines during the period of October to November 1944.
FERGUSON Ian Cochrane	T/Lt RNVR	HMT *Property* (ex-*Portrush*) (M/S)	6 Jun 44	DSC	Minesweeping – DSC awarded for leadership, skill and devotion to duty in an important minesweeping operation. Humber Approaches 28 Jun 44.

Name	Rank/Role	Ship	Date	Award	Citation
FIDDLER Albert	Seaman (HSD)	HMT *Valesca* (M/S)	3 Apr 45	MID	Minesweeping – MID awarded for great gallantry and endurance in clearing the estuary of the Scheldt of mines during the period of October to November 1944.
FIRMAN Terence	Wireman	HMT *Prowess* (M/S)	3 Jul 45	MID	Minesweeping – MID awarded for consistent zeal, courage and good seamanship in arduous operations along the coasts of Southern England and Northern France.
FISH James Henry	T/Lt(E)	BYMS 2279	11 Dec 45	DSC	Minesweeping – Wind-up ops Europe 1945.
FISHER Ambrose Ernest	T/Skipper RNR T/Skipper RNR T/Skipper RNR	HMT *Corena* HMT *Marand* BYMS 2078	1 Jan 41 11 Jun 42 16 Jan 45	MID MID MID	Minesweeping – First MID awarded New Year Honours 1941. Second MID awarded King's Birthday Honours 1942. Third MID awarded for gallantry and skill in minesweeping operations off the coast of France. Cherbourg Approaches.
FISHER Ernest Leonard	Chief Enginemen	BYMS 2149	14 Jun 45	MID	Minesweeping – MID awarded King's Birthday Honours 1945.
FOGGITT John Farbridge	A/Lt Cdr RNVR	BYMS 2034	11 Apr 44	MID	Minesweeping – MID awarded for courage and skill in a successful mine clearance operation.
FORD Douglas	T/Lt RNVR	HMT *Bay*	15 Aug 44	MID	Minesweeping – MID awarded for courage and undaunted devotion to duty. Mine Disposal at sea 21 Apr 44.
FORSTER George Anthony	Chief Engineman	BYMS 2189	3 Apr 45	MID	Minesweeping – MID awarded for great gallantry and endurance in clearing the estuary of the Scheldt of mines during the period of October to November 1944.

Name	Rank/Rate	Ship	Date	Award	Citation
FOUNTAIN James	T/Skipper RNR T/Skipper RNR T/Skipper RNR	HMT *Resparko* HMT *Ben Meidie*	1 Jan 41 27 Jan 42	DSC Bar to DSC	Minesweeping – DSC awarded New Year Honours 1941. Bar to DSC awarded for minesweeping in bad weather.
FOUNTAIN Robert	LS	BYMS 2071	16 Jan 45	MID	Minesweeping – MID awarded for gallantry and skill in minesweeping operations off the coast of France. Cherbourg and Approaches.
FOX Alfred	Second Hand	BYMS 2189	3 Apr 45	DSM	Minesweeping – DSM awarded for great gallantry and endurance in clearing the estuary of the Scheldt of mines during the period of October to November 1944.
FULLER William Richard	T/Lt RNVR	HMT *Goth* (M/S)	7 Dec 43	DSC	Minesweeping – DSC awarded for steadfast courage and skill in a dangerous and important minesweeping operation. Op ANTIDOTE Galita, Algeria to Sousse, Tunisia May 1943.
GALLOWAY George Edward	Chief Engineman Chief Engineman	BYMS 2211 BYMS 2211	16 Jan 45 3 Apr 45	DSM MID	Minesweeping – DSM awarded for gallantry and skill in minesweeping operations off the coast of France. Cherbourg. MID awarded for great gallantry and endurance in clearing the estuary of the Scheldt of mines during the period of October to November 1944.
GANT James	Chief Engineman	HMT *Harris* (M/S)	3 Apr 45	MID	Minesweeping – MID awarded for great gallantry and endurance in clearing the estuary of the Scheldt of mines during the period of October to November 1944.
GANT Laurence	Seaman	HMT *Calvay*	3 Apr 45	MID	As Above

Name	Rank/Rate	Ship	Date	Award	Citation
GEMMELL David McLure Sturgeon	Chief Engineman	BYMS 2282	4 Sep 45	DSM	Minesweeping – DSM awarded for courage, resolution and skill in minesweeping operations clearing a channel from the Humber to Heligoland and thence along the North German Coast to Cuxhaven, Hamburg and Bremerhaven during May 1945.
GIBSON-FLEMING Robert	T/Lt RNVR	BYMS 2252	3 Apr 45	DSC	Minesweeping – DSC awarded for great gallantry and endurance in clearing the estuary of the Scheldt of mines during the period of October to November 1944.
GOOD-BRAND John Wilson	Chief Engineman	BYMS 2175	15 May 45	MID	Minesweeping – MID awarded for gallantry, perseverance and devotion to duty in minesweeping operations under enemy fire in the Adriatic Aug–Dec 1944.
GOODLEY Kenneth Ivor	Telegraphist RNVR	HMT *John Cattling* (M/S)	3 Jan 41	MID	Minesweeping – MID awarded for good services in HM Minesweeping Trawlers and Drifters.
GOSLING Ernest Patrick	Wireman Leading Wireman	HMT *Lord Grey* (M/S) HMS *Liberty* (Algerine Class M/S)	1 Jan 41 13 Nov 45	MID DSM	Minesweeping – MID awarded New Year Honours 1941. DSM awarded for devotion to duty and outstanding endurance during mine clearance operations which entailed the working of very long hours in the Elbe and Weser rivers over the period March–June 1945.
GOWEN William James	Engineman	BYMS 2078	16 Jan 45	MID	Minesweeping – MID awarded for gallantry and skill in minesweeping operations off the coast of France (Cherbourg Approaches).

Name	Rank/Rating	Ship	Date	Award	Citation
GRANLUND Henry Paddison	T/Sub Lt RNVR Lt RNVR	HM *Trawler Brock* (M/S) MTB *218*	3 Jan 41 20 Jan 42	DSC MID	Minesweeping – DSC awarded for good services in HM Minesweeping Trawlers and Drifters. MID awarded for action in Dover Strait 3 Dec 41.
GRANT William James	Engineman	BYMS *2213*	4 Sep 45	DSM	Minesweeping – DSM awarded for courage and determination while serving in HM Minesweepers in clearing a passage into Rotterdam, Yjmuiden and Den Helder thereby making possible the swift relief of Holland (Operation Fireball).
GREAVES Reginald William Francis	Signalman	HMT *Elbury* (M/S)	5 Oct 43	DSM	Minesweeping – DSM awarded for courage and skill in many successful minesweeping operations in Mediterranean waters Jan–May 1943.
GREEN Albert	T/Lt RNVR	BYMS *2044*	4 Sep 45	MID	Minesweeping – MID awarded for courage, resolution and skill in minesweeping operations clearing a channel from the Humber to Heligoland and thence along the North German Coast to Cuxhaven, Hamburg and Bremerhaven during May 1945.
GREEN Percy Joseph	Second Hand	HMT *Sarpedon* (M/S)	3 Jan 41	DSM	Minesweeping – DSM awarded for good services in HM Minesweeping Trawlers and Drifters.
GREENHILL Francis William	Stoker PO	HMT *Brock* (M/S)	3 Jan 41	DSM	Minesweeping – DSM awarded for good services in HM Minesweeping Trawlers and Drifters.
GREGSON George	LS	HMT *Varanga* (M/S)	6 Jun 44	DSM	Minesweeping – DSM awarded for leadership, skill and devotion to duty in an important minesweeping operation (Humber area 28 Jan 1944).

Name	Rank	Ship	Date	Award	Citation
GREGSON Joseph	Chief Engineman	BYMS 2070	16 Jan 45	MID	Minesweeping – MID awarded for gallantry and skill in minesweeping operations off the coast of France (Cherbourg and approaches).
GRISEDALE James	Seaman	BYMS 2174	15 May 45	MID	Minesweeping – MID awarded for gallantry, perseverance and devotion to duty in minesweeping operations under enemy fire in the Adriatic Aug–Oct 1944.
HALL William Nowell	T/A/Lt Cdr RNVR T/A/Lt Cdr RNVR	HMT *British Withernsea* (M/S) HMT *British Withernsea* (M/S)	1 Jan 44 8 Feb 44	MID DSC	Minesweeping – MID awarded King's Birthday Honours 1944. DSC awarded for bravery and skill (Nore Command).
HAMILTON James Simpson	Chief Engineman	BYMS 2055	16 Jan 45	MID	Minesweeping – MID awarded for gallantry and skill in minesweeping operations off the coast of France (Cherbourg and approaches).
HARDY Leonard Sidney	T/Lt RNVR	BYMS 2213	30 May 44	MID	Minesweeping – MID awarded for enterprise and devotion to duty in minesweeping.
HARRIS George Ellis	Engineman Chief Engineman	HMT *Cornea* (M/S) MMS 175	11 Jul 40 3 Apr 45	DSM Bar to DSM	Minesweeping – DSM awarded King's Birthday Honours 1940. Bar to DSM awarded for great gallantry and endurance in clearing the estuary of the Scheldt of mines Oct–Nov 1944.
HARWOOD William Thompson	Chief Skipper RNR	HMT *Sawfly* (M/S)	6 Jun 41	DSC	Minesweeping – DSC awarded for courage and endurance while minesweeping.

Name	Rank	Ship/Unit	Date	Award	Citation
HILLDRITH Ernest	T/Skipper RNR	HMT Glen Kidstone (M/S)	1 Jul 41	MID	Minesweeping – Awarded for outstanding zeal, patience and cheerfulness, and for never failing to set an example of wholehearted devotion to duty, without which the high tradition of the Royal Navy could not have been upheld.
HODGKINSON Donald	Wireman	HMT Rotherslade	6 Jun 44	MID	Minesweeping – MID awarded for leadership, skill and devotion to duty in an important minesweeping operation. Humber 28 Jan 44.
HODGSON Robert Foylon	Lt RNR	BYMS 2020	15 May 45	DSC	Minesweeping – DSC awarded for gallantry, perseverance and devotion to duty in minesweeping operations under enemy fire in the Adriatic Aug–Oct 44.
HOGHTON Richard de Vere	Lt RNVR	HMT Loch Eribol (M/S)	13 Apr 43	DSC	Minesweeping – DSC awarded for bravery and skill while employed on the hazardous duties of keeping the seas clear of mines. North Sea 18 Jan 1943.
HONOLD George William Edward	T/Skipper RNR T/A/Skipper Lt	HMT Sycamore (Tree Class M/S) MMS 141 – 131 Auxilliary Minesweeping Sqn	9 May 44 1 Jan 45	MID MID	Minesweeping – MID awarded for enterprise and skill minesweeping. Op SMI 23. Second MID awarded New Year Honours 1945.
HOPE Reginald Alexander	PO Wireman	BYMS 2211	16 Jan 45	MID	Minesweeping – MID awarded for gallantry and skill in minesweeping operations off the coast of France. Cherbourg and approaches.
HUGHES David Reid	Second Hand	BYMS 2070	16 Jan 45	DSM	Minesweeping – DSM awarded for gallantry and skill in minesweeping operations off the coast of France. Cherbourg and approaches.

HUNT Reginald Thomas	Seaman	HMT *Valesca* (M/S)	3 Apr 45	MID	Minesweeping – MID awarded for great gallantry and endurance in clearing the estuary of the Scheldt of mines during the period of September to November 1944.
HUTCHINSON Lewis	T/Lt RNR	BYMS *2011*	23 Jan 45	MID	Minesweeping – MID awarded for courage and skill in hazardous minesweeping operations off the Adriatic coast of Italy.
IVES Harry Edman	CPO	HMT *Inersay* (M/S)	19 Mar 46	MID	Minesweeping – MID awarded for great skill, efficiency and endurance during minesweeping operations off the Japanese-held Islands of Car Nicobar in July 1945. Op Collie.
JACKSON Fred	Lt RNV(W)R Lt Cdr RNV(W)R	HMT *Colonsay* (Grimsby M/S Base) S RNV(W)R	4 Sep 45 2 Jan 50	MID MBE	Minesweeping – MID awarded for courage, resolution and skill in minesweeping operations clearing a channel from the Humber to Heligoland and thence along the North German Coast to Cuxhaven, Hamburg and Bremerhaven during May 1945. MBE awarded New Year Honours 1950.
JAMES Sidney	Leading Wireman	BYMS *2209*	24 Apr 45	DSM	Minesweeping – DSM awarded for outstanding skill, determination and despatch in carrying out minesweeping operations, frequently under fire, off the East Coast of Italy. Ancona Jul–Aug 1944.

Name	Rank/Rating	Ship	Date	Award	Citation
JENKINSON James William	PO	BYMS 2209	24 Apr 45	DSM	Minesweeping – DSM awarded for outstanding skill, determination and despatch in carrying out minesweeping operations, frequently under fire, off the East Coast of Italy. Ancona Jul–Aug 44.
JOHNSON Ernest	PO	HMT *Ensay* (M/S)	18 Sep 45	MID	Minesweeping – MID awarded for bravery, determination and great devotion to duty in minesweeping operations in the Adriatic over a period from April to May 1945.
KAY Phillip	Skipper RNR	HMT *Stella Orion* (M/S)	3 Jan 41	DSC	Minesweeping – DSC for good services in HM Minesweeping Trawlers and Drifters.
KEEPING James Harold Henry or Harold James Henry	Leading Wireman	HMT *Clythness* (M/S) MMS *1051*	29 Sep 42 4 Sep 45	MID MID	Minesweeping – First MID awarded for bravery and skill while minesweeping in HM Ships Clythness, Kingscourt, Lynx, Onetos, Ronso, and HM Motor Minesweepers. Dover Jun–Jul 42. Second MID awarded for courage, resolution and skill in minesweeping operations clearing a channel from the Humber to Heligoland and thence along the North German Coast to Cuxhaven, Hamburg and Bremerhaven during May 1945.
KIRKHAM John	A/Chief Engineman	BYMS *2041*	3 Apr 45	DSM	Minesweeping – DSM awarded for great gallantry and endurance in clearing the estuary of the Scheldt of mines during the period of September to November 1944.

LANE Harold Arthur	Wireman	BYMS 2211	6 Jun 44	DSM	Minesweeping – DSM awarded for leadership, skill and devotion to duty in an important minesweeping operation. Humber area 28 Jan 44.
le MASURIER Robert Hugh	T/Lt RNVR	HMT *Welbeck* (M/S)	13 Apr 43	DSC	Minesweeping – DSC awarded for bravery and skill while employed on the hazardous duties of keeping the seas clear of mines. North Sea Aug 42.
LEAVOLD Frederick Samuel	Seaman Cook	HMT *Brock* (M/S)	3 Jan 41	MID	Minesweeping – MID awarded for good services in HM Minesweeping Trawlers and Drifters.
LEEDS Herbert William	T/Lt RNVR T/Lt RNVR	BYMS 2174 BYMS 2174	15 May 45 14 Jun 45	MID MID	Minesweeping – First MID awarded for gallantry, perseverance and devotion to duty in minesweeping operations under enemy fire in the Adriatic. Second MID awarded King's Birthday Honours 1945.
LEWIS George Ernest	LS RNPS	HMT *British* (M/S)	8 Feb 44	DSM	Minesweeping – DSM awarded for bravery and skill in minesweeping. Nore Command.
LEWIS Thomas John	T/Sub Lt RNVR	BYMS 2035	3 Apr 45	MID	Minesweeping – MID awarded for great gallantry and endurance in clearing the estuary of the Scheldt of mines during the period of September to November 1944.
LICKFIELD John Stanley	Signalman	HMT *Negro* (M/S)	5 Oct 43	DSM	Minesweeping – DSM awarded for courage and skill in many successful minesweeping operations in Mediterranean waters.

222

Name	Rank	Ship	Date	Award	Citation
LOCK William George	T/Lt Cdr RNR	HMT *Ronaldsay* (Isles Class M/S)	9 Jun 42	MID	Minesweeping – MID awarded for bravery, determination and fortitude in important minesweeping operations. Orkney and Shetland Oct 41.
LOYNS Bertie Horace	T/Lt RNR T/Lt RNR	BYMS *2209* BYMS *2209*	23 May 44 24 Apr 45	MID DSC	Minesweeping – MID awarded for Operation Avalanche (Salerno landings). DSC awarded for outstanding skill, determination and despatch in carrying out minesweeping operations, frequently under fire, off the East Coast of Italy. Ancona Jul–Aug 44.
MABBOTT William Livingstone	PO	HMT *Probe* (P Class M/S Trawler)	3 Jul 45	MID	Minesweeping – MID awarded for consistent zeal, courage and good seamanship whilst serving in HM 104th and 31st Minesweeper Flotilla and the 159th Trawler Group and in HMCS Blairmore in arduous operations along the coasts of Southern England and Northern France. Opening of Le Havre and Seine.
MacKAY Donald	Seaman LS	Not listed BYMS *2211*	17 Mar 42 6 Jun 44	MID DSM	Minesweeping – MID awarded for minesweeping in North Sea. DSM awarded for leadership, skill and devotion to duty in an important minesweeping operation.

MacLEOD Donald	LS	HMT *Prowess* (M/S)	3 Jul 45	MID	Minesweeping – MID awarded for consistent zeal, courage and good seamanship whilst serving in HM 104th and 31st Minesweeper Flotilla and the 159th Trawler Group and in HMCS Blairmore in arduous operations along the coasts of Southern England and Northern France. Opening of Le Havre and Seine.
MANTRIPP William Wilfred	2nd Hand	HMT *King Emperor* (M/S)	1 Jul 41	DSM	Minesweeping – Awarded for outstanding zeal, patience and cheerfulness, and for never failing to set an example of wholehearted devotion to duty, without which the high tradition of the Royal Navy could not have been upheld.
MARK Alleyn Oliver	T/Lt RNVR	BYMS 2052	15 May 45	DSC	Minesweeping – DSC awarded for gallantry, perseverance and devotion to duty in minesweeping operations under enemy fire in the Adriatic. Aug–Oct 44.

Name	Rank	Ship	Date	Award	Citation
MARTIN Alister Angus	Cdr RNR	HMT *Taipo* (M/S)	4 Oct 40	MID	First MID awarded for sustaining air attack.
	Cdr RNR	LP Trawlers Unit Officer	1 Jan 41	DSC	DSC awarded New Year Honours 1941
	A/Capt RNR	HMS *Rothesay*	31 Mar 42	MID	Second MID awarded for courage, skill and endurance while minesweeping in dangerous waters. Minefield clearance Nore Dec 41–Jan 42.
	A/Capt RNR	HMS *Rothesay*	7 Dec 43	Bar to DSC	Bar to DSC awarded for steadfast courage and skill in a dangerous and important minesweeping operation. Operation Antidote.
	A/Capt RNR	HMS *Rothesay*	14 Nov 44	MID	Third MID awarded for outstanding courage and devotion to duty in minesweeping operations in the Mediterranean. Second bar to DSC awarded for Operation Dragoon.
	A/Capt RNR	HMS *Fabius* (Taranto)	27 Mar 45	Bar to DSC	
			12 Jun 45	DSO	DSO awarded for gallantry, outstanding skill and devotion to duty in minesweeping operations over dense and shallow minefields in the opening up of Greek ports in the Gulf of Corinth. Patras and Itea.
MARTIN George	LS	HMT *Westray* (Isles Class M/S)	18 Sep 45	MID	Minesweeping – MID awarded for bravery, determination and great devotion to duty in minesweeping operations in the Adriatic over a period from April to May 1945.
MARTIN Leonard	Seaman	HMT *Fezenta* (M/S)	6 Jun 44	MID	Minesweeping – MID awarded for leadership, skill and devotion to duty in an important minesweeping operation. Humber 26 Jan 44.

225

MATHIE-SON Kenneth	Stoker First Class	HMT *Proof* (M/S)	3 Jul 45	MID	Minesweeping – MID awarded for consistent zeal, courage and good seamanship whilst serving in HM 104th and 31st Minesweeper Flotilla and the 159th Trawler Group and in HMCS Blairmore in arduous operations along the coasts of Southern England and Northern France. Opening Le Havre and Seine.
MAWSON Vivian Adams	Prob/T/S/Lt Lt RNVR	HMT *Berberis* (M/S) BYMS *2161*	3 Sep 40 23 Jan 45	MID MID	Minesweeping – First MID awarded for coming under air attack. Second MID awarded for courage and skill in minesweeping operations in the approaches to Le Havre.
MAYHEW Arthur Frederick David	Cook	HMT *Hoy* (M/S)	14 Nov 44	MID	Minesweeping – MID awarded for outstanding courage and devotion to duty in HM Ships Brixham, Bude, Hoy, Polruan, Rothesay and Sharpshooter in minesweeping operations in the Mediterranean.
McBRIDE Joseph Henry	PO RNPS	HMT *Epine* (M/S)	13 Apr 43	DSM	Minesweeping – DSM awarded for bravery and skill while serving in HM Ships Alafoss, Sidmouth, Bridlington, Blackpool, Bangor, Eastbourne, Sargasso, Dhoon, Loch Levan, lowther, Welbeck, Star of Orkney, Epine, Feasible, Miranda, Loch Eribol, Welsbach and William Bell while these ships were employed on the hazardous duties of keeping the seas clear of mines. North Sea Sep 1942.

McGRATH Desmond	T/Lt RNVR T/Lt RNVR	BYMS 2157 BYMS 2157	16 Jan 45 13 Jun 46	MID MBE	Minesweeping – MID awarded for gallantry and skill in minesweeping operations off the coast of France. MBE awarded King's Birthday Hnours 1946
McMULLAN Walter Joseph	T/Sub Lt RNVR	HMT *Galvani* (M/S)	1 Jul 41	MID	Minesweeping – Awarded for outstanding zeal, patience and cheerfulness, and for never failing to set an example of wholehearted devotion to duty, without which the high tradition of the Royal Navy could not have been upheld.
MELHUISH William John	Chief Engineman	BYMS 2053	15 May 45	DSM	Minesweeping – DSM awarded for gallantry, perseverance and devotion to duty in minesweeping operations under enemy fire in the Adriatic. Aug–Oct 1944.
MILLS Charles William	Engineman RNPS	HMT *Dhoon* (M/S)	13 Apr 43	DSM	Minesweeping – DSM awarded for bravery and skill while serving in HM Ships Alafoss, Sidmouth, Bridlington, Blackpool, Bangor, Eastbourne, Sargasso, Dhoon, Loch Levan, lowther, Welbeck, Star of Orkney, Epine, Feasible, Miranda, Loch Eribol, Welsbach and William Bell while these ships were employed on the hazardous duties of keeping the seas clear of mines. North Sea Aug 1942.

MILLS Kenneth Edward	A/Leading Wireman	BYMS 2236	20 Nov 45	MID	Minesweeping – MID awarded for courage, efficiency and devotion to duty in the establishment of navigational aids in the approaches to the Rangoon river, in minesweeping and in the survey of the river prior to the assault on the city, May 1945.
MITCHELL Edward Matthew	Seaman	HMT *Negro* (M/S)	5 Oct 43	DSM	Minesweeping – DSM awarded for courage and skill in many successful minesweeping operations in Mediterranean waters while serving in HM Ships Negro, Elbury, Achroite and Triton and HM Motor Minesweepers 47, 68, 80 and 171. Feb–Jul 1943.
MITCHELL Frank	Second Hand	HMT *Berberis* (M/S)	5 Sep 44	MID	Minesweeping – MID awarded for skill and devotion to duty in HM Ships Bunting, Firefly, Edward Walmsley and Berberis in minesweeping operations. Nore area May–Jun 1944.
MITCHELL Stanley Samuel	Lt RN	BYMS 2061	14 Jun 45	MID	Minesweeping – MID awarded King's Birthday Honours 1945.
MOODY Freer	Engineman Engineman	HMT *Amroth Castle* (M/S) HMT *Valesca* (M/S)	1 Jan 45 3 Apr 45	MID DSM	Minesweeping – MID awarded New Year Honours 1945. DSM awarded for great gallantry and endurance in clearing the estuary of the Scheldt of mines during the period of October to November 1944.

Name	Rank	Ship	Date	Award	Citation
MOORMAN William Joseph Henry	Boatswain Lt RN	HMT *Meonstone* (M/S) HMS *Speedwell* (M/S)	5 Jul 40 21 Apr 42	DSC2 MID2	Minesweeping – DSC for capture of Italian submarine Galileo Galilei off Aden 19 Jul 1940. MID awarded for good services in HMS Speedwell following towing of torpedoed merchantman SS Harmatris 17 Jan 1942.
MORE-LAND Walter	Seaman RNPS	HMT *Filey Bay* (M/S)	7 Dec 43	MID	Minesweeping – MID awarded for steadfast courage and skill in a dangerous and important minesweeping operation while serving in HM Ships Acute, Albacore, Brixham, Cadmus, Circe, Clacton, Elbury, Espiegle, Fantome, Felixstowe, Filey Bay, Goth, Hazard, Negro, Polruan, Rothesay, Rhyl, Speedwell, Stornoway, and other ships (Op Antidote).
MORRISON Angus George	Second Hand	HMT *Stella Orion* (M/S)	31 Dec 40	DSM	Minesweeping – DSM awarded for good services in HM Minesweeping Trawlers and Drifters.

Name	Rank	Ship	Date	Award	Citation
MOTSON Norman Wingfield	T/Lt RNVR T/Lt RNVR T/A/Lt Cdr RNVR T/A/Lt Cdr RNVR T/A/Lt Cdr RNVR	HMT *Ben Glas* (M/S) HMT *Ben Glas* (M/S) MMS 29 HMS *St Tudno* (M/S depot ship) HMS *St Tudno*	11 Jun 42 1 Jan 43 14 Nov 44 3 Apr 45 4 Sep 45	MID MID MID MID DSC	Minesweeping – First MID awarded King's Birthday Honours 1942. Second MID awarded New Year Honours 1943. Third MID awarded for Op Neptune. Fourth MID awarded for great gallantry and endurance in clearing the estuary of the Scheldt of mines during the period of September to November 1944. DSC awarded for courage and determination while serving in HM Minesweepers in clearing a passage into Rotterdam, Yjmuiden and Den Helder thereby making possible the swift relief of Holland.
MUDD George Harry	T/Sub Lt(E) RNVR	BYMS 2001	26 Dec 44	MID	Minesweeping – MID awarded for Op Neptune.
MULCARE Arthur Leonard	Lt RNVR Lt RNVR	HMT *Remexo* (M/S) BYMS 2173	1 Jan 44 16 Jan 45	DSC MID	Minesweeping – DSC awarded New Year Honours 1944. MID awarded for gallantry and skill in minesweeping operations off the coast of France. Cherbourg harbour and approaches.
MULLOCK Charles Goss	Chief Engineman	BYMS 2221	3 Apr 45	MID	Minesweeping – MID awarded for great gallantry and endurance in clearing the estuary of the Scheldt of mines during the period of September to November 1944.

Name	Rank	Ship	Award	Date	Citation
MURRAY John Finlayson	Chief Engineman	BYMS 2194	MID	4 Sep 45	Minesweeping – MID awarded for courage, resolution and skill in minesweeping operations clearing a channel from the Humber to Heligoland and thence along the North German Coast to Cuxhaven, Hamburg and Bremerhaven during May 1945.
MURRAY John Geddes	LS LS	BYMS 2175 BYMS 2175	DSM MID	15 May 45 14 Jun 45	Minesweeping – DSM awarded for gallantry, perseverance and devotion to duty in minesweeping operations under enemy fire in the Adriatic. Aug–Dec 1944.
PARKINSON John	Stoker Second Class	HMT General Botha	MID	1 July 41	Minesweeping – MID awarded King's Birthday Honours 1941 for outstanding zeal, patience and cheerfulness, and for never failing to set an example of wholehearted devotion to duty, without which the high tradition of the Royal Navy could not have been upheld:
PARKINSON Joseph	Second Hand RNR	HMT Fyldea (M/S)	DSM	31 Dec 40	Minesweeping – DSM awarded for good services in HM Minesweeping Trawlers and Drifters.
PORTER John Henry George	AB	HMT Galvani (M/S)	DSM	1 Jul 41	Minesweeping – Awarded for outstanding zeal, patience and cheerfulness, and for never failing to set an example of wholehearted devotion to duty, without which the high tradition of the Royal Navy could not have been upheld.

REYNOLDS William James	Seaman	HMT *Stella Orion* (M/S)	31 Dec 40	MID	Minesweeping – MID awarded for good services in HM Minesweeping Trawlers and Drifters.
ROMYN Leopold Dickson	A/Skipper RNR	HMT *Rolls Royce* (M/S)	? 24 Oct 41 23 Jan 42	DSC MID Bar to DSC	Minesweeping – MID awarded for good services while minesweeping. Bar to DSC awarded for courage, resolution and devotion to duty while minesweeping.
ROY William Robson	Seaman	HMT *Craig Millar* (M/S)	1 Jul 41	MID	Minesweeping – Awarded for outstanding zeal, patience and cheerfulness, and for never failing to set an example of wholehearted devotion to duty, without which the high tradition of the Royal Navy could not have been upheld.
SHAW John Hampden	Telegraphist RNV(W)R	HMT *Fyldea* (M/S)	30 Dec 40	MID	Minesweeping – MID awarded for good services in HM Minesweeping Trawlers and Drifters.
SKINNER Samuel George	Engineman RNPS	HMT *Liberia* (M/S)	1 Jan 43	DSM	Minesweeping – DSM awarded 1943 New Year honours for gallantry or outstanding service in the face of the enemy, or for zeal, patience and cheerfulness in dangerous waters, and for setting an example of wholehearted devotion to duty, without which the high tradition of the Royal Navy could not have been upheld.
SLATER Joseph	Engineman	HMT *Stella Orion* (M/S)	31 Dec 40	DSM	Minesweeping – DSM awarded for good services in HM Minesweeping Trawlers and Drifters.

APPENDIX FOUR

The Royal Naval Patrol Service Association

On 5 November 1975, the Royal Naval Patrol Service Association was launched. The first reunion took place in October 1976 and since then an annual reunion has been held each October. Each reunion features a parade, service of remembrance, wreath laying ceremony and march past, all topped off with a dinner.

The national office and the RNPS museum are based at the Sparrow's Nest in Lowestoft, the wartime home of the service and the former HMS *Europa*. The museum is housed in the Stannard Room on the first floor of one of the original buildings of HMS *Europa*. In the museum there are details listing the 850 or more individuals of the service that were awarded honours during the Second World War. The museum also has a mock up of a wheelhouse, thousands of photographs and hundreds of models of the various vessels used by the service.

Admission to the museum is free; it is open on Monday, Wednesday and Friday mornings (subject to the availability of volunteers).

Overlooking the Sparrow's Nest is the impressive RNPS Memorial on the cliff top in Belle Vue Park, Lowestoft. It was erected by and is maintained by the Commonwealth War Graves Commission. Around the base of the memorial are the names of the

2,385 men of the service lost during the Second World War.

Royal Naval Patrol Service Association is a registered charity, No. 273148

The RNPS Association can be contacted at:

RNPS Association
Sparrow's Nest Gardens
Whapload Road
Lowestoft
NR32 1XG

Telephone: +44 (0) 1502 586250

To email the Association HQ for any purpose:
rnps_HQ@lowestoft.org.uk

Bibliography

Brookes, Ewart, *Glory Passed Them By*, Jarrolds, 1958

Brown, Jimmy, *Harry Tate's Navy*, self published, 1994

Elliott, Peter, *Allied Minesweeping in World War* Two, Patrick Stephens, 1979

Featherbe, F C, *Churchill's Pirates*, North Kent Books, 1994

Foynes, J P, *The Battle of the East Coast*, self published, 1994

Graves, Charles, *Lifeline*, Heinemann, 1941

Hampshire, A Cecil, *Lilliput Fleet*, New English Library, 1957

Her Majesty's Stationery Office, *His Majesty's Sweepers*, Ministry of Information, 1943

Hurd, Sir Archibald, *The Battle of the Seas*, Hodder & Stoughton, 1941

Kerslake, S A, *Coxswain in the Northern Convoys*, William Kimber, 1984

Lund, Paul and Harry Ludlam, *Trawlers Go To War*, Foulsham, 1971

Lund, Paul and Harry Ludlam, *Outsweeps*, Foulsham, 1978

McAra, Charles, *Mainly in Minesweepers*, Leach, 1991

Minett, Eric, *The Coast is Clear: The Story of the* BYMS, self published, 2005

Sutherland, J and Diane Canwell, *The RAF Air Sea Rescue Service 1918–1986*, Pen & Sword Books, 2005, pbk 2010

Sutherland, J and Diane Canwell, *Air War Malta*, Pen & Sword Books, 2008

Sutherland, J and Diane Canwell, *Air War Over the Nore*, Pen & Sword Books, 2010

Toghill, Gerald, *Royal Navy Trawlers, Part One: Admiralty Trawlers*, Maritime Books, 2003

Toghill, Gerald, *Royal Navy Trawlers, Part Two: Requisitioned Trawlers*, Maritime Books, 2004

Walmsley, Leo, *Fishermen of War*, Collins, 1941

Index